BOOKS BY JOSEPH MONNINGER

NEW
JERSEY

NEW JERSEY

◆◆◆ JOSEPH *◆◆◆*
MONNINGER

ATHENEUM ◆◆◆ 1986 ◆◆◆ NEW YORK

Library of Congress Cataloging-in-Publication Data

Monninger, Joseph.
   New Jersey.

   I. Title.
PS3563.0526N4   1986   813'.54   85-48153
ISBN 0-689-11770-1

Published simultaneously in Canada by Collier Macmillan Canada, Inc.
Composition by Maryland Linotype Composition Co., Inc.
Manufactured by Fairfield Graphics, Fairfield, Pennsylvania
Designed by Laura Rohrer
First Edition

To Bill, Chuck, John, Cathy, Joan, and Mike

O running stream of sparkling joy
To be a soaring human boy!
Charles Dickens, *Bleak House*

PART
1

❖❖ 1 ❖❖

MY NAME is Max Darrigan.
My mother died in the first year of my life. I killed her, I'm sure, though no one has ever accused me of it. Left alone, my father took on the task of raising me. He was a large man. The hair on his chest, when seen from the side, formed a halo around his upper torso. It was the same hair that pushed the weight of his T-shirts off his body, cushioning it and making it wonderful to lean against. Cotton and hair are what I remember of him. He was good with his hands, though he worked with his mind. He taught school at Westfield High—algebra and geometry—and left early each morning with a bag lunch and a stack of work sheets. He returned in late afternoon, hoping for enough time to putter.

During my earliest days and during stretches of the summer, when he traveled, he left me with Honey, our black maid. Of course, Honey was more than a maid to me. She was a huge woman with Spalding speed bags for breasts, large skirts, a loud laugh, and a gap where her two front teeth should have joined. I loved Honey and she knew it.

The days I spent with Honey were rich. She knew enough about housework not to take it very seriously, and so the small jobs she had to complete became games in her hands, events to look forward to rather than avoid. Singing, she threw rugs over the clothesline in the backyard, then stood in front of them, a baseball bat in her hands, saying, "Come on, kid, try me." She would dig a tennis ball out of her apron pocket, roll it to me, then tap the ground in front of her. She mapped out the strike zone behind her by using the various patterns on the rug.

"See that thing there that looks like a lion's head . . . then over there, to that picture of a queen . . . then down to the other lion's head, back up again? You get it past me, that's a strike."

She rapped the bat again, making mock-snorting sounds, the black high-topped sneakers she often wore tearing at the grass, all the while shouting, "Come on, Maxy kid, put one in."

She could hit, and more than once she ripped a line drive off my shins or stomach, then ran over to soothe me, gently walking me back to the pitcher's mound, putting the ball back in my hand, petting me, giving me tips.

"Don't just lay it in there, buster. Put a little hook on it . . . something. I'll rap that pitch of yours all day long."

I didn't strike her out until I was eleven—although she had let me do it a few times and had faked badly in the process—and by that time I could snap off a good curve. She was the first person to press a baseball bat in my hand, the first one to change my stance. She knew how to bone a bat. She knew how to dunk a new glove in a bucket of cold water, tie a softball in the center for a good pocket, smear it with oil, then put it in some dark corner of a closet until it dried and aged to a fig-colored web that fitted smoothly on my hand.

In the afternoons, when I was small and even sometimes afterward, we went for walks. We started off a different way every day, but we always ended by following Bayberry Road up to Cherry Stable. Her husband, Zeke, worked in the stables as a swipe, and it was Honey's duty to bring him lunch. And so we walked, she in front, stopping and pulling me along, her wide behind swinging gently, while I asked countless questions.

Cherry Stable was halfway to the Watchung Reservation and it seemed a great distance. I suppose it was only a mile or so, but it was a journey to us. We followed a hiking path the horses sometimes used, and we walked through pine forests, fitting our

4

feet to the hoof slices in the dirt. A stream ran beside the path part of the way, and Honey let me have free rein on these stretches. She often stopped to sit with me, guiding me to different pockets of water where I might find tadpoles or minnows, whistling me up when it was time to go or when she became impatient.

After the stream we walked in silence. Honey's breathing was loud, but it sounded like something from the forest. She loved the sun and always tried to find warmth, at times crossing and zigzagging on the path to catch a shoulder in a beam of light. Now and then she pointed something out to me, lifting one of her big arms, her fleshy triceps floating and shaking, while her finger sighted down on a squirrel or robin or rabbit, and I was forced to follow the line of her finger until I could pick out from the underbrush whatever it was she saw, record it, then nod that we could go on.

This was her lesson: silence in the face of nature. She had few names for the things we saw. She was content to walk slowly, to amble in her zigzag fashion, catching light, breathing deeply, her feet leaving sneaker tracks beside the hoof marks.

She began to speak again when the forest gave way. Near the end of the trail, but before Cherry Stable, there was a small wildlife museum called Trailside, which displayed different species indigenous to the Watchung Reservation. Outside the museum was a poorly run zoo that was, I suppose, the object of a million elementary school field trips. The cages were small, and the animals all showed some trace of neurosis: The coyote paced back and forth, its tail gnawed; the raccoon dipped its food into a pie tin containing its water; an owl blinked in a shadeless roost, a dead mouse half dissected on the cement floor below. The zoo had a high, wild smell that broke the hold of the forest. Children were frequently clustered around the cages, shrieking now and then, jumping back if the animal they watched snarled or came too close. During the summer we sometimes found Cub Scouts camped nearby in an open field, working diligently on some survival drill fifty miles from New York City.

Some days Honey stopped and sat on a bench and allowed me to roam the zoo. I'm sure she didn't think much of the zoo, but it gave me a chance to bump shoulders with other children as I squeezed in next to the railings that sectioned off the cages.

5

I knew the animals by heart, but my knowledge didn't help me. I was an outsider; I belonged to no group, and so my presence was endured but not invited. When the children read the small histories painted on the green boards beside each cage, I listened as attentively as the rest, pretending ignorance, giving up my own knowledge in the hope of belonging. Sometimes the adults were kind to me. A few women, elementary-school teachers who were well groomed and oddly virginal, occasionally allowed me to tag along for the lectures given by Park Officer Nenduck. Once or twice I managed to strike up temporary friendships with the butt pinchers and peanut butter-breathed boys who always coagulated at the back of the groups. After a while, after the red-tailed hawk or beaver, the group broke off, and I would be left dangling, alone again to examine for the fiftieth time the hedgehog mound or otter slide, while the boys I had just befriended ran off to sweet yellow buses, souvenirs of rose quartz tight in their hands.

It was then I listened for Honey's whistle, and I was always grateful when it came. "Come on," she said, her arm or hand touching me briefly on the shoulder, "Zeke will be waiting."

We followed the Braille Path to the stables. The Braille Path was designed for blind people, with a wooden rail down the center. The wood was smooth from so many hands, and Honey let me shut my eyes and trace it. The railing stopped at different places along the trail, and there were small signs, again in braille, which reported to the blind people's fingers what they might have seen had they been sighted. At other times the railing led to different bushes, which the blind were encouraged to smell and touch.

"Go ahead," Honey said, and I bent forward, hugging some green thing to my chest, using my senses in a new way until I knew the smell of hawkweed, sumac, or bayberry. Some of the bushes had signs in front of them, both in braille and in ordinary letters, and Honey quizzed me, asking at each stop, "What's that? Don't open your eyes now, just tell me."

I had learned the intervals of the bushes and soon memorized the stops, but I tried to play the game as honestly as I could, feeling for the texture of the leaves and bark, deciphering the

6

smell from the smells around it, rubbing my cheek against the green.

"Rhododendron," I'd say.

"That's right," Honey agreed, and then I'd be off again, wobbling ahead, my hand gliding on the railing.

The forest gave way a second time to the stables, and I knew by the increase in light that we were there. The horses' smell came, too, thick and fine, and we moved to it. Honey hurried at this point, remembering, I suppose, that Zeke was waiting, that he had been up early and hadn't eaten since.

"Go ahead now," she told me, and I ran up the small slope to the open stable yards, feeling the soil change under my feet, picking up sounds and colors that seemed too loud and bright after the forest.

A jumping ring circled in front of the barn, but I seldom found Zeke there. The ring was for girls in brown breeches or tall suburban women in crisp shirts and velvet riding hats. I had the notion, even then, that riding horses had nothing to do with Zeke. The actual sound of it—the rich clopping, the whinnies, the girls shouting and speaking to their mounts in serious voices—had nothing to do with Zeke. He was a swipe, a barn creature, and his sounds were muted, low. I identified him with the soft grunts of horses after exercise, the slurp of horses over oats or hay, the leather tap of tack swinging against wooden walls.

And so, most days, I found him at the back of the barn, bent over some harness or rein or cleaning out the stalls with a shovel. He hummed when he worked and also carried a loud pocket watch that I heard when things were still. He wore overalls and thick boots that always had a little manure matted to the crease where the sole and leather joined, and his feet often trailed wisps of hay that had knotted in the manure—bows and beards of hay that gave his feet an animate quality all their own.

He was tuned to the barn, to its sounds and moods, and he always detected me before I sneaked up on him. He would start talking before he even saw me, saying, "I'm about ready to eat some of this hay myself. I wish that Max would get here with something else, but if I have to, I'll eat hay."

I'd run to him then, staying to the center of the barn, away

7

from the lazy horse heads that looked over their stalls, shouting, "Honey's coming. She's almost here."

Zeke was different from most adults. He didn't insist on his game, and he gave it up as soon as he saw me.

"What took you all so long?" he asked, putting down his shovel or leather work. "It's almost two."

"We came straight up."

"You stop at the zoo?"

"For a minute."

Zeke had a small table in the back of the barn, which he used for lunch. The tabletop had been cut and gouged for years, and its tiny nicks and slices made it useless for writing. Zeke's paper work—hours for billing, veterinary visits, his own schedule—was neatly arranged on clipboards and hung from nails on the back wall. A pencil or pen always dangled from a long rawhide strap, and I was allowed to play with it, swinging it back and forth while Zeke cleaned the table, brushing yesterday's crumbs into his palm, then onto the floor.

Finally Honey appeared, large and dark in the center of the doorway, blinking for a moment to let her eyes adjust. She didn't like horses, and she stayed close to the center of the barn, her head straight forward, her sneakers soft on the old boards. She raised whatever she had brought in front of her, wagging the paper bag a little, while Zeke slid into his spot behind the table and leaned his head against the wall.

He rarely ate bread, and so Honey normally brought cheese and sausage. It was his favorite lunch, and he ate it with grace, cutting thin slices of cheese with his buck-handled knife, sliding the meat between the cheese, and eating it in small, delicate bites. I envied the knife, of course, but I also admired his style—the slow, leisurely way he went at food, his ability to eat just enough, the peel of the blade next to his dark fingers. He talked to Honey in quiet tones, now and then whistling to the horses that stared at us over their stalls. He wasn't foolish about animals, about his horses, though he granted each a personality and worked around their eccentricities.

Lunch had no proper ending. He merely slowed, his knife idle for a moment, while we sat on his bench, the three of us staring straight out at the bright square of sun outlined by the door. The

8

horses would breathe, and Honey would breathe, and Zeke would turn his knife on something he was whittling. I would push off onto the floor and lie there listening to the scrape of steel on wood, the low-throated chuckle of pigeons high in the rafters, the hazy drone of mosquitoes and flies. Some days I fell asleep, drifting off to the heat and warmth, but better still were the days I remained quiet, somewhere near sleep, my senses open, my blood sinking to stillness. I would hope that none of the riders would return while I was there, pushing away the silence, forcing Zeke to stand and go out into the yard, lifting the spell that we barely understood yet entered into so easily.

❖❖ 2 ❖❖

FOR MY father teaching was not simply a job. Teaching was his vocation, his calling, his approach to life. He was also his own best student and therefore supplied himself with a constant stream of information. It was nothing to see him have one, two, even three books going at a time. He subscribed to ten or twelve magazines, ranging in subject from the natural sciences to the latest on the space program, and for most of his life he clipped articles, stashing them away in manila folders for later reference or sending them to former students as a codicil to some earlier discussion. It was never in his mind to give information in order to impress someone or to make someone squirm at his own ignorance. No, he explained, he generously dished up what he knew, correcting opinions only so far as it brought both parties closer to a truth.

Perhaps he should have been a more important man; perhaps he should have achieved more. His flaw, however, was his great gift. He lacked discipline in his approach to things. He couldn't organize, could never deduce what was required of him. Asked for a trickle, he delivered a deluge, drowning the questioner in a bath of pertinent facts and side issues, his own answer becoming more viscous with each new clarification. He knew too much, or maybe he simply lacked some valve, some device that would switch off at an appropriate time. He could not judge a mind outside his own.

From the beginning I knew I had to share my father with other people. I knew he was well respected, maybe even loved, at the high school. Students honked when they drove past the house, waving to him, sometimes pulling over to talk with him, shouting over the grind of the power mower that they were off to the Magical Forest, the Watchung Mountains, the Red and Green Road. Two or three times a year he received letters from former students—normally in their freshman year at college—thanking him for his contribution to their lives, wishing him well, telling him in whatever way they could that his work had meant something. He was "Teacher of the Year" one spring and had the yearbook, the *Weathervane*, dedicated to him one June.

During the summer months he was free to follow his own mind and interests. This was never easy since he tried to take on too much, tried to consume too much. Although he was rarely bored by his students, he was nevertheless limited, and in his release from them each spring he became a little reckless, a little driven. He visited museums, walked through zoos, looked up local historians, and started numerous projects. He also read intimidating volumes, fat red leather books propped open on one another, their wide flanks molting, their weight enough to make the binding glue of the bottom volume crackle on quiet evenings.

During summers he also traveled, often paying Honey to come spend the night with me. He had converted our old station wagon into a camper vehicle and used it as a field study base. He kept sleeping bags rolled up and ready behind the driver's seat and a hibachi in the tire boot. The rest of the car was crowded with charcoal briquettes, coffee cans rattling with rock specimens, weeds and wild flowers pressed between old sheets of newspaper, sea shells, crab legs, the paw print of an animal lifted, as if in plaster, from the damp spring mud banks of a river or lake. Two spools of rope lay coiled near the back, ready to pull out for a clothesline or a lean-to. In the front, near my feet when I went with him, he stored at least a dozen grapefruits for each trip. They

rolled across the floorboards, the gentle tick of their skin a re-
sponse to every curve or bump in the road, until he bent and
stabbed one up to his lap, the yellow juices trickling over the
back of his hand. He cut the grapefruits on the move, his sharp
knife slicing them into quarters so that he could eat them with
his hands, his lips pulling the pale yellow pulp into thoughtful
slivers as he kept his eyes on the road. At the same time he
listened to *Talking Books*, recordings of great works of literature,
which he received from Washington free of charge. The humped
console of the car glistened with the sides of many cassettes, their
titles as exotic and rich as the scent of grapefruit. His taste ran
to adventure, so we listened to *The Sea-Wolf*, or *Kon-Tiki*, or
Moby Dick. He had a special fondness for dog books, and these
he borrowed from the children's list, checking off his favorites
each month so that we always had copies of *Lad: A Dog*, or *White
Fang*, or *The Call of the Wild*. He particularly loved the scene in
The Call of the Wild when Buck and Spitz chase an arctic hare
over the tundra, then fall together in combat, the wolf pack closing around them, waiting for the first weakness.

"The stars and the night and the crispness—can't you see it,
Max? There's something wonderful about that scene, something
you can go to sleep to if you're having trouble falling off."

He said this as he played it back, listening for the fifteenth
time, his knife nicking through another grapefruit, his body
leaning slightly to take the voice on more directly, to be closer
to the scene.

There was more than a little of the prospector about him, the
tortoise hobo who cannot entirely relinquish his home. I knew,
even at an early age, that my father did not camp but squatted.
He had a rare knack of traveling to see. He cared nothing for
comfort, nothing at all for real leisure. In fact, he took pleasure
in sleeping beside a golf green or nestled in a sand trap, while
above him, in a tall Holiday Inn or Howard Johnson's, people
paid twenty or thirty dollars a night for the same view. He knew
side streets and back alleys, wooded lots where he wouldn't be
disturbed for a night. He felt rich when he slept under the stars.

I loved him and admired him and went with him when I could.
It was impossible not to love him as he crouched over his hibachi,

his eyes blinking at the smoke, his saggy rain hat over his hand as a potholder. To be in his company was to be invited into a large, wonderful sphere where things would be explained, where any thought was a good one, where questions were better than answers.

❖❖ 3 ❖❖

I T WAS June and I was thirteen when I took my last
L real trip with my father.

"What do you say we head off to Point Pleasant?" he asked me
one evening after a Pony League game. "It's a good beach, and
there are lots of rides. Would you like that? We can call it a
celebration. We'll get rid of the stuffiness from a year of school."

We were eating Toasted Almond Good Humors. We had lost,
12 to 7, against the Senators. I had not played well. I had struck
out twice against Jimmy Meluso, the Senators' pitcher, a tall,
stringy kid who threw too hard. I was afraid of Jimmy, afraid
that in his wildness, which was legendary around the league, he
would drill me in the back or head with one of his fast balls. I
had been happy to ground out weakly to second base.

"Are you serious?" I asked, not positive he meant it. I knew
this was a trip for me. Point Pleasant was not a destination he
would pick on his own.

"Sure I'm serious."

"When?"

"Well, how about right now?"

"You're kidding."

"No, I'm not. Try me. The car's all ready, you know that. We'll run home, get some clothes, and we're off."

"I have a game on Sunday."

"You'll be back."

"Are you serious?"

"Of course I'm serious. If we hurry, we'll be there in an hour."

He took a large bite from his Good Humor. The cords of his hooded sweat shirt bobbed back and forth as he turned to watch a group of kids hitting fly balls to one another. I waited a moment longer, trying to decide if he was serious or not.

"You could bring a friend if you like. How about Harry? You like him, don't you?"

"Not Harry."

"Well, someone else then. How about Mike? He played pretty well tonight, didn't he?"

"I'd rather just go alone," I said. "With you, I mean."

I never felt entirely comfortable having my friends around him, and I avoided inviting them to the house. My father was too unpredictable. He had a teacher's familiarity with kids, and he behaved too naturally, too freely. He was likely to say or do something to embarrass me, not because it was inappropriate but because it was actually too appropriate, too on target. In seeing through us, he somehow made himself transparent.

He considered. "Come on then. Let's go."

We drove home. I ran upstairs, showered, filled a gym bag, then came back down the stairs. He was packing the rear of the station wagon when I stepped outside, his body disappearing inside the car to push things into deep corners. He wore sneakers, khakis, and a tan Windbreaker over his sweat shirt.

"You have your things? What are you bringing?" he asked.

"Just jeans."

"And a swimsuit, right? You're going to swim, aren't you?"

"Sure."

"You have a heavy jacket?"

"Yes."

"Then we're set. I've got sleeping bags, money, keys, what else?" he asked, tapping his pockets. "Nothing else? Let's go then."

We drove across town. At that time of night the sprinklers were on, and I heard water flicking across lawns, the pitch changing

only when the looping streams fell on concrete. The grass smelled
rich and sad. In the center of town the Rialto played *The Sound
of Music.* A transparency of Julie Andrews was somehow pinned
to the lighted marquee, her arms open, her mouth wide in song.
A long line of people waited to go in, a few of them eating ice
cream, some smoking. Mr. Strunk, the only black cop on the
force, directed traffic, crossing kids from Baron's Drugstore to
the Rialto. His white gloves made quiet arches in the fading light.

At the light across from Sycamore I watched a crowd slowly
leave another Little League field. The first stars were already out,
and a breeze blew softly across the diamond, lifting the dust in
small orange whirlpools. Two little boys ran in opposite directions around the bases, racing to see who would reach home first.
A third boy dangled from the top of the backstop, his fingers
digging at a ball stuck there.

We followed Central Avenue to the Garden State Parkway.
The station wagon could not go fast, and my father never pushed
it. We rolled down the windows and let air blast through. My
father's jacket caught the wind, his sleeve billowing to an enormous size, his chest filled out and rippling.

We listened to *Where the Red Fern Grows.* It was the story of
a boy and his two red tick hounds, hunting for raccoons in the
Ozark Mountains. The section being narrated was about a raccoon contest that almost ended in disaster. The two hounds had
treed a coon, but a blizzard moved in, and the boy couldn't find
the dogs until morning. Remarkably the hounds hadn't left the
coon. They remained by the tree until they could barely move,
their fur glazed with ice.

"You think that could really happen?" my father asked, going
over the Amboy Bridge.

"I don't know. Do you?"

"I've decided to believe it. That's what counts."

We continued listening. He had an old change counter like the
ones ice-cream men wear at their waists so that he could punch
out the correct amount without looking. He took an unjustified
pride in it, as he did in most gimmicks, and that evening, as we
traveled, he punched out a quarter when we approached each toll
booth and held it close to the windshield so I could verify it by
the toll plaza light.

16

"A quarter?" he asked each time.

"Yes."

"Shhh, this is a good part."

When we steered off the Garden State, the smell of the sea seemed to come up all around us. It took only a moment for the houses to become less substantial. They were built of clapboard and painted soft pastel colors, the wood bowed and weathered, the paint often chipped to shells. The black asphalt road sparkled and glittered, tiny pieces of silicon catching the first throw of our headlights. Sand pooled in the gutters.

"Smell it?" my father asked, turning the tape recorder off. "You could follow your nose now, couldn't you? This is the only smell that never gets old. You can always smell the sea, even if you live right next to it."

"Is it far?"

"Ten minutes. Not much more. Hungry?"

"A little."

"We'll find a spot, then take a walk on the boardwalk. What do you say? Sound good?"

"Sure," I said.

He drove through the small town of Point Pleasant and found Route 35 along the ocean. A Ferris wheel appeared occasionally between the trees, the tremendous circle of light spinning in its own halo. The sea rolled to our left, its sound like traffic, only smoother, and on some corners we could see the white foam running forward and back, framed by the gray wood of the board-walk. Here and there couples walked toward the lights. Near Ocean Avenue one man stood on a bench, looking out to sea, while his wife pinched her cardigan closer to her throat, her free hand holding onto a wrinkle in his trousers.

My father parked illegally. He pulled his two right tires up on the curb so that the car tilted to one side. When I tried to open my door, it wouldn't stay. I had to use my feet to keep it from smashing me while I struggled out, jerking myself into position as the door swung back. My sneakers sank into sand and crab grass.

"Oh, boy," my father yelled, "grab your jacket, hear? It will be a little chilly up on the boardwalk."

I reached in through the back window and took my sweater.

My father reached in and found an old parking ticket under the floor mat. He slipped it under the windshield wiper.

"Sometimes this works," he said. "If they bother to look, they get a little angry. It's a gamble."

"We could drive around the block a few times."

"No, too much bother. Come on. How about a sausage sandwich? I've been thinking about one since we decided to come down here."

We crossed the street and climbed up onto the boardwalk. Two bikes passed, tires thumping the boards one at a time. We walked to the opposite railing, drawn to our first full view of ocean. The wind increased, sand spraying against the boardwalk and pinging against the fenders of the cars parked behind us. A few candy wrappers swirled in the hollow of a lifeguard stand, lifting and dropping on tiny gusts of wind.

"This ocean is a mess, but it's still wonderful, isn't it? They haven't killed it yet, have they?" asked my father, touching my shoulder.

"Is the pollution bad?"

"This close to New York and Jersey City and Newark? I should take you to New England so you could see what real water smells like. But for now, well, this is fine. It's still the ocean. I like it better in some ways for being close to so much junk."

"Did you come here with Mom?"

"No, I don't think so. I don't remember if we did. We went to Sandy Hook a lot. It was closer and less of an amusement park."

"Did she like the ocean?"

"Not so much. She liked lakes more."

He reached in his pocket and took out his glasses. I never understood why he needed glasses at one moment and not another, but he put them on and took them off frequently. It was as if the world slipped out of focus for hours at a time.

Afterward he put his arm around me quickly and squeezed my shoulders.

"Come on," he said, "let's get some sausages."

We walked near the railing, our eyes on the water. A sea gull lifted once, startled from its sleeping perch, then veered sharply over our heads and disappeared in the darkness. Two girls passed us from the other direction, both of them eating cotton candy.

18

A tiny dog trailed after them, its back legs moving almost sideways to the rest of its body. It sniffed us quickly, then let us pass.

The barkers started the moment we passed the first stand. They were not sharp, not fully honed for the season. There was an easiness about them, a feeling of spring training, and often their final pitch became mumbled or lost in the mechanical whir of a ride or the shout of a second barker.

We ate at Pete's Italian, a hot-sausage stand in the center of the arcade. Pete wore a white T-shirt dotted with tiny flecks of tomato sauce. He stirred a large vat of sauce with an enormous ladle, a crumpled paper napkin serving as a potholder.

"Two sandwiches, please," my father told him.

"Everything?" asked Pete.

"What's everything?"

"Everything's everything. Peppers, gum balls, Good and Plenty, you name it. Come on, you look like a sport. What do you say?"

"Everything."

"Good. What a decision. What the world needs, a man who can make a decision."

Pete whistled. A young woman wearing a hair net brought two deli rolls and sliced them through. She had a faint mustache and squinted to cut the rolls.

"With," Pete told her.

She reached under the counter and came up with peppers, lettuce, tomato bits, grated cheese, and slices of olives. She fashioned a bed out of the materials, then held the top half of the bread while Pete ladled out two sausages per sandwich.

"Clean," he said while she put them on paper plates. "Don't worry about a thing. Some people eat this stuff and the whole time they're expecting to bite into a rat or something. You eat this right up and don't worry about a thing. We keep a clean place here."

We ate standing at a Formica counter, dabbing at our mouths with balls of paper napkins. "Mmmmmm," my father said, his glasses glinting orange and yellow from the blinking lights outside. His fingers moved up and down the sides of the sandwich, lifting as if on the stops of a flute.

"Yours good?" I asked.

"Real good. Yours?"

19

"Great."

"You like that, son?" Pete asked me.

"Yes."

"Good. Nothing but the best in here. That's why I've been here fifteen years, every summer. I get fine-quality meat—none of this ground crap you get most places. And this happens to be a good batch. It's like vintage, you understand me?"

I nodded. My father finished the last of his sandwich and bought us two Cokes. He sipped until I finished.

"What now?" he asked. "You want to try some rides?"

"If you do."

"It's up to you. Here," he said, digging in his pocket. "Here's ten dollars. You spend it any way you like, okay? That's the deal."

He held the ten dollars out to me. I stared at the money, wanting to refuse it. My father was never free with money—he could never afford to be—and I knew I couldn't accept it without accepting the responsibility to spend it wisely, to spend it as he would.

"Why don't we just go on a few rides?" I asked.

"No, this is better. This way you can do what you like. Go ahead. Take it."

"Take it, kid," Pete said from behind the counter. "It's not every day someone offers you money."

I took the money and pushed it into the pocket of my jeans. My father tapped me on the back.

"There you go. Any way you like."

I finished my sandwich and took a long drink of Coke. My father stood next to me, his hand resting lightly on my shoulder. He seemed to be thinking about something, and it was a full minute or two before he remembered me.

"Ready?" he asked.

"I guess so," I said.

We said good-bye to Pete and went out. The boardwalk was more crowded. Raw bits of music mixed in the wind. I heard the Temptations singing "My Girl." The Ferris wheel continued to roll, and for a moment it looked like a giant paddle wheel. I imagined us all standing on the deck of a riverboat, the wheel churning us slowly westward, the waves across the ocean simply a wake.

20

We moved to the left, staying close to the buildings. There were four or five wheels of fortune in a row, all ticking out numbers, the barkers shouting about prizes already captured. We stopped for a moment to watch a heavy woman throwing Ping-Pong balls at a table fenced off like a boxing ring. The table was lined with cupcake tins, and at the bottom of the different pockets there were cigarette prizes. The woman pitched until she won a carton of Kents, her beefy arms flapping, her purse dangling from her left forearm.

"A winner, a winner," the barker yelled when she won, but we didn't stay to see her receive her prize.

We walked the length of the boardwalk, then worked back down the other side. I was always conscious of the ten dollars. Several times we stopped at rides or booths, standing in the press of people, and I slipped my hand into my pocket and covered the single bill. It was impossible to draw it out, even though my father asked me frequently if I wanted to take a try.

"How about here? You want to try it?" he asked.

"No, no, I'll wait."

"Better pick something soon. You've got some money to use up."

"I will."

I finally bought a box kite at a large tourist shop specializing in beach articles. The kites were kept in a barrel near the door. I bought it knowing it was the kind of purchase my father would like. I bought it, too, supposing it would rid me of the obligation to spend the rest of the money.

"What did you get there? A box kite? God, I haven't flown one of those in years," he said outside the store. From this I knew it was a good purchase, one he approved of, and he took the kite from me and examined it.

"The nice thing about a box kite is that it doesn't need a tail," he said. "With the other kind, the classic design, you always have trouble with getting the right balance. Not these, though. Good. We'll fly it tomorrow, okay? Now, what about some rides?"

"I'm a little tired."

"Tired? At your age? How about one ride at least?"

I touched the money in my pocket. The coins gave me away.

"You're not worried about the money, are you?" my father asked. "Is that it?"

21

"No."

"You sure?"

"Yes."

"No, you're not. It's the money, isn't it?"

He reached in his back pocket and pulled out his wallet. He plucked a ten-dollar bill from it and held it up to the wind, the sides flapping back against his hand. It made a small, vibrating sound like a sail fluffing or the edge of a newspaper pushed too close to a fan.

"Watch," he said.

"Dad, don't."

"It's just because I'm a teacher, Max. Money isn't anything at all. Nothing at all."

He let the ten go. I took a step after it, but it flew over the boardwalk and out to sea. I watched it, not quite believing he had let it go. At any moment I expected him to move to the stairs leading to the beach, but he simply watched the bill until it disappeared.

"It isn't anything," he said again, though whether it was to me or not, I couldn't tell.

❖❖ 4 ❖❖

THE TEN dollars was forgotten as soon as we returned to the car. We found a second parking spot a block or two down the beach and set about unloading what we needed for the night. We made a small pile of sleeping bags and ground cloths on the sidewalk, then debated whether or not to bring the hibachi.

"What do you think? Would you like a fire, Max?"

"If you don't think it will draw too much attention."

"No, I don't think so. Not at this time of year."

He took out the hibachi and loaded it with briquettes. Some of the briquettes were already soaked with gasoline, but he added lighter fluid anyway. He nodded at the sleeping bags.

"You bring those, Max, and I'll carry the hibachi."

"Where are we sleeping? On the beach?"

"You'll see."

I followed him up and over the boardwalk. My sneakers filled with sand the moment I stepped onto the beach. The wind was very strong, blowing out to sea, and I clutched the sleeping bags closer. My father stopped every once in a while to make sure I stayed with him. Now and then he lifted the hibachi to his shoulder and carried it there.

We walked to the edge of the beach. A long rock jetty cut out into the water. The rocks were black, blacker even than the night, and when the waves broke, the foam was remarkably white. The sea pulled back and forth through some of the most distant rocks, and the sound created was a hollow hum, a wonderful rush of air that came to us as we stood on the beach.

"Be careful climbing. The rocks are slippery," my father said, his khakis flexing to pull him up the first row of rocks. He climbed with the hibachi well out in front of him, using it for balance.

I followed him. The rocks were covered with algae near the bottom but became dry as I climbed higher. The hum grew lower, its pitch harmonizing with the rinse of waves over the ridged sand. The breeze blew more strongly with each rock I climbed, and I had the sensation of entering a current of air and wind that somehow mirrored the strong tides of the ocean. I stopped for a moment, listening to the wind around me, slowly becoming aware of the magnificent view the jetty afforded. I heard my father call something, but he was too high, his voice caught up in the air swirling around me.

I climbed a few more rocks and gained the top. My father stood on a square cement platform, the hibachi still in his hands. His jacket whistled and flapped in the high wind, and his hair pulled back from his forehead. I knew, in one glance, that he was happy.

"How's this? Isn't this wonderful?" he shouted to me. "Feel the air? And all this water . . . everywhere . . ."

I stepped across the last few rocks and tossed the sleeping bags onto the cement slab. The slab was obviously the foundation of some old structure. It was not large, and I guessed it had held a jetty light at one time.

"Helllllloooooo," my father hooted into the wind. "Hellloooo, Neptune. Helloooooo, Proteus!"

He slapped me on the back. Then, impulsively, he hugged me. I hugged him back. We stood for a moment in the raw wind, holding each other as if we could be lifted and taken out to sea.

"Come on, now," my father said, breaking away, "say hello. Shout something. Come on."

"Helloooo," I shouted, feeling a little self-conscious, and felt my voice pulled away the moment the word left my mouth.

24

"A fire now. Can you look around and see if there's any drift-wood? We'll use the coals to get everything started. If I set it down here, the flames will be out of the wind."

My father squatted and put the hibachi in a small hollow at the base of the cement slab. There was enough room to sit on either side of the fire, though I didn't see how we could possibly sleep out of the wind.

I left him and went across the rocks, searching for driftwood. I didn't expect to find anything, but now and then I discovered small pockets of wood and dried seaweed. The wood had been thrown up by storms and stayed there, unclaimed, looking like small nests for sea birds.

It took me ten minutes to gather an armful. My father hovered over the fire, his body shielding it from the wind. His face glowed yellow and red. His jacket still chattered.

"Do we need more?" I asked.

"No, that should do it. Come here and get warm. You might try spreading out the sleeping bags. We can sort of sit in them, if you know what I mean."

I unrolled the bags and put them on either side of the fire. They did not spread out completely. I saw that it would be a fine place to sit but that sleeping would be cramped and uncomfortable.

I moved closer to the fire. Already the coals were bright red. My father reached behind him and put two driftwood logs across the bed of the hibachi. Flames rolled quickly around them, and a few sparks lifted into the wind.

"Have you been here before?" I asked.

"A couple times just to sleep. I was out here one day, climbing the rocks, and I saw this cement slab and figured it was a good place to sleep. I saw a shark here, too. I didn't notice it at first. A fishing boat came in, you know, the kind that goes out for bluefish, and a bunch of guys were leaning off the back rail. I figured they were drunk or maybe even sick, but pretty soon I saw that the mate was cleaning the catch and throwing the guts and heads back in the water. There was a bunch of sea gulls diving at it, but there was also a shark. It had a big fin, and I guessed it was a blacktip from the look of it. I remember how the men were mesmerized by that fin and how the fin just swam

25

slowly after the boat, ready for anything that happened, ready to eat up whatever fell in. A couple of the men pretended to push each other, but it really wasn't a joke because they always grabbed the railing very quickly."

"Did the shark go all the way in?"

"It went as far as I watched. I waited, thinking it would come back after a while, but I didn't see it. There were swimmers just around the other side of the jetty."

The wind curled back on us and blew smoke up and over our heads. Then, just as fast, it reversed and blew directly out to sea once more. Sparks lifted and blew down the rocks, rolling sometimes for two or three jumps until they finally died in the wind. The rocks hummed beneath us.

"Clouds," I said.

"You think it will rain? I wanted to show you some stars tonight, but you're right. It's a storm moving out to sea."

"What if it rains in the middle of the night?"

"We get wet. It doesn't matter, does it? Are you warm enough?"

"I'm fine."

The fire had started to throw some heat. The logs smelled of salt water and algae. Occasionally I caught the scent of the rocks themselves, a hard, definite smell. My father stayed with the fire, feeding it small splinters from a log at his side. We sat for a very long time without saying anything. I climbed into the sleeping bag and put my head back against the rock.

I fell asleep in a long series of nods, my eyes snapping open with a gust of wind, the run and tug of a wave. Each time I opened my eyes I saw my father next to me, looking out to sea, his fingers working idly over the log. Once he reached out and brushed my hair back, but that was only to assure me he was close, that he would not leave. He hummed softly, though it was no tune I could recognize, while I dreamed of the shark, the slow stitching of its fin across the stern of the ship, now and then waking to find my father's humming joined with the low drone of the sea beneath us.

❖❖ 5 ❖❖

THE RAIN came just before dawn. I woke to find my father already up. He had knocked out the hibachi on the rocks below us. Drops of rain hissed as they found the dying coals.

"How long have you been up?" I asked.

"It just started. Come on, we'll head back."

"Where? To the car?"

"No, no. Don't worry. It's really going to open up, so hurry."

He rolled his bag quickly and covered it with a ground cloth. I pushed out of my bag and did the same. My limbs felt stiff and cold. The rain came down harder.

"Ready?" asked my father. "Be careful now, the rocks will be even more slippery. Take it easy."

I carried the bags again, following him down the rocks. It was still very dark, but I sensed it was near dawn. There were no waves at all now, and I thought to ask him if the tide had gone out but then gave it up and concentrated on climbing. I almost fell once, my sneakers slipping on a piece of kelp, but I caught myself and actually ran a few steps forward.

My father waited on the sand below.

"Come on," he said, "I have an idea."

"It's clearing over there," I said. "At least I can see the moon and some stars."

"Oh, it will be a good morning. I'm sure of that. We could stay up and watch the sunrise if it weren't raining."

He started off again, walking parallel to the waves. It was very quiet on the beach. A few gulls called from far away, but by some trick of sound I couldn't tell whether they were out on the sea or somewhere on the jetty.

My father stopped when he came to an old rowboat. It was upside down next to a pod of green garbage cans and a lifeguard stand. A long rope anchored the boat to an orange buoy farther up the beach.

"If we can climb under, we can sleep here," my father said.

"Wouldn't it be easier just to go back to the car?"

"This will be more comfortable. Give it a try. I'll lift the boat and you climb under. See if there's space for both of us."

It was raining too hard to argue. My father put the hibachi down and lifted the near side of the boat. He grunted softly and dug into the sand. The boat came up, the sand dry beneath it.

"How's it look?" he asked.

"It's big enough."

"Well, climb under. We can dig under the sides a little."

I went under the boat, and my father eased it down on top of me. It was extremely dark except where the oarlocks forced the boat off the sand. My father began digging on the outside, pulling away sand until he could begin handing me things. He passed the hibachi and sleeping bags to me, then wriggled in himself.

"It's close in here, isn't it? After all the wind on the jetty, this feels awfully stuffy. Can you hand me one of the sleeping bags?" he asked.

"How are we going to spread them out?"

"Well, I'm afraid you're on your own. I can't be of much help. Try to wrap it around you some way. I can't see to help you."

I took one of the sleeping bags and did as he said. It was damp, and sand stuck to it whenever I moved. A mosquito or two buzzed in the darkness. I felt too tired to care if they bit me. I managed to get the bag around my shoulders, though the rest of my body rested on the sand. My father kicked the side of the boat several times trying to get comfortable.

28

"You okay?" he asked after a few minutes.

"Yes. I guess so."

"You don't sound very sure. Does it bother you to sleep under here?"

"No, it just seems sort of strange."

"It's adventure. Adventure's never easy. Five years from now you'll be laughing about it. That's one of the things you have to learn: Things have a reflection. You can look at them from the past or the future. It's up to you."

"We're still under a lifeguard boat."

"You're a realist, Max. Your mother was the same way. I don't know how you put up with me."

"It isn't you. It's the lifeboat."

"See? See how you stick to the facts?"

He laughed softly, then said, "Just try to sleep for a while. It's almost sunrise. We'll have a nice breakfast, and then we'll get some sleep in the sun. That's the way to do it. And we can fly the kite, too. What do you say?"

"Okay."

We were quiet for a long time after that, but I couldn't sleep. I listened to the mosquitoes buzz closer, then fade away. The sea gulls cried, and the rain was loud and steady on the wood hull of the boat. My father snored gently, his jacket whistling whenever he moved.

I squeezed out as soon as I was certain the sun was up. It was just dawn and the beach was clear. A few birds ran in and out at the water's edge, but the tide was low, and the waves only lapped. A blue ring of oil marked the high-tide line, the iridescent bubbles quite beautiful in the soft light.

I sat on a strut of the lifeguard stand until my father's head appeared. He squeezed halfway out from under the boat, then stopped and pulled the sleeping bags free.

"It's a pretty morning, isn't it?" he asked me while I took the bags from him. "Low tide?"

"Yes."

"It will be a pretty day. Feels like it's going to be close and sticky."

He had lost his hat under the boat, and he fished with his free hand to retrieve it. I sat back on the strut and watched him. I

29

couldn't look at him without some admiration, yet it was undermined by the sight of him pressed against the boat. His face, twisted as it was by the efforts of his hand, was serious and somehow tragic. He needed to shave, needed to brush his hair back off his face, needed to splash some water on his eyes. A small patch of dirt smeared the sleeve of his Windbreaker; a circular island of sand stretched from his eyebrow to his hairline, the grains sparkling in the lines of his forehead. The joy of the night before, the sense of wind and sea, was entirely gone. He resembled too closely a hobo, a vagabond crawling out of a dark corner.

He finally found his hat and stood up, dusting at his pants. He grabbed my arm and yanked me to the water. He stopped at the high-tide line and kicked off his shoes.

"You, too. Come on. It's good for you."

I kicked off my shoes and ran ahead. The wet sand was very cold. I ran fast, jumping a little at the tiny pools and funnels of water pulling back from high tide. My father ran behind me.

"Just wash up," he yelled. "Don't get too wet."

"Hello, Neptune," I shouted. "Good morning!"

"Good morning, Proteus!" my father cried after me. "Good morning, Ocean!"

His voice carried far beyond my own. I heard it over the small waves and listened while gulls called back. My father splashed up next to me, his feet throwing a solid spray of sand.

He bent to the water and washed himself. He cupped his hands in the tidal pools and threw the salt water at his face. He blew air out of his nose and mouth, snorting on purpose, letting the water soak his hair and collar.

I washed as he did. The water numbed my wrists and fingers, but it felt wonderful on my face. I continued long after my face was rinsed. A dull headache pumped slowly to my temples.

"Breakfast now, huh? Flapjacks? That's the one meal Americans cook like no one else on earth . . . breakfast."

"Is there a place around here?"

"Sure. I know of a great place."

We went back and collected everything and carried it all to our car. We put it away quickly, then drove out Route 35 until we found a restaurant, called Billy's, that catered to party boat crews.

Two or three tables of men looked up as we came in, and my father nodded to each in turn.

"They're going out," my father said as we sat at a small table near the front. "That means good weather."

"They go out for blues?"

"Blues and flounder and hake. It all depends on how far out they want to go."

The waitress came and took our order. We both had flapjacks and bacon. My father ordered a pot of coffee for himself and milk for me.

We didn't speak. I was very tired. I watched the men come and go. They ate quickly, almost as if taking on fuel, and the two waitresses served them as fast as the food was ready. At some point my father went outside and bought a paper. He handed me the comics and sports page, but I was too exhausted to read. He laughed and poured himself coffee. When he put on his glasses, a small trail of sand scattered over the table.

It was still early when we finished. My father told me to slip my suit on under my jeans. I went out to the car to get my gym bag and took it into the bathroom with me. I dressed in the stall. My father came in a few minutes later, but I didn't wait for him.

I stood outside until he was done. Across the street, on a small lagoon, one of the party boats prepared for the day. A young man stood in the middle of the street, waving cars into a parking lot. He wore a sign like a sandwich board that read: CAP'N JACK/ HALF DAY/ ALL DAY/ FLOUNDER HAKE BLUES. One car stopped and turned in as I watched. The young man slipped a flyer under the windshield wiper, and someone in the car handed him a Pabst Blue Ribbon. He snapped the lid and raised it as a toast while they rocked into the lot.

"They drinking this early?" my father asked from behind me. He carried his pants over his shoulder. His legs looked far too white. "You know, they'll go out for blues and come back drunk and sick, with a stinking burlap bag full of bluefish fillets that everyone pretends to like but no one manages to eat. It happens without fail. Everyone says how much they love the stuff, but then you give it to someone, and it sits in the freezer like a silver cricket bat for the next year and a half. It's crazy."

31

"Did you ever go?"

"Once or twice. I took so many pills against seasickness that I always fell asleep. The whole day I'd go around groggy and worrying that the next roll of the ship was going to make me ill. It never did, though. I was lucky."

We climbed into the car and drove back to the beach. Our parking spot was still empty. We took the sleeping bags again and walked up on the boardwalk. At the bottom of the wooden staircase a teen-ager stood at the entrance to the beach. He had a table all set up, and on the table were small tags—red, green, blue. A sign behind him said today was a RED day. He was busy arranging umbrellas. There was a pile of air mattresses on the sand beside him.

"Good morning," the kid said as we came down the stairs at him. "Good day for the beach, huh?"

"Morning," my father said.

"Two?" the boy asked.

"Two what?" my father asked.

"Two tags. Today's red. You can buy a week's ticket—that's a green. The blue tag was yesterday."

Out of the corner of my eye I saw my father smile. It was a smile I knew. The kid seemed to understand it also. He wrinkled his nose, which was pink and peeling from the sun, and put a hand up to shade his eyes.

"Do you own this beach?" my father asked.

"Mister . . ." the boy started.

"I was already on this beach this morning. You didn't own it then. Or maybe you own the sunlight. Is that it?"

"Mister, I'm just working here. Everyone has to pay. Jenkins owns it, not me."

"You really believe this man Jenkins has the right to own a beach?"

"Dad," I said, "I'll pay. Let me use the money you gave me."

"That's not the point, Max," he said quickly. "I may even pay this young man myself if he gives me a good enough reason. But I want to know first why he thinks he, or anyone else, can own a beach."

The kid dropped the umbrella he was holding and walked

32

squarely behind the table. He was well built. His ribs had small lines of gristle at the very top, a webbing of muscle that kept his solar plexus sharp and visible.

"You have to pay, mister. You can argue all you want, but you have to pay. If not, I get the cops."

"Get the cops then."

"You don't think I will?"

"You might. But you'll remember it a long time if you do."

It was such a curious thing to say that it stopped the boy. He looked again at my father. My father stared at him for a moment longer, then pulled me softly by the arm onto the sand. There was nothing triumphant in what my father did. He was very solemn.

"Dad, did you have to make such a big deal out of it?" I asked as soon as we were out of earshot.

"Was I right?"

"I don't know. But why'd you have to take it out on that kid? He didn't deserve that."

"If he works for the man who pretends to own it, then he does. Think of it, Max. If there's a storm and the ocean whips up and wipes out the boardwalk, do you think this Jenkins is responsible?"

"No."

"Then he obviously doesn't own the beach, does he? If someone drowns here, can he sue him? Of course not. The most he can own is access to the beach, and even that's debatable."

I was too tired to argue with him. I shook my head and spread out the sleeping bag. The sun was warm. I took off my shoes and stretched out. My father sat down beside me and read the paper.

I'm not sure how long I slept before I heard voices. I knew at once what they were. I looked up to see a policeman standing over my father, his blue uniform out of place on the beach. A ring of children had followed the policeman and now stood ten feet behind him, their feet digging listlessly into the sand.

"Two dollars," the policeman said.

"But you haven't answered me."

"You don't get it. I don't have to answer you. That's not my job."

"Why isn't it your job? A law is only an answer to a question."

33

"Come off it, mister. Who the hell do you think you are? You Perry Mason or what? You want to come to the beach, you pay two dollars. You don't want to, don't."

"That's a wonderful argument . . . very forceful."

"And don't get smart. You've got a boy here. Either pay for him or take him out of here."

I turned my head away and closed my eyes. More than anything I wanted my father to be quiet. I thought of the money in my pocket but knew I could never use it.

"Listen," the policeman said when my father didn't move or answer, "is this really worth getting arrested for?"

"You tell me. Is it worth the law's time to arrest me?"

"Oh, Jesus, you're something. Kid, hey, kid, wake up. Can you do anything with your old man here?"

I rolled over onto my back and sat up. The sun was very bright now. I saw a yellow flicker of sunlight on the policeman's black shoe.

"We should go, Dad," I said.

"There, see?" the policeman said. "Listen to your son. He's making sense."

My father looked at me, then stood and began rolling up the sleeping bag. I folded his newspaper and put it under my arm. He put his pants over his shoulders, the legs dangling like the straps of a parachute.

We walked off the beach ahead of the policeman. The children went off to play. My father stopped at the entrance and put two dollars on the table. His glasses caught the light and flashed for an instant. He smiled at the kid manning the entrance, then walked slowly up the stairs. He waited for me at the top and put his arm over my shoulders when I got there.

❖❖ 6 ❖❖

IT WAS only a week or two later that my father took
up his summer project. I had no idea, when he started,
how this move would affect me. I watched him as he paced the
perimeters of our yard, stopping occasionally to hammer wooden
posts into the ground, slowly stringing twine in a neat grid across
the lawn. He concentrated when he worked, and I watched without speaking, content to follow his thick arms flexing, his brown
hair blowing, all the while trying to unravel the meaning of his
movements.

He worked one solid day, and at the end of it he had a plot of
land carefully charted. I'm not sure what I thought the plot
signified. Perhaps, like most of the neighbors, I assumed my
father meant to put in a garden. It would have been a large
garden, too large for only the two of us. Yet there was something
else, something exotic about the plot of land that suggested
grapes or figs, perhaps a small bottling plant in our cellar where
we would put up the first of the New Jersey chablis. It was not
impossible—my father was handy.

In the evening of that first day my father gathered me into our
station wagon, and we drove downtown. We parked in the municipal lot and climbed out.

"Over here, I think," my father said. We walked off toward the stores.

"What are we getting?"

"You'll see."

We walked into the Old Colonial Stationery Shoppe. The store smelled of paper and pencil shavings. It was crowded with paper —folders, reams of mimeograph paper, three-by-five cards, note-books, writing pads, address books. My father seemed too large for the room. His jacket carried the scent of the outdoors.

The woman who waited on us knew my father. She was old, too old for him. She wore bifocal glasses that severed her eyes when she looked at me. She called my father Mr. Darrigan and asked a few questions about the high school. Perhaps she expected a large order—graph paper for his algebra class, stacks of master carbons—but she showed no surprise when he asked to see her ledgers.

"Leather or paper-bound?" she asked.

"Leather, please."

We spent a considerable time looking at ledgers. There was a fine selection, although the pages looked much the same. The more sophisticated versions had lines in red and blue, but that was the only difference I saw. My father finally chose a beautiful book covered in green leather.

We paid and left. The woman walked us halfway to the door, then let us go. I was curious, of course, to know the meaning of the ledger, but it was obvious my father wanted to keep it a secret. I knew from experience I couldn't pry him open. He would tell me when the time came.

I didn't have to wait long. The next morning he was up early. I heard him in the kitchen, the light still weak outside, as he knocked a fry-pan against the metal grill of the range. I heard the refrigerator door open and shut, open and shut, and I smelled bacon and the slightly rancid odor of frying eggs.

I dressed quickly and went downstairs. He had just finished turning an egg when I came in, the spatula dangling from his hand, a tiny fleck of yolk bright yellow against the chrome of the blade. He wore an old pair of blue jeans and a green plaid flannel shirt. He whistled and winked when he saw me.

"Did I wake you?" he asked. His voice was soft.

"No, I was getting up. What's going on?"

"You'll see."

He put breakfast on the table, and we ate without speaking. The bacon was underdone, and I took this to be a signal: Something was about to happen, and we couldn't wait for bacon. I spotted the ledger on an empty chair in the dining room. A square white sticker was glued to the front cover. My father had written something across it, but I couldn't see what it was from where I sat.

We finished quickly. I had already assumed his pace, though I still had no idea where we were going with such energy. He didn't wash the dishes. He set them in the sink and ran water over them until they sank from sight.

"Come on," he said, slipping his glasses on and leading me out of the house.

He went to the garage and rolled open the door. Dust pinged against the steel bumper of the station wagon. The door was hardly opened before my father began pulling down rakes and hoes, stacking them in a neat pile in the corner. He grunted as he lifted the wheelbarrow down, and he had to press himself against the fender of the car in order to wrestle it out to the light.

"Run in and get the ledger, will you?" he asked me.

I ran and brought it back to him. By the time I returned, the tools were arranged in the wheelbarrow. He put the ledger on top and lifted. He rocked the wheelbarrow over the tiny curb of the driveway, then rolled it down the gentle slope of the back-yard. We passed Honey's pitcher's mound and ducked under the clothesline. The wheelbarrow gradually gained momentum, and he jogged behind it, laughing.

"Know what we're doing yet?" he asked when the yard leveled off.

"No, not exactly."

"This is going to be a dig. An archaeological dig."

"What are we looking for?"

"Odds and ends. Something. Actually there's a good chance there was a colonial dump around here. I know this was once farm country, and I think they used some of the flatter lands for disposal. Anyway, dumps can be very interesting. But really, who knows? We'll probably just find enough to keep us interested. There's always the slim chance we'll strike it rich and find some dinosaurs. You never really know what's underneath you until you look. Everything else is just so much theory."

He plucked the ledger from the wheelbarrow, then dumped the tools on the grass. He knelt and wrote a note in the ledger, his leg squared for a desktop. I sat behind him in the empty barrow and waited.

In time he looked up.

"You ready, Max?"

"Sure."

He stood and pushed the wheelbarrow to the southeast corner of the plot. I carried a hoe. He stretched a piece of chicken wire over the wheelbarrow, then used an edger to cut a perfectly square piece of sod. He lifted the sod like a scalp and put it on top of the chicken wire.

"Shake it through," he told me.

"How?"

"Here, watch."

He rubbed the sod along the chicken wire, grating it like some rich cheese. The grass crumbled apart, but the thick roots tangled around the wire filter until he was obliged to push them through with his fingers. Nothing foreign appeared. It was a suburban cross section, a simple swatch of grass.

"There, like that," he said.

"What are we looking for?"

"Whatever there is."

And so the pattern was set. It was our first entry: "Square one, SE corner, A1, level 4 inches: Westfield, New Jersey." The soil under the grass was black and rich. A few worms turned at the light, sinking like U nails back into the ground.

We uncovered the entire plot that day, though we went no deeper than four inches. We worked quietly, seriously, our movements becoming refined. We might have set out a fine garden, but my father was interested in removal, not production. He scrupulously recorded our three finds: a comb, the nozzle off the power mower, and a tiny silver hand from a watch. He liked the watch hand best of all. It was made of metal, and neither of us had a clue to its origin. He examined it for some time, clicking his tongue, squinting at it, before finally giving it to me to put in the shoebox we used to hold our samples.

We put the tools away at last light. I went to bed early and read for a while. Alone in my room, I smelled the scent of earth riding on the spring air. I imagined the dirt as a drum skin, and I pictured dinosaurs beneath it, rolling slowly, sometimes cresting on the flat patch of dirt until their backs pushed up and through, their spines large knots of bone that would catch and hold my father like the gears of an ancient machine.

❖❖ 7 ❖❖

DURING the next week or two, with my friends at camp or off on vacation, I worked with my father. It was good work, and fun to be with him. He put me on a small salary and made me keep short but regular hours. I enjoyed packing our lunch out like miners, wheeling the tools through the early dawn. I liked having my father to myself. I liked being near him.

In July we carried a picnic bench to the dig and lowered it in to use as a step. With the bench something changed. The dig was no longer casual, no longer a place we came to without expectations. We were traveling and we both knew it.

We found things along the way. Sifting through the dirt, grating some of the soil across the screen set against the wheelbarrow, we came across minuscule finds. They were rarely exceptional, yet they were enough to keep us interested. We found several coins, a hairpin, a metal fork tine, and a cache of bullet shells evidently emptied from a rifle all at one time. Once we found part of a doll's leg, and another time a tin soldier. These were momentous occasions, and my father and I worked harder afterward. The finds convinced us that small children had been raised here, and my father promised to do research on the house's history when the weather became too cold to dig.

Honey watched. She mistrusted the dig, and her observation was not innocent. It grew increasingly concerned as we went deeper. I tried, whenever I could, to head off their exchanges. I wasn't positive why I felt the need to protect my father, but I was certain of Honey's disapproval when she clucked her tongue at the sample boxes and refused to look inside them. She was exact. She was a measure against which my father's behavior would eventually be judged, and I attempted to keep them apart. I was an ambassador to both parties, soothing each one in turn, explaining the other's position even when I did not fully understand it myself.

My father, however, was only too willing to explain any aspect of the dig to her, and I grew uneasy each time he went into an explanation, knowing that he was simply confirming Honey's opinion of the entire project. Her questions were traps. Although they were not maliciously set, they were still anchored to solid sense, a practical vision of the world my father could not accommodate.

"Just tell me when you're going to stop." She always interrupted when he began to talk about the dig. "The rest is a bunch of malarkey."

"It's not malarkey, if you'd just listen."

"Tell me what you've found."

"You know what we've found. You've asked Max . . . hasn't she, Max?"

"Don't bring him into it. He's just going along with you. Tell me what you've found."

"Odds and ends."

"Odds and ends. You've moved this mountain of dirt for some odds and ends? You're telling me that's sensible."

"I never said sensible."

"At least you admit that. All I'm asking is for a finish date. You tell me that and I'll leave you alone. You can dig to China for all I care."

"It depends on too many elements. I can't tell you when I'll call a halt. I can't predict it."

41

"Well, I can predict one thing, Mr. Darrigan: The police will shut you down. You don't have a license or anything else. If the police don't shut you down, I will. That isn't a threat; it's a promise."

During July our dig began to draw some attention. I'm positive Honey had nothing to do with it, although I'm equally sure it was she who eventually called Uncle Jack and Aunt Gertrude and asked them to intervene. No, the attention was a simple thing. It might have started the day Bob Marrone, our next-door neighbor, stopped by to examine our work. He said he and his wife had been watching for weeks, and they both had to hand it to us—digging a pool by hand was quite a project.

Or perhaps the attention might have started with my father, when he mentioned the dig to a fellow teacher or to a student, who in turn told another and another. Westfield was not large, and it wouldn't have taken much to begin a rumor.

Either way, it was in early August that the news finally spread to the *Westfield Leader*, our local paper. The *Leader* was primarily concerned with the latest sales and real estate values around town. It also included a small editorial section, and every week there were one or two articles about leaf-burning ordinances, dump regulations, zoning restrictions, or school-crossing safety improvements. Stan Smith organized the page and also wrote the "Chatter Column." The "Chatter Column" was a scratching post for suburban news. In it he mentioned the horsy brides who stared out from their engagement photos, the birch-breasted women of such and such a club, the Junior League, the PTA, the PTO, the teachers' union, and the garbage pickup. To appear in Stan's "Chatter Column" was a dubious honor. It was the first thing people turned to when they received the paper, all of them hoping to find a friend in mild disgrace, news of divorce, lechery, some failing.

Stan visited our dig in early August and stayed only a half hour. He wore a brown suit that seemed, even to me, too heavy for the summer weather. When he climbed down onto the picnic bench, he removed his jacket and carried it cradled over his arm.

I remember this most distinctly: He wore wing tips, and the soles of his shoes made no mark. I was accustomed to seeing my father's boot tread, my own sneaker pattern, as they wove together over the soft dirt, but Stan passed unmarked over the floor of our pit.

"What have you found so far?" he asked as he moved around the dig, his eyes scanning the walls. He stopped and squatted next to my father, who was examining a hole we had just excavated.

"Not too much," said my father. "Just bits and pieces of things."

"And what are you looking for exactly?"

"Oh, nothing exactly. The past . . . it isn't that specific, you see."

Stan Smith stood and smiled. I didn't like the look of him, and I wished my father could explain himself better.

Stan stayed a little longer, then made some polite excuse when my father offered to show him our samples. I was pleased Stan refused to look. I knew he had not taken us seriously, and I couldn't avoid looking at us through his eyes, to see my father's clothes, his dirty nails—to see both of us diving in day after day, paddling with shovels deeper and deeper into my father's project.

I didn't blame Stan Smith. He needed copy, and besides, I don't know what else he might have said. That we were making scientific history? That, barring all else, we were at least constructing something, anything—a pool, a root cellar, a bomb shelter?

No. What he said, softly, with reasonable kindness, was that my father was a crackpot. Stan made no attempt to see any real virtue in the dig. It wasn't interesting, he said, precisely because there was little chance we'd find anything of interest. In addition, he pointed out that it was a safety hazard, a public menace —something about contaminating the water table—and a futile way for one of the high school's most respected teachers to spend his summer.

My father's reaction frightened me. He said almost nothing when he read the article. I realized, watching him, that he was beyond being touched by ridicule.

But the article wasn't dismissed so easily by others. Honey took it up and made a point of asking my father about it.

"What did I tell you? You better fill in that hole pretty soon, Mr. Darrigan," she said. "Folks are starting to talk."

"Let them."

"It's no way for a boy to spend a summer . . . down in a hole like that."

"He's getting paid. Besides, Max doesn't mind, do you, Max?"

"No, it's okay."

"It's a mistake," Honey said.

"Rest it awhile, will you, Honey?"

Once, after the article had appeared, Zeke came by with Honey. He didn't say anything except to make some excuse about walking Honey into town. But I knew Zeke well enough by then to see a look of confusion in his eyes. He paid attention when my father spoke to him, even pretending some interest, but I noticed his eyes kept ranging to me.

Other people took up the article in different ways. Some high school students began sneaking into our yard late at night and burying things. The first time this happened my father was ecstatic. He thought we were on to something as a skeleton began to take shape six feet down. It was a fragile bone structure, and my father spent an hour one morning working it slowly free, dusting it with his brush, blowing on it to remove the silt. Twice he mentioned to me that we might need to call someone, to get hold of an expert who could give us the proper means of handling the extraction.

He cried when he found the box top carefully buried beneath the skeleton. The bones were from a local Kentucky Fried Chicken. They had been stripped of all their meat by chemicals, then smashed to provide some intrigue. My father had all the bones out and was fitting them together when he discovered the corner of the Kentucky Fried Chicken box top. He pulled the box up slowly, dusting it for the barest instant as if this, too, might be a find; then he pushed it behind his leg and tried to hide it from me. But he cried softly, gently, the kind of crying that only heavy work and disappointment can draw out of one, and his voice locked when he asked me to run up to the garage for a garden trowel.

When I returned, the skeleton was gone. We never spoke of it again.

The hours he spent in the pit increased. Our meals were hasty and poorly prepared. Sometimes Honey came and spent most of the day in the kitchen, cooking up dishes we needed only to re-heat, baking pork and chicken pies, forcing us to interrupt our work in order to take a decent meal. I normally made an excuse to get away from the dig when she was there. It was starting to bore me. We found so little that I couldn't maintain an interest. Our finding nothing had just the opposite effect on my father. It made him more frenzied, more productive. It had gone out of proportion.

I talked to him once about it shortly after Stan's article had appeared. It was at the end of the day, and we both were tired. My father sat on the picnic bench, eating a grapefruit, and the smell of the juice, the sight of him thinking quietly made me feel nostalgic and empty. I realized then that I had had enough. I wanted us to stop.

"Leaves will start to turn in a few weeks," I said. I sat down next to him. He passed me a slice of grapefruit, but I shook my head.

"It's getting colder. It will be fall soon," he said.

"Do you think it's time to stop now?"

"For the night? Or forever?"

"I thought forever."

"You don't enjoy the work anymore?"

"It's not that, Dad. We're not finding that much, that's all. I guess I think it's sort of over."

"What are you trying to say? You want to stop? Is that it?"

"Yes."

He patted my thigh. When he saw his hand left a small stain on my blue jeans, he tried to wipe it off. He only managed to smudge it more, so he finally patted my thigh again.

"It probably is time you stopped, Max. School's almost here. You've hardly had a chance to be with your friends."

"How about you?"

"Oh, I'll probably go on a little longer. I have a theory we're just about down to a good level."

"Maybe you should stop, too. Maybe we should just call it quits."

"Oh, just a little farther, I think. But you go ahead. I've loved working with you so long. I don't think I could have at your age."

He was very calm. He smiled at me. Then he said something

curious. "Who is going to spot the birds for me? How will I remember to look up?"

He put his arm around me and pulled me close. I felt the roughness of his hands, the heat of his body. He kissed my forehead, squeezed me for a moment; then he let me go.

❖❖ 8 ❖❖

IN THE next few weeks my father's efforts tripled. He
felt the pinch of autumn approaching and even talked
of ways to cover the pit. Throughout it all he never tired. He was
possessed of enormous energy, tremendous vigor. He drifted in
and out of the house, dirty, always dirty, his hands rubbed sore
and red from tools, his hair unkempt, his eyes glassy and intensely
aware. He glowed during those days; his eyes glowed during the
afternoons, glowed through the evening and into the first real
darkness as he talked of the dig, showed me samples, wired lamps
in order to see better, longer. I recall his chest heaving, his
breath, and his desire to take it all in, too impatient, too demanding.

The kitchen table was his office, and he stayed there into the
night, the moth beat his company, the lights around him harsh
and hot. Some mornings I found him curled over his ledger, a
small beach of sugar spilled near his forearm. Other mornings he
would already be out, his shirt off, his grunts growing more and
more serious as he approached the depth of his own height.

It was Honey, out of love for me, who made him pause. She
knew I was neglected, though I doubt she ever held it against
my father. I sustained no injury. In fact, I gained weight and

PART ONE

muscle that summer, and I slept well, knowing my father was
there, always up and about to protect me. No, it was merely that
Honey saw what I had seen some time before: There was no
room for me in my father's obsession.

Honey called Uncle Jack, and that, as she knew it must, began
a series of visits, consultations, and arguments. Jack was my
father's older brother, and he lived with his wife, Gertrude, near
Stockton, New Jersey.

The first time Jack visited the dig he tried to jolly my father
out of continuing. Uncle Jack was subtle to a point, and he
followed my father down into the trench, showing some mild
interest, bending with him to inspect an unusual rock, the hole
that had once held a bone, an arrowhead, smiling and slapping
my father on the back, saying over and over, "Isn't that something?"

But they knew each other too well for it to go on. Uncle Jack
finally grew bored, and he began a quick interrogation that made
my father uncomfortable.

"You going to fill it in when school starts?"

"No, I don't think so. It's becoming more interesting."

"Ahhh, sure you are. What do you want to keep on with it for?"

"Why not?"

"Why?"

"I asked you first."

"Now, don't be silly. What good is a hole in your yard? Fine,
I'm glad it kept you occupied for a summer . . . you schoolteachers
have a racket. But, tell me, when is it going to end? You've got
a few people worried around here."

"Who?"

"Honey, for one. And look at Max. He looks like a graverobber."

"He's all right."

"Ahh, you say. What about him? Max, you think your dad
should fill this in?"

I didn't speak, but I knew what my answer would have been.
It would have been "Yes, fill it in, cover it up." I was tired of dirt,
tired of hearing my father's shovel, tired of seeing the intent look
on his face. Most of all, I was frightened of the atmosphere surrounding the house, the slow dread that deepened beside him in

48

the pit. I wanted to tell him to return, to come back before he went too far.

Uncle Jack read me and climbed wearily out of the pit. It required a ladder now, and he pushed his knees down with his hands, climbing slowly, his pipe burning in his mouth. I expected to see him angry, but he wasn't flushed at all. He appeared sad and serious.

"How deep then?" he asked when he gained the top, turning back to watch my father climb out. "When will it be enough?"

"I don't know."

"That's a hell of an answer."

"It's the only one I have."

Uncle Jack shook his head and knocked out his pipe on the heel of his shoe. A second later he blew through the stem, and the pipe made a loud, liquid sound.

"You know," he said to my father, "this is going beyond seeming crazy. It's starting to be crazy."

"Well, I can't help that."

"Sure you can. Of course you can."

Uncle Jack stepped forward and began pushing dirt into the pit. He stooped over and shoved rapidly, hands locked together like a plow. My father moved toward him, but Uncle Jack stopped and slapped his hands together.

"That's all there is to it. You stop, you fill in the dirt, you get this boy a haircut, you clean your house, you get ready to teach, and you cut out this crazy business. See? It's that easy. I don't want someone in my family going crazy. Not my brother, not me, not anyone I know, understand?"

To Uncle Jack's credit, that evening was the only time he lost his temper. The other times he visited—and it was often in the days before school began—he spoke calmly, watching my father sharply for new signs of instability. He never went near the pit, but I know Honey kept him informed of its progress. I suppose he didn't want to acknowledge the pit, thinking, perhaps, that if he ignored it, my father might follow his example. Still, he listened to my father talk of it, only now and then attempting to turn him back to reason.

I didn't know what arrangements were made between Honey

49

and Uncle Jack, but I knew I was to be taken away. I was not frightened by the prospect. My father was retreating, going each night to a more distant past of his imagination, and I understood he needed time to find his way back. I accepted the decision as a mature approach to the situation, and I confess to having felt a little pride that I took the verdict so well. It made me feel older to understand something about my father he did not understand himself. I never doubted he would straighten out once school began.

"Uncle Jack is taking you out to the country," Honey told me. "At least for a little while, until this all settles down."

"When will I come back?"

"In a while. Probably for school."

Honey finished packing. Suddenly she hugged me. We stood for a long count in the center of the room, her weight rocking me gently. It had been some time since she had held me so tightly. Afterward she let me go and touched my hair.

"Max?" she said as I started out of the room.

"What?"

"Don't hold this against your daddy, you follow me? It just happens this way sometimes."

"All right, Honey."

"And, Max? It isn't God's fault either."

That night my father came to my room and woke me. The edge of my bed went down, and then he was there, sitting quietly, his muddy fingers black against the turned-down sheet. I smelled him, smelled the grass stains on his cuffs, the wild night scent on his sleeves whenever he moved. There was only a little light from the hallway, but it was enough to see by, enough to watch his hand raise as if to comb back my hair.

"Come on, Maxy," he said.

He stood nearby while I slipped on my baseball jacket. I pulled my jeans on over my cotton pajama bottoms.

"Ready?" he asked.

"Yes."

We went outside. It was a beautiful night. Stars were up, the trees were thick, and the white rail fence that bordered our yard was a perfect boundary. Nothing would come over it, and I had a feeling of safety, of quiet.

50

"Jack picking you up tomorrow?" asked my father.

"I guess."

"Well, well."

In silence we climbed down the ladder. I felt my father everywhere—behind me, beside me, his breath warm nearby. We stood for a moment without moving; then he leaned past me and pulled the ladder away from the wall. He lifted it and carried it to the southeast corner, almost directly across from where it had been. Some dirt crumbled away as he propped it against the wall. He whistled to me when he was sure it was solidly wedged.

I went to him. He took my hand and squeezed it.

"I want you to climb up and look at the wall there. Go ahead," he said when I hesitated. "I found something the other day. I wanted you to see it."

I stood on the bottom rung and looked at the blank wall. I couldn't see much in the dark, but then my father flashed a small light at a hollow just to the right of the ladder.

"What is it?"

"Look and see."

I climbed another rung, then leaned to my right. I had to reach in almost to my elbow. My fingers brushed something wooden, but there didn't seem to be any way to take it out, no way to tell what it was.

"What is it?"

"It'll come out. Just keep at it. I didn't see it myself at first."

I put my eye near the hole and tried to look in, but my head blocked the light whenever I looked, so I was obliged to reach in again with my hand. This time I got my fingers over the edge of what felt like a box. I pulled it toward me.

The front end slipped out and the entire thing would have fallen if my father hadn't reached up to block it.

"Do you see it?" he asked. He was very excited.

"What is it?"

"It's an old wooden box—probably used for flour. A child must have hidden it. There's a diary inside, a pack of cards, and a tin soldier a great deal like the one we found . . . other odds and ends. I'm guessing, but I bet a boy buried it. Maybe he buried the diary and held it ransom over his sister."

He opened the box. I bent close to him, watching his hands

51

sift through the contents, his muddy fingers somehow recalled to sensitivity.

"We dug right past it. It was at one and a half feet, just outside the G three grid square, almost exactly where you found the penknife. I saw it the other day when I was planing off the walls."

"It's a diary?"

"I think so."

He rocked back on his haunches and laughed aloud. I laughed with him, not knowing why or what else to do. When we stopped, he looked at me seriously.

"Remember we found something, okay?" he said.

"I will."

"You might need to."

"All right."

He walked me back inside, carrying the box under his arm. We didn't say anything at all.

❖❖ 9 ❖❖

UNCLE JACK smoked pipes. He wore corduroy. He was a businessman, though he reminded me a great deal of my father. He was vague and dreamy; his presence in the house was very soft.

He was also something of a dandy. He wore his hair combed back, the lowest strands just nipping the sharp crease of his oxford collars, and he had a shiny, fine forehead that flexed and danced when he chewed. He paid me a quarter to do his shoes and even went so far as to have an automatic buffer installed in the bottom of the closet. Every morning he stood, fully dressed, extending one foot forward to the buffer, a look of contentment on his face. Then, lightly, he switched feet, his lips moving silently as the furry buffer ran up and down his laces, while Gertrude, getting dressed herself, shook her head and put on her practical clothing.

Gertrude countered Jack's vagueness with her own practicality, her own agenda of window washing, table decorating, and putty scraping. Their house was never completely finished. It was always in a state of flux—first a new paint job for the living room, then a new wallpaper for the upstairs bedroom. The furniture, stripped and refinished time and time again, took on a certain historical interest. Peeling away lacquer and varnish, Gertrude counted her own years on table legs and seat backs.

It was Gertrude who held the house together. Often I thought that she was the element missing in my father's life. With her, or someone like her, there would have been no dangerous edges, no soft margins. She was constant and sure, orderly without being too occupied with cleanliness. She prided herself in seeing through things, in calling bluffs, in getting fair prices for fair quality. This was not stinginess, but rather her own respect for shrewdness, for the reality of any exchange. While Jack went to the store and brought back blood oranges, mangoes, and papaya, she followed behind and lined his purchases with walls of beefsteak, pot roast, and chicken legs. Likewise, she took stamps at the counter and pasted them into books, stockpiling large cartons of them before she chose the stainless steel mixing bowls, the garden hose, or the donkey-shaped plant trolley. She knew how to save and budget. She guarded and kept account of Uncle Jack.

I missed my father very much and worried about him constantly, yet I was sure the arrangement was temporary. School, I knew, would bring both of us back. During phone conversations at night he filled me in on the progress of the dig, though I was tentative about asking for details since Jack and Gertrude were normally close by.

Although I was comfortable with Jack and Gertrude, I missed Honey, too, and I was lonely. By the second week in Stockton I spent more and more time by myself. Jack and Gertrude's yard had a small brook running through it. The brook was mossy and filled with rocks, and the air around it was always cool and moist. Trees grew nearby, their roots digging into the bank, and during those late days of summer their branches arched and twined together overhead, creating a leaf cave, a boulevard of quiet and peace. I lay on the bank and read dog books, pausing now and then to think of my father. I stayed purposely away from *The Call of the Wild* and *Where the Red Fern Grows*, trying instead to read new books I might bring back to him.

I also climbed trees. I was too old for it and knew it, but I did it anyway. I staked out various branches and spent entire afternoons clinging to them, sleeping with the branch notched between my shoulder blades, a hand out to a thin twig in order to main-

54

tain my balance. I grew to trust myself in trees, grew to enjoy the sickening feeling of waking in a near fall, clutching for a purchase, my teeth grinding over the knowledge that my own pain was close, that I might fall, break something, and that I had only my animal wits to protect me.

On warm summer nights I liked to slip out of the house to spend extra time in the trees. The first time I was properly prepared. I had loaded up on food, securing caches in different notches, decorating the tree with peanut butter and jelly sandwiches, cheese slices, cookies. That night, when I slipped out and began climbing, I found ants trailing over the food, their line of bodies moving like black veins in moonlight.

On the second night I met Martin.

It had started the same way as the first; only this time I didn't plant food. I went out near nine and ran across the lawn. The stream was only a gurgle in the dark, and I had to navigate slowly, straining to hear the quicker breaks of water, to see the white-skulled rocks. When I reached the tree, I bent close and smelled the bark. I put my nose near a crack and inhaled, breathing in the tree odor and thinking of Honey and the Braille Path, taking in the earth smell and the dampness the tree collected each night from the brook. Afterward I started to climb.

When I reached the top, someone asked, "You the new kid?"

The voice was quiet. I couldn't tell where it came from, so I leaned against the trunk and wrapped my hands together.

"You the new kid?" the voice asked again.

I was near enough to the top of my own tree to see that no one else was in it.

"Who's there?" I asked.

"Over here."

"Where?"

"Over here."

I looked to my right. There, sitting quietly in a second oak, was Martin. He had a pair of binoculars trained on me. He sat on a small platform constructed of two boards placed between branches. I wondered why I hadn't seen them before.

"You the new kid?" he asked once more.

"Yes."

"Your name Max?"

"Yes."

"Your dad go crazy?"

"No."

"That's what Mrs. Darrigan told Tilly, my mother. She said your dad was crazy. My mom wanted me to come over and meet you."

"What are you doing up here?"

"What do you mean, what am I doing up here? I came up here because I saw you go up. Aren't you a little old for climbing trees?"

"Aren't you?"

"Forget it. Did he? Go crazy, I mean?"

Martin swung his binoculars away from me. He scanned the neighborhood.

"He didn't go crazy. . . ."

"Wait a second."

He raised his hand to quiet me. I looked to see what he was watching, but I couldn't make out anything. A wind came up and blew the trees, and I saw Martin swing back and forth, his hair lift and flap across his face.

"I was at camp," he said after a while, putting the glasses on his lap. "I just got back. Marcie got sick, so we all had to come back early."

"Who's Marcie?"

"Marcie's my sister. She's nuts; that's why I asked about your dad. Marcie has an imaginary friend named Wily who drinks tea with her all the time. You've got to be careful of stepping on Wily."

"What are you looking at?"

"Everything. Anything. You never know what you're going to see. Jackie Buck—she's a cheerleader—she lives over there. You wouldn't tell about the binoculars, would you?"

"No."

He said something else, but I didn't hear him. The wind blew a little stronger, and the leaves turned white all around Martin. He pointed to the ground and began climbing down. I noticed he wore the top of a baseball uniform. It was blue and white and had the number 3 on the back.

I climbed down after him. When I arrived on the ground, he was already near the base of his own tree, unwrapping a pack of

56

bubble gum. I saw I was taller than he was. He was short and squat; his shoulders hunched slightly forward. He wore the binoculars around his neck, and his uniform glowed in the dark.

He paused long enough to break off a piece of gum for me, but when I reached for it, he jerked his hand away, then laughed. It was a crazy laugh, contagious and catching, and it was my first glimpse of Martin the wise guy, Martin the card.

"Here," he said a second later. "My brother, Stu, licks the whole pack so he won't have to give any away. He's a muscle man."

"A muscle man?"

"He lifts weights and uses all those machines you get from the back of comics. He's got an atomic chest smasher now. He's stacked."

"Is he strong?"

"He almost killed Bobby Fielder. He got him in a headlock and wouldn't let go. Bobby Fielder's mom wanted to sue my parents because she says Bobby still gets migraines. Bobby came after Stu with a pair of hedge clippers, though, so the suit was called off."

Martin was interesting. He was a talker, and he began the lengthy process of filling me in on the family history. I listened with fascination. Martin was unlike anyone I had met. He had grown up in New York City, and he had a city kid's mentality. His father, Gil, was some sort of computer expert, the type of man who wears vest sweaters and puffy blue shirts and walks around all day in slippers telling people how he quit the rat race. He had made a killing on some technical innovation that no one understood or ever heard of, but it had enabled him to retire and, more important, had enabled him to wrestle away a sort of genius status from everyone who knew him. Gil had moved the whole family out to Stockton, bought a station wagon, put in a woodstove, scattered wood chips in the garden and driveway, and now spent most days with a bow and arrow, playing archery golf.

Stu had a mild case of epilepsy that had not been diagnosed properly. He'd been kept back a year and was in Martin's grade, our grade, although he turned out to be an excellent student. To compensate for being held back, he had turned to his muscles.

He lifted weights twice a day, demanding smaller and smaller shirts from his mother as his muscles increased. He performed odd feats of strength for the kids at school. He could climb anything and often did, showing up outside second-story windows or creeping through the rafters in the gym after swinging with ease up the rope. He bent forks into knots, snapped yo-yos in half, ripped open lockers, lifted "human rafts" of six or seven boys who entwined themselves at his feet, launched bowling balls half the length of the alley whenever he went to the lanes, karate-chopped number two pencils, and tried to get any victim he could in a vicious headlock. He was a bulldog in a fight. He was the local tough, the hero, because he would hang on to his opponent's head though he sustained a severe beating, occasionally glancing up with a crazy wink and squeezing the head a little more.

Marcie was just the opposite. She was like Tilly, a bookish girl who wore stretch pants too high over her round stomach and pulled her fleshy buttocks into two large globes. Her clothes, like Stu's, were always tight. She read constantly and lived in a paper world, yet her love of books had nothing spiritual about it. Seeing her, you had the notion she read to acquire an advantage. Usually she read aloud to Wily, her imaginary friend, and Wily herself was as spooky a concoction as anyone could have invented. Wily —to hear Marcie tell it—was fatter than Marcie herself. Wily ate constantly, stuffing anything she could find into her wide, sullen mouth. Wily was a whiner, a nail biter, a sulking baby; she was, in Martin's vernacular, a "disgusto," a peevish, ignorant brat. Still, Marcie and Wily were inseparable, and it was impossible to organize a game of any sort without including Wily.

Martin was the classic middle child. He wore his baseball uniform to excess, and it was only after I had known him for a month that he admitted it was out of love for Babe Ruth. It was odd to see him give Babe's farewell speech into a pop bottle, his breath wheezy, his face suddenly squashed and porcine, his voice mimicking the loudspeaker echo that the Babe himself had to contend with that day. Then, running, he minced away in Babe's stride, tipping his hat, waving to the crowds up and down the right-field line. Martin seldom relived the Babe's glory days; he was in love with the pathos of the Babe, in love with the gentle decline of the

58

beer-drinking, hotdog-eating, swaggering Babe. When, on rare occasions or on the annual Yankee Old Timers' Day, they showed film clips of the Babe on TV, it was always the final episodes of his life that won Martin's attention. He loved the grand swing and loved, perhaps still more, the even grander misses.

❖❖ 10 ❖❖

MARTIN and I gradually fell into a pattern during the next few weeks. Each day around noon Martin took me to McAfferty's, the local corner store, and ordered from the candy section strange snacks of Fire Bombs, Turkish Taffy, Lick-A-Mades, Pez, Tongue Twisters, rock candy, and Necco wafers. We consumed these meals in Martin's favorite hiding place, the willow, which was, as its name suggests, a large weeping willow positioned near the corner of his yard. It was bare beneath the willow, the earth hard pressed, and Martin had salvaged an old hammock from someone's garbage dump and strung it up between two of the lowest branches. This was his throne, his camp, and he permitted me to hang with him there, our bodies crosswise to the hammock so that our toes and heads dangled while our bellies rested securely in the sarong of material. In the coolness, in the shade, we ate our candy meals, always on the lookout for Stu, always ready to give Marcie a hard time if she appeared, content as two thick-stomached snakes to suck our pops and fizzes, content to talk.

He liked to hear about Honey and the stable, and he liked to hear about my father.

"So he's still digging?" he often asked, pretending interest in my phone call of the evening before but really intent on using this as a way to go back over the summer.

"Until school, anyway," I told him.

"Find anything new?"

"Not that he said."

"You think the box thing is real? Do you? I'd ask him straight out if I was you."

"I think it's real."

"Why didn't he show it to you right away, though?" he asked, his lips folding around another Tootsie Pop. "Why the big hold-up?"

"Maybe he was waiting for the right time."

"The right time is in the middle of the night? He's a little cracked, though, right? You'll admit that, won't you?"

"Maybe a little. I don't know."

Martin frequently persuaded me to admit more than I wanted to admit. He had a manner of asking questions that made it seem as though he were not interested personally but asking for the sake of science or truth—for the sake of the tale. I never felt he was judging my father except as a character in a story, or I would have stopped at once.

There were days when we did not keep the willow to ourselves. Stu came and went as he pleased, even making us hop off the hammock if he chose to stretch out. Usually he was too nervous to rest and instead talked from the tree branches above us, dangling from his knees upside down or snapping off chin-ups, explaining the anatomy of his arm, the flex of his muscles, occasionally squatting before us and making his pectorals jump up and down in rhythm to "My Darling Clementine."

Stu could be harsh. He did not like strangers until he had head-locked them into submission and wrenched from their skulls the obligatory "uncle," so we sometimes had the diversion of following Stu into the street to watch him initiate the newest paperboy. His name must have been famous among the boys who delivered the *Stockton Daily*, because whenever Stu appeared, the new boy seemed to recognize him as if from a wanted poster and began pedaling for his life. Stu, who was as quick as he was strong, took off in pursuit, chopping off the squared edges of corners, gaining on the boy block by block until he finally ran beside the bike, his

61

wild pink tongue clenched in his teeth, calling in his oddly feminine voice, "Stop right now or I'll squeeze your brains onto the lawn."

The boy, terrified, would sometimes try another burst of speed, but Stu would grab the handlebars and begin hopping up and down, digging his heels into the pavement, gradually bulldogging the bike.

"Sorry, sorry, sorry," the kid would say, though he had done nothing wrong, while Stu led the bike slowly off the road.

"Jeez, Stu." Martin would try to intervene, but Stu simply shook his head. Once the bike was settled, Stu tried to force the boy into starting the fight. He insulted the boy, taunted him, stuffed grass down his back until the boy had no choice but to fight back or lose all self-respect. Stu would pounce, leaping and lassoing the boy with his lobster arms, judo-tripping him neatly to the ground. Then Stu's eyes would go bright, his tongue would come out, and he would begin the slow grind, the exquisite exercise in dominance.

"Give?"

"Give what?"

"Do you?"

"Yes."

"Say uncle."

"Uncle."

Stu would let go, and the boy would remain on the grass, the top of his head white, the lower portion red. Stu was kind then, collecting the spilled papers, setting the kickstand straight, sometimes digging into his pocket for a piece of gum for the boy. There was nothing personal in Stu's attacks.

After Stu had left, the boy would get up, holding his head in real pain, and climb onto the bike like an old man. He pedaled away with a deep sadness, while Martin and I returned to the willow to scold Stu within the limits of safety.

Sometimes Marcie was there, kneeling in the dust and serving tea to her imaginary friend, Wily. Martin would grab my arm and hold me outside the drapery of the willow, put his fingers to his lips, and we would listen to Marcie, her voice high and obnoxious, her sentences often containing sweet French phrases she had read somewhere.

"*Voulez-voulez le thé?* Say, *bientôt, n'est-ce pas?*"

Martin would put his hands to his mouth and begin making kissing sounds, finally shaking the tree and saying, "Wily, put your clothes on and go have some tea with Marcie. Go ahead, quit kissing me."

Marcie would screech and Martin would smash through the tree, pelting her with pricker balls as he came. Marcie was Martin's only cruelty, and he couldn't keep from throwing things at her as she hunkered into a lard ball next to her tea table, sniffling and trying to keep her cups straight. It was her softness that triggered his fury, and so, when she sank down, he was compelled to dance closer, to thunk the pricker balls against her that much harder, to kid her about Wily's playing strip poker.

If Martin was Marcie's only enemy, he was also her only real friend. Often his reaction to her was just the opposite, and he would treat her with courtliness, talking freely to Wily, accepting cups of tea, asking Marcie what she had read recently. It was curious to watch, almost unearthly—the two of them, both redheads, sitting on opposite sides of a tiny table, the saucers set for three. Martin was always serious on these occasions, and he never laughed about them afterward. It was as if he understood Marcie's world for brief times, and I wondered if there might not have been a miscarriage between their births, if these teas might not be some sort of memorial to someone they had both met at different times in their mother's womb.

❖❖ 11 ❖❖

M Y FIRST thought on seeing my father was: His hair
is cut.

I remember that much vividly, remember standing in front of
him as he loomed in the kitchen, the light behind him, his hair
too short. He had come for my birthday, and though he had presents in his arms, my attention rested on his hair. It was not because his hair was shorter than normal, but because it had been
clipped as indifferently as one might cut back a hedge.

It would have been an awkward moment regardless of the
haircut. We were jammed together in the kitchen, and the walls
were too bright, the floor too bare, the sunshine too brilliant. My
father turned twice with my presents, looking for a place to put
them down. One finally skidded off the pile and landed on the
floor, making a loud smack against the tile.

He put them on the dishwasher at last. Gertrude and Jack
stepped back, leaving an aisle clear. I knew I was supposed to go
to him, but in that first instant I was too filled with emotion to
know how to go about it. Finally I stepped forward, and he
hugged me, and I hugged him back.

"How are you? How are you?" he kept asking as he let me go

and straightened up, the high cut hair on his neck and around his ears showing too much skin.

"How's the dig?" I asked.

Before he could answer, I heard a car door slam. My father reached forward and pushed me toward the door, nudging me to go ahead. I almost bumped into Uncle Jack, but I sidestepped him and got my first glimpse of Honey standing near Dad's station wagon.

"Come here, sweetheart," she said.

I ran to her. My emotions rushed up, and I was crying before my forehead touched her shoulder. I hadn't known how much I missed her, hadn't remembered her as perfectly as I could have, and now I was shocked to be so near her, to hear her voice saying over and over, "That's all right. It's all right."

She rocked me, squatting to prop herself on the fender of the station wagon, wrapping me in her arms, sighing. She rubbed my hair, then began a laugh deep in her stomach that cheered me at once, rose in me as it rose in her until she pushed me off, stuffing things into my hands.

"Carry this inside now, go ahead. You're the birthday boy, aren't you? Or are you too old for that now?"

Inside, Gertrude had herded my father off to the screened porch at the side of the house. I put the packages on the kitchen table, then went back to Honey.

"My, this is pretty here. It's real pretty, isn't it?" Honey said.

"It's nice."

"You like it here?"

"Is he sick?"

She took one long look at the trees around us, then sighed.

"No, no, darling," she said. "It's just going to be a little while before you can go home. He's having some problems."

"What kind of problems?"

She thumbed back the hair on my forehead. "He's lost a little touch with things, I think. He's not taking care of himself."

"Has he gone to the doctor?"

"No, he won't do that. They're after him to fill in the dig. He's fighting it. But I called a doctor—your Uncle Jack hasn't told you all this?"

"No, not everything. Tell me."

"He's having episodes. Psychotic episodes—at least that's what the doctor said they sounded like. It's a sort of breakdown. He's going to have to pull out of it. He may need help."

"Who cut his hair?"

"He did it himself."

She hugged me again, very tightly, almost as if she could depend on the hug to stop my line of questioning.

"I should be home with him," I said, moving away a little.

"To do what? Max, honey, you can't save him. Believe me, you can't. I'm watching him. I promise you I'll watch him, but he's got to come out of it himself. Or maybe it just has to bottom out somehow. I don't know what will happen. We'll see if school does anything, okay? Hold on until then."

"Is he going to die?"

The actual sound of the question, spoken aloud, came out as a quick, short sob. It caught me unaware. I covered my face but felt the muscles in my cheeks and forehead moving in tiny spasms against my fingers.

Honey didn't say anything. She put her arms around me and held me. She held me until the smell of her dress, the weight of her arms worked their calming effect.

"Is that what you've been afraid of all this time?" she whispered. "Is that what you've been thinking? Oh, honey, he's not dying. He's having a hard time right now, that's all. That doctor I talked to, he said there are lots of people that have things like this. It doesn't mean he's crazy or dying or anything else. He'll be okay. Like I said, it may have to bottom out, it may be painful to watch, but it's just a sickness. Things have piled up on him. He feels lonely, and then this dig came along. It adds up. He needed something else in his life, but this dig wasn't it, and now he's stuck on the idea. He can't pull back, he's gone in too far, and I think he's frightened to stop. But just hold on and keep loving him like you do. You're the best thing in his life right now."

Honey moved me away gently. She nodded, even though I hadn't said anything. She touched my hair again.

"Don't blame yourself, sweetheart. You wouldn't blame yourself if your dad had a cold, would you? Now, use this mirror here, and then we'll go in."

66

I bent to the side mirror on the station wagon and wiped my face. She kept her hand on the small of my back.

When we went in, we found the others had moved out to the picnic table at the side of the house. The sun was already setting, and we sat in a pocket of shadow, Honey suddenly formal, Uncle Jack smoking, Gertrude hovering with lemonade, and my father staring a little too blankly at all of us.

It was my father, of course, we all watched. He was behind everything, a part of each sentence and sip of lemonade. We watched his stiff movements, stared at the thin lines of dirt that had collected in the creases of his hands, felt the tight rub of his shirt around his throat. His attention wavered, although it was obvious he tried very hard to be with us, to remain interested in the flow of conversation around him. He was very animated at moments, then stopped too suddenly, leaving those listening caught on an emotional wave they could not sustain alone. A small, quiet smile rested on his lips. He ate nothing.

The afternoon turned slowly to evening. Uncle Jack told jokes that hung and cluttered the air, while Gertrude could not allow herself to rest. She rushed my birthday cake, bringing it out before we all were quite ready, the candles pale in the last of the sunshine.

"Make a wish," Honey said. "Go ahead. Anything you like."

"You're getting to be an old man, Max," Uncle Jack said. "Fourteen and in high school."

Most of my presents were practical. I received socks and shirts, a pair of school pants, some pencils and pens for class. Uncle Jack came through with four tickets to a Yankees versus Red Sox game. He spent a long time explaining how he'd gotten them, but I didn't follow it. Instead, I watched my father, who pushed three rectangular boxes toward me.

"I don't know if you'll like these," he said. "Honey didn't think, well . . ." he said, then was quiet.

I opened the first package. It was a scale model of a *Brontosaurus*. I smelled glue. Inside, there was a sheet of instructions and a second sheet giving a brief history of the *Brontosaurus*. It was a model for a much younger child.

"You don't have to open the other two. One's a *Stegosaurus*. The other's *Tyrannosaurus rex*. I thought you might . . ."

67

"I like them."

"But you don't love them. Are they too young for you? I didn't know if they were or not."

"No, I'll make them. I will. I've read about them."

"Have you?"

"Yes, in school. I have."

"This whole family's going backwards, huh?" Uncle Jack interjected. "What about the future? Doesn't anyone think of that?"

He meant it as a joke, but nobody laughed. Gertrude ran her fork over the center of her plate, stirring the crumbs without any intention of eating them. Honey began stacking the dishes.

Oddly enough, it was my father who saved us. He took me for a short walk down by the brook, and in the darkness there he found a long, beautiful feather from a blue jay.

"Maxy, get me a firefly," he said, picking up the feather.

I looked at him for a second, then jogged off to a patch of deeper shadow. It only took a minute to catch a firefly, and I brought it back in my cupped hands, careful not to crush it.

"Have it?" he asked.

"Here."

I passed it to him with some difficulty. Our hands cupped each other's. We stood close enough so that I heard the soft pull of his tie and collar as it grated on his neck. When at last he had the firefly, he crushed it in the center of his palm. I wanted to say something, to tell him I hadn't caught it for that, but there was something in his manner that prevented me from speaking.

He took the feather and dipped it into the phosphorus. Then, bending close, he painted the lines of my cheekbones, dabbing softly with the feather, slowly smearing the phosphorus into two small pools.

Without speaking, he finished with the feather and tossed it away, then bent to me and kissed my cheeks. When he stood up, his lips were gold.

❖❖ 12 ❖❖

SCHOOL started and nothing changed. The weather turned early, and it became cold and raw at the beginning of October. Leaves far up in the trees caught the earliest winds and colored soonest, forming a kind of halo. It surprised us when a weather report said the foliage moved south a hundred acres at a time. The season had seemed to come on us tree by tree.

Most evenings I called my father. When I got him on the line, he was frequently vague and distant. His voice drifted in and out, almost as if riding some electrical impulse I could not feel at my end. Then, on other nights, his voice would be charged and full, excited by some new aspect of the dig or by the legal battle that occupied more and more of his time. Twice he asked me about my school, yet never spoke of his own.

It was Honey who told us finally that he had applied for a leave of absence. She did not know the terms and did not know if it had been granted, but she told us he had not gone into the school at all. He hurried now, she said, to go deeper in the dig since the legal question was beginning to haunt him. A court order was expected any day.

Uncle Jack visited him regularly on his trips to New York, attempting each time to win him back to reason. These trips wore tremendously on Jack. He looked tired most of the time. Getting out of the car, he pulled himself up, his hand on the roof, his legs slowly swinging to the ground. Often he sat for a moment before climbing all the way out, his arms disappearing to distant parts of the car to retrieve his briefcase or tap out his pipe. He always closed the car door gently.

On weekends during the first cold weather Jack chopped wood. For me, this was the true sound of my father's descent, the actual pulse of his sinking. The chopping started early in the morning, almost with the sun, and continued on, rising with the light that hit the house and working nearly to a comforting pitch before the final throb of stacking and collecting, preparing for a winter somewhere in the future. Later he came into the kitchen, stamping his thick boots, trampling down the newspaper Gertrude had set out for him, his soles raising page after page until they flapped like bat wings beneath his feet. After pulling off his boots, he slapped his hands together, pounding his work gloves, then threw out a few jabs, starting his sock dance, sparring with air, making quick, foolish passes at Gertrude as she carried food to the table.

"A right, a right, another right," he called, dancing still, his socks too slick for the floor. Gertrude was drawn in, and she made a few half-hearted jabs at his stomach, flicking her lazy knuckles at him while he jumped backward, fending her off easily, raising his voice and lifting his own hand in a victory stance.

"Still undeefeeeeted heavyweight champion of the worllllld."

Finally he sat, his clothes giving off puffs of fresh air; his cheeks were always red and wet, and his sleeves often carried small curds of ice, which dropped on the maple table and melted there.

Gertrude, during that change of season, took it on herself to fix elaborate meals. Each weekend morning we ate a banquet. Uncle Jack ate heartily, digging into whatever was served, pouring out long glasses of milk around the table, while Gertrude jumped up and down, her eye always checking for refills, her spatula constantly at her side.

"Good?" she liked to ask.

"Oh, boy!" Jack said. "Oh, boy, oh, boy, it's delicious. I haven't eaten a breakfast like this since I was a kid. It might change my whole way of life."

"So it's good?"

70

"Oh, boy!"

That was the pattern, and afterward we helped clear, passing our plates under the warm stream of water at the sink, carrying out garbage, capping the milk, wrapping leftovers for the next day. Jack, more affectionate than I had ever seen him, frequently stood behind Gertrude and put his arms around her waist while she dug her hands into the dishwater. He kissed her often on the neck, and I was charmed by Gertrude's subtle turn, her coquettish bend as she accepted the kiss without encouraging more. Jack would turn to me and wink, then back away, holding out his arms, bending slightly at the waist.

"Dance, my dear?"

"Jack . . ."

Once or twice he persuaded her to dance, and she put her dishtowel aside as carefully as if it were an expensive purse, shaking her head all the while, eventually lifting her arms and folding into Jack.

He had no shoes on, so the dance was rocky and sloppy, but there was nevertheless a certain grace, beauty to their waltz. Gertrude's hands dripped suds, and without effort I imagined this to be the long drape of a lace hem. Jack hummed and Gertrude followed, sometimes saying, "Stop, we should stop now," but continuing on, entering the dance bit by bit, swept away by Jack's gentle guidance.

After the dance Jack went out again. I normally went with him unless I had something planned with Martin. I went partially to be near him but also because by working with him, I could hear about my father.

He wasted no time in starting. "Put it up on the block," he would say, and I set up on the stump whatever log he pointed out, then backed off far enough to be safe. Jack tapped the wedge into a crack in the wood, slowly shifting his hands down the ax handle, gradually picking up force and weight until the wedge was driven through into the white meat. Once it was firmly embedded, he stepped back and, in the same motion, began his roundhouse swing. With a combination of wood springing and metal clanging, the log ripped open, hanging sometimes by a string of fiber as the wedge rolled free and thudded with a heavy dullness to the ground.

71

"How's that?" Jack asked, already beginning the rocking again. "Good shot."

"Practice is all. Your grandfather could do this all day."

"Could he?"

"Everyone's grandfather could do it all day. That's the secret, you see? If everyone's grandfather and grandmother could do all the things their children say they could do, then people of our generation ought to go and jump off the nearest cliff. The whole human race is headed downhill, if you believe them."

"You think?"

"Oh, I don't know. I'm just talking. Set up another log, will you?"

This is how I came to know Uncle Jack. I watched as he took pleasure in the physical work, piling wood, his breath curling and heating as the sun rose to midday. On cold days he quit at noon, but on milder evenings he returned to the woodpile, his jacket buttoned tight, his swing less sure, his unevenness causing the wedge to miss and slip. At times, almost unaware of me, he stopped after a particularly poor swing to massage his hands. He flexed them, stretching them, testing the pulls and gaps in his skin, then gripped the handle more tightly. When I helped him put the tools away, I found blood there, cooled yet indelible. I fitted my hand to whatever pattern I discovered, finding in the mesh of my hand and his a tribute to my father, to lineage.

It was near the middle of October, on a weekend evening, when he stopped with me out on the porch after cutting wood. He touched me softly on the arm, and I knew he had something important to say. It was very quiet. I smelled pot roast and potatoes and carrots cooking. Now and then we heard Gertrude stirring, her spoon tinging on a metal pot, and once the oven door opened and closed. Two crows came to pick through the wood chips we had made, their heavy beaks tossing the white slivers in a tiny spray across the grass.

"Max, we may have to commit him," Jack said after a while. He took in his breath very fast.

"He's not hurting anyone," I said, staring at the crows.

Jack didn't speak for a long time. He looked down at his hands, his thumb probing his blisters. I began to cry then, and I couldn't stop myself. I tried to think of ways to defend my father, but it was impossible. I put my hands over my eyes and pressed, but I continued to cry.

"He's hurting himself now," said Jack finally, his voice not quite sure. "He's fighting this legal thing, and he doesn't have a chance. The school's in an awkward position, too. They don't want to fire him, but then, legally, they don't have any real alternative. As it stands, he simply hasn't reported to work."

"Can't they just give him a leave? Can't they just do that? He was the best teacher they had."

"They can. They're sort of doing that right now. But you see, they really need a doctor's certificate, or statement, or something. The principal, Mr. Hunnerson, has been very kind, but you can't expect him to let it go on forever. Your dad didn't give them any warning about this leave, and they were caught without a teacher. You see how it is, Max."

Gertrude came out and stood beside me. She didn't say anything. She put her hand on the small of my back, in exactly the place Honey had held it.

"I was just saying to Max—"

"I know," she said. "I know what you're talking about."

"What would it mean?" I asked, though the voice did not seem to belong to me. A strange buzzing sensation snapped in a quick line across my forehead. Things around me did not quite feel real.

"Well, it would mean that he'd be taken under medical care."

"And you'd stay right here with us. Don't ever worry about that, Max. We want you here."

"This isn't my home," I said, and was instantly ashamed of it, though I couldn't control my voice to explain.

"I know it isn't," Gertrude said. "It never will be. I know that, and Jack knows that. Your home is with your dad. But for now, just for now, we want you here."

Her hand moved on my back. I knew this had been prepared. I knew Uncle Jack had searched for that phrase about medical care long before he had ever said it to me, and it disturbed me that the spiral my father followed could be so predictable.

"What does Honey think?" I asked after a little while.

"She thinks it's time."

"Could I see him once before it happens? I might be able to talk to him."

They looked at each other. Jack started to say no, but Gertrude cut him off.

"It's his father," she said.

"But he's not himself, Max. You have to remember that," Jack said. "It's not fun anymore, what he's doing. It isn't pleasant."

"All right. I understand."

"I hope you do."

The conversation had no place to go. Gertrude touched me again and went inside. Jack and I stood for a little while longer, watching the crows hunt for insects.

❖❖ 13 ❖❖

I WAS STANDING close to the dig when my father
came out.

"Max, there you are," he shouted.

He hurried over and hugged me quickly. I noticed at once that
he had tried to clean himself up for my visit. He had on a fresh
flannel shirt, and his hair was washed. His khakis were dirty, but
they were no worse than they might have been in the old days.
He looked like a teacher, like a man dressed to putter in his yard.

"Where's Jack?" he asked. "Didn't he just drop you off?"

"He had some things to do," I said, lying. "He'll be back around
nine or so."

"Well, what do you think? Is it getting impressive, or what?"
he asked, nodding at the dig.

I didn't say anything at first. I couldn't quite grasp how far he
had gone. As many times as I had tried to prepare myself, as often
as I had listened to Uncle Jack's accounts, I had never pictured
the yard in such a state of destruction. My memory of it had
stopped with my time there. I had never pictured the dig continuing, its gradual expansion and possession of the yard.

Even now it was hard to take it in. The dig seemed an actual
force, a suction that drew everything toward it. The surrounding

grass, high and uncut, appeared to be the only thing fighting against its gravitational force. The bushes near the back of the house leaned outward, almost as if their roots had been undermined. They seemed ready, at any moment, to let go entirely, to leave the house and follow the natural pull. A block of sidewalk had chipped and broken, and it reminded me of films I had seen of earthquakes or some sudden wrenching in the earth. It warned of disaster, of peril, and the image was enhanced by three yellowed *Westfield Leader*s lying nearby.

A rainstorm had caved in one side of the dig, and dirt stretched in a long tongue across the floor. Nothing of the early orderliness remained. The square shape of the dig had bowed and flexed; the sides had lost their plumb, and one now angled sharply inward, the slope as steep as a pyramid. The ladder was gone. Now, it seemed, my father entered on the crest of the crumbled side like a surfer or skier, the dirt loose and scrabbling under his feet, the descent a glide and a stumble.

"It's caving in," I said after a moment.

"I know. I'll have to get some timber to shore it up, but right now I'm in this damn legal battle. We'll see. But you're right, it needs some work."

"Are you finding anything?"

"You won't believe it."

"What is it?"

"Wait and see. I have lunch ready. What do you say we go for a little ride? Just like old times?"

He nodded twice before I said anything; then his hand touched my shoulder. His fingers were very gentle, and he rubbed me softly, almost as if combing back a cowlick or smoothing away questions of any kind.

"Sure," I said.

"It's such a day. What do you say we go for a picnic? We can go to the Magical Forest. How would that be?"

"Great."

"Okay then, we're set."

There was an awkward moment before I realized the car was packed, the picnic already waiting in the back. But my father made no motion to get in. Apparently he was willing to let me decide the course of the day.

76

"Should we go then?" I asked.

"Sure, sure, I was waiting for you. Whatever you say."

Finally we climbed in and started up New Providence Road. There were no grapefruits by my seat, but the tapes were still on the console. I looked them over quickly.

"Nothing new," my father said, only, it seemed, to fill the silence. "We need some new books, though, don't we?"

"I read one just a few weeks ago. It was about a dog named Kazan or something. He belonged to a Mountie."

"Those are the best kind. Anytime you have a Mountie in a story, you've got something."

He reached across and slapped my knee. He left his hand there. We passed the Children's Country Home and followed signs for Summit.

"Now tell me, how's school?" he asked as we crossed Route 22 and headed up past Our Lady of Lourdes. "You enjoying it?"

"It's okay. I like it."

"They giving you any of that new-kid stuff?"

"No, not too bad. They know I know Stu."

"Tell me about those guys. You like them a lot, don't you?"

He looked at me and smiled. His hand pressed my knee. It surprised me that he would remember who Stu was, who the Kellermans were.

And so I told him. I told him about Uncle Jack and Aunt Gertrude, about Martin, about Marcie and Gil and Tilly. He listened very carefully, asking intelligent questions, connecting ideas rapidly and correctly. As we climbed higher in the mountains, passing the turnoff for Overlook Hospital, then the Trailside Museum, I felt better and better. I talked for five or ten minutes, filling him in on everything that had happened. He explained a little about the dig, but not too much. When he spoke of it, he seemed very much in control, very cautious. I was aware that the conversation consisted as much of what was avoided as what was said, yet it didn't disturb me. Each time he came accurately back to the subject, each time he treated the dig with sufficient detachment, I collected the statement and held it.

Near Berkeley Heights we were caught in a line of traffic heading for a football game. The car ahead of us was covered with crepe paper and pompoms, and two or three cheerleaders hung out the windows, yelling at the car in front of them. A car honked behind us, then gave up. One cheerleader jumped out of the car and circled it, then climbed back in, her skirt momentarily swirling, her saddle shoes flashing white in the sunlight.

We sat for a few minutes, then moved very slowly. The road was lined with trees, all at their peak. A huge maple stood bright red above us, and deeper in the woods we saw pale birches, their leaves gone, their barks stark and white against the dark forest floor.

We intersected with the band at a side street. The Berkeley Heights band, called the Highlanders, wore kilts and tartan caps. They had a bagpipe brigade, and it was this we heard as we came across them.

"Roll down your window, quick," my dad said.

There were six bagpipes. The music carried through the mountain air and echoed faintly, beautifully, drifting down toward Route 22. There was a little drumming, but only a little. The band marched to the whine of the bagpipes, cutting down through a mountain path to take a shortcut to the stadium. The music rose and fell, and even when I thought it was gone, it surprised me by rising once more, drifting back through the trees.

"Do you miss teaching, Dad?" I asked.

He looked at me.

"No," he said after a little. "No, I don't."

"How will you live?"

"I have some savings. It isn't much, but I'll be all right."

Without looking at me, he asked a question. "Are they all talking about me?"

"Who?"

"You know who. Are they?"

"Pretty much," I said. "You don't give them much to go on."

"It's none of their business what I do."

I nodded. I wanted to say, "It's my business," but I didn't. I suddenly felt very close to crying. I knew he wouldn't surrender to them. He would continue to take an abstract, intellectual approach, while all around him people judged his behavior according to their own practical terms. He couldn't see it, or more likely, he refused to see it, and I knew I somehow did not count in this.

78

I hated him for ignoring me, hated him for disregarding what was practical and evident to everyone around him.

We didn't speak until we arrived at the Magical Forest. My father parked the car near an open field just off the Red and Green Road. He sighed and tapped his hands on the wheel but made no motion to get out.

"Hungry?" he asked.

"A little."

"I brought that kite along. I thought maybe you might want to fly it?"

"The kite I bought down the shore? I'd forgotten all about that."

"Yes. Would you like to?"

I nodded. He reached over and rubbed my hair, then jumped out, suddenly animated once more. He opened the back and pulled out the kite, tossing me a ball of string.

The Magical Forest was all pine. The trees grew in rows, and any way you stepped you saw them from a different perspective. Now the rows appeared diagonal; now, square. The field near the parking lot had a softball diamond and an ancient backstop. My father carried the kite to the backstop and began piecing it together.

"All wooden joints. See? No glue needed. Pretty sharp, isn't it? Come here and help, Max."

I squatted next to him but didn't help. He had the kite together inside a minute.

"There's a good wind coming up. You're going to have to run that way, down toward the forest," he said.

"All right."

He made a few last adjustments. I was slowly catching his excitement. He lifted the kite and inspected it, turning it slowly from side to side.

"Airworthy, I'd say. Ready, Max?"

"If you are."

I let out some string and backed off ten or fifteen yards. My father held the kite at chest level, ready to toss it.

"Ready?" I called.

"Go ahead."

I ran. I lifted the string above my head. I felt the kite lift, then lift once more. The pines changed color in the shadows, and the strange trunks seemed now lined diagonally, now in perfectly straight lines. The kite suddenly caught an updraft and pulled more string off the ball. I slowed and turned to face it. It rose at the slightest finger pull.

"Bravo!" shouted my father. He ran down the open field, his heavy boots clumping, his hair back, his hands out for balance. He looked awkward and frail and helplessly childlike. He turned to watch it and nearly stumbled, but he continued running, hurrying toward me, his sense of wonder his greatest obstacle.

❖❖ 14 ❖❖

WE HAD cold cuts and potato salad for dinner. My father arranged it all on the counter in the kitchen, jars of mustard and mayonnaise spread in a half circle around him. His knife clinked against the glass, and occasionally he took a sip of beer. Watching him from behind, I saw he had lost weight. His pants sagged; his belt, I had noticed earlier, was pulled to a new notch, one I'm sure he had dug himself. The belt, tightened so, left no room for his shirt, and as a result, it bunched above his khakis. He kept a large handkerchief in his back pocket, and he reached for it often, his hand tucking it back expertly when he finished.

I drank a soda and waited. I knew he was excited. Twice he had begun to tell me of his find, but each time he caught himself.

"You like pickles, don't you?" he asked now over his shoulder.

"Yep."

"On the sandwich or on the side?"

"On it."

"Good. That's the way I like it. It gives a little crunch to a sandwich, doesn't it?"

He finished and carried the tray to the table. The sandwiches were very large. He had wedged a bag of potato chips between another beer and a second can of soda for me. The top of the bag unrolled little by little on its own, the plastic opening in quick bursts against the cans.

"Dig in now. You must be hungry."

"I am."

"We have everything?" he asked, patting his pockets and looking around. "You all set?"

"Sure. Have a seat."

He sat down quickly, but I could tell he wasn't going to rest there. He sat cocked on the chair, his weight too far forward. He was ready to move, ready to go on with his work, and I imagined him taking his own meals on the run, gobbling things down in the time it took him to get back to the dig.

"Are you going to tell me about the dig now?" I asked. "You said you found some things."

I took a bite of sandwich and waited. He swallowed a large gulp of beer, then grinned.

"I've found something pretty fascinating. Do you remember that box I showed you?"

"The wooden one?"

"Yes. You remember. I showed you a diary inside it? Well, it wasn't the diary of a boy, that's for sure."

"Whose was it?"

"Well, that's a story in itself. It took some research, let me tell you. This house has quite a past, a past we didn't know anything about. It's very old; it dates from before the Revolution, did you know that?"

"You said so once or something. I think I knew."

"Well, it does. The foundation was built around 1680. I'm not positive, but it's from around that time."

"And the diary's from then, too?" I asked, taking another bite.

"Oh, maybe. How's that sandwich?"

He took another sip of beer. He was enjoying himself. He smiled at me and ate a potato chip. He hadn't touched his sandwich.

"It's good. Whose diary is it then?" I asked when I finished chewing.

"It's a woman's diary. I should have known from the handwriting. It was too orderly, too neat to be a boy's. It's from just before

82

1700, from the time this whole area was farmland. We were the west fields of Elizabeth, really very rural."

"And the woman lived here?"

"And the woman lived here."

He was doling the story out very slowly, and I could tell he wanted me to guess or at least to see how he had pieced the information together. In a way, I understood this to be my payoff for having worked most of the summer. He tried to give me some of the pleasure of discovery, even though I had no idea where he was leading.

"So the woman kept a diary? Is that it?" I asked eventually.

"Yes, but what a diary! It was remarkable, absolutely remarkable. It's an amazing document of colonial life. An astonishing document."

"But what was it about?"

"About madness, and death, and sadness. And it was wrong. It was mistaken in its premise, and I've proved it."

"Dad, you're not being clear."

"I'm not being clear on purpose. I want to get your interest, then take you on a little journey."

"Where?"

"Here, in the house."

He nodded very slowly at me. I had no idea what he was talking about, and I suddenly felt afraid. I felt afraid for him, afraid to see his mind clouding and moving in ways that did not seem rational. His ideas and theories reminded me of a plant, a vine searching through a garden for a new patch of soil. I could not answer, could not respond to him without feeling I was giving him another place for his ideas to take root. I ate slowly, purposely giving myself time.

"Interesting?" he asked, eating more potato chips.

"I don't know. It might be."

He laughed.

"Max, you beat everything. I tell you that there is a wonderful document uncovered literally in your own backyard, and you're still skeptical. Isn't that it? Are you done with your sandwich?"

"Just about."

"Come on then. You can come back to it. I promise this will interest you more. Come on."

He stood up and pointed with his beer at the living room beyond.

"Where are we going?" I asked before I stood.

"Upstairs. You'll see."

"Where upstairs?"

"You'll see. Come on."

He frightened me. I did not think he would harm me, but I was afraid of what he might want to show me. All the weeks and months of his work had come to this, and it terrified me to think what it could be.

He led me upstairs. It had been two months since I had been upstairs, but it didn't feel at all strange. I might have been going to bed, except for my father in front of me, constantly turning to make sure I was still with him. Each time he turned, he grinned, but he succeeded only in making me feel more uncomfortable.

"In my room?" I asked when we reached the second floor.

"No, in mine."

"Where?"

"I'll show you. This is it."

We went down the hall and into his room. A grandfather's clock, one my mother had brought to the house from her family, ticked quietly in the far corner. The room itself was surprisingly clean. Everything was folded, and the bed was made, but whether it was done only for me or as a matter of course, I couldn't tell.

He went into the bathroom. It was very small. Purple tile covered the floor. A square shower stall, closed in by frosted glass, took up one whole wall. The rest—the towel rack and sink—lined the wall opposite the door.

"This is it," my father said, raising his beer.

"This?" I asked, trying to keep my voice even.

"See anything?"

"What should I see?"

"Oh, I guess you won't see it. I saw it only because I was looking for it. I knew it had to be here."

"Dad . . ."

"I know, I know. I'm sorry. I'm trying to be too dramatic. Here, hold my beer. Now watch."

He took a step toward the sink, then reached up to the mirror that covered the medicine cabinet. He made a quick motion, a

84

lifting and twisting, and suddenly the entire cabinet came off in his hands. A few bottles rattled inside, but it was obvious he had done this before and knew they wouldn't break. He put the frame of the cabinet on the toilet and leaned to peer into the hole in the wall.

"The past," he said.

"What past?"

"Take a look. It may surprise you."

I went close to him and looked inside. I couldn't see much, but it was true there was certainly a room there. It was very small and very hot. The air was not good; it smelled of dust and droppings and summer sun on shingles.

My father was very calm. He put a hand on my shoulder, and I knew it was to share the moment with me. He whispered.

"I had done some research, and I knew it was here somewhere. It had to be. This is the back of the attic. The chimney runs through it back there. The diary talked about the room, but it was weeks before I could figure it out. I found it only because of a freak accident. I was changing razor blades, and when I dropped the blade into the slot, it didn't go down very far. I heard it hit right here, right on the floor here. I knew I had found it then."

"But I still don't understand."

"It's in the diary. Wait, I have to show you one more thing."

He bent and picked up a flashlight that I hadn't seen before. My first impression had been correct. The room was tiny. It was, perhaps, five feet to the roof at its highest point. Wooden beams ran diagonally down, the slats running crosswise.

"See it?" he asked.

"No. I mean, yes, I see the room. What about it?"

"See it, though? You haven't spotted it yet?"

Then, suddenly, I saw what he had been hinting at all this time. There, two feet above the floor, dangling from the chimney, was a metal shackle. I drew in my breath when I saw it. The metal was rusted. The circular cuff was orange. Even the wooden floor beneath the cuff was rimmed by old stains and deep scratches turned white with age and decay.

"Who was kept here?" I asked finally.

"A boy. A boy a little older than you."

"Who kept him?"

"His father, then his mother. His mother wrote the diary, and then, maybe just before she died, she buried it outside. The boy died before her, but she lived with the shame of it for at least three years. She was alone. She also feared they might think she was a witch."

"But why was he kept here?"

"He was mad, although I've even proved that wrong. I think, from what I can piece together from farm records and accounts, that he was accused of killing livestock in the area. The boy, that is. His parents locked him up here to prevent the townspeople from killing him."

"How can you know that?"

"I don't know, precisely. I'm putting some of it together, but it works, doesn't it? Doesn't it seem plausible?"

"Maybe. I can't tell."

"I did research some records, and I came up with a few things. There was a period when this might have happened. An account was made concerning a number of sheep and cows being killed in the surrounding area. The slaughter was at first attributed to a bear or a wolf."

"And you're saying the boy did it?"

"No," my father said, his hand drumming lightly on my shoulder. "No, I'm saying he was accused of it. The local farmers wanted someone to blame—or maybe they simply responded to the boy's strange behavior. Whatever it was, I proved he couldn't have done it."

"How?"

"I tried it myself. I waited until sunset, then tried to get to the farms and back before daylight."

"You mean you ran through the streets?"

"No, mostly I went over the Watchung Reservation."

"Dad, that's crazy."

"Why? I had to prove it one way or the other. What I wanted to find out is whether or not the boy was imprisoned for any good reason. Imagine these people locking him up and leaving him there, and all the time he didn't even do it. I don't think he could have done it."

"Dad, isn't a lot of this just, well, circumstance or something? Couldn't it all have another explanation?"

86

"Like?"

"Like, I don't know. Maybe they kept prisoners here or something. There has to be another explanation. Besides, you shouldn't be running all over the Watchungs trying to prove something like that. People are saying things."

My father tapped me twice more on the shoulder, then flicked the flashlight off. He reached down and picked up the medicine cabinet and fitted it back into its place. Suddenly he seemed tremendously weary. When he finished, he took out his glasses and wiped them clean on his handkerchief.

"Let's finish that sandwich," he said.

"Dad, I didn't mean to upset you. I just thought there might be other possibilities."

"I know. You're right, of course. There could be."

"But this might be one. This could be just the way it happened. What else do you think might have happened?"

He didn't answer. He watched me for a long time; then he smiled. As soon as I saw it, I shook my head. The smile marked me clearly for what I was. I was part of "them" now, those people trying to corner him.

❖❖ 15 ❖❖

JACK picked me up and took me back that night. He didn't ask much, and I didn't volunteer a great deal. I kept the room to myself, thinking that if I couldn't quite go along with my father, I could at least not work against him.

It was right after the first snowfall that Jack told me the papers were all in order and he was going ahead with the commitment. He didn't dwell on the details, and I didn't ask. Still, at night I pictured my father standing in the dig as the men came to get him. I imagined him looking up to see them there, their smiles sad and intended to be reassuring, their eyes searching to see if he might grab a tool and decide to be dangerous. I knew without question that he would not fight; I knew, also, that he was beyond all argument. It would have been too easy for him to have broken their arguments to pieces, to have protected himself with words, if words had held any meaning. But the power to convince anyone by thought and reason was gone, and I knew my father would give in when the time came, going as docilely as we had returned to our sandwiches the night he showed me the hole in the wall.

I waited. Each morning I looked at Jack to see if he had gone ahead, but he stalled. He himself was frightened of what he was about to do. Perhaps he was waiting to see if my father pulled out of it with the snow. In any case, two or three days went by, and Jack said nothing.

It was on a Saturday that he finally received a call from the hospital. I listened to it from the living room and heard Jack's voice become serious. He spoke very low, stopping at times to listen to what seemed a long story. Finally he hung up, and there was a long silence before he called me into the kitchen.

"Max?" he said. "Could you come in here, please?"

I found him at the kitchen table with a cup of coffee still in front of him. Gertrude had gone grocery shopping, and I knew she wouldn't be back for another hour or so.

"That was the hospital," Jack said.

"I thought so."

"They called about your dad. There's a problem."

"What now?" I asked. I felt close to crying. I wanted whatever was going to happen to be over and done.

"They went for him, and he wasn't there."

"What do you mean?"

"I mean, he was gone. The house was empty."

"Where is he?"

"I don't know."

"Did he leave—I mean, is he gone for good?"

"I don't know."

Jack looked at me.

"Do you know where he went?" he asked.

"No."

"Are you telling me the truth? Did you tell him what we were going to do?"

"No, I didn't."

"Swear to that?"

"Yes."

He continued staring at me. He stared for a long time, then said finally, "I have to call them back."

"What will they do?"

"I don't know. I can check the bank on Monday and see if he's touched his money."

Jack shook his head; then he did a curious thing. Just the beginning of a smile appeared on his lips, and he quickly covered it by taking a sip of coffee.

"Gone, just like that," he said.

"He suspected something," I said.

This time Jack really smiled, and I smiled with him. It was a relief to both of us. Jack called back and told the hospital people what he knew, and they asked if he wanted to turn the matter over to the police. Jack looked at me and told them no.

On Monday we found out my father had taken nearly ten thousand out of his savings account. He'd gone without a note or any clue whatsoever to where he was going. He had taken the car and all the camping gear he owned.

I did not know how to take his leaving, although I was glad he had escaped the hospital. I knew, now, how to picture him. I could imagine him in the car, traveling over long roads, stopping to ask questions of strangers or to inspect an outcropping, camping at night beside the old station wagon. He would bend sometimes to stab a grapefruit, eating it with one hand while he listened to the story of Buck in the Arctic woods. Perhaps when he came to the part about Spitz going down and the other dogs closing on him, he likened the situation to his own and marveled at his good fortune in getting away.

But I missed him and cried for him for weeks after he disappeared. And sometimes, late at night, I wondered if he had gone at all. In dark moments I wondered if he hadn't just escaped into the house, crawled into that tiny room and closed the door behind him.

PART

2

❖❖ 16 ❖❖

O N A DAY during spring vacation of my junior year I visited Honey. We did not go to my house. Instead, we walked up toward the Trailside Museum. The brook beside the path was still frozen, and now and then Honey picked up a small pebble and threw it, bending a little at the waist to hear it hit and skid. She liked it when I did it even better because it left her free to listen. She stood with her hands on her hips, her breath a fog, her ski cap pulled down, laughing as I skipped pebbles on the ice.

"Always reminds me of Hans Brinker and the silver skates," she said. "I don't know why."

"Did you read that one to me?"

"I think so. They skated on canals, didn't they? Someone told me there used to be canals in New Jersey. Did you ever hear that? I didn't know whether or not to believe them."

"I don't know."

"He was a Dutch boy, wasn't he? I mean the boy in the story, not the person who told me about the canals. I just remember parts of the story, not the whole thing—funny how it works like that."

"I know."

She walked ahead, still finding the sun when she could. Her pace didn't seem as fast, and I was surprised at how easy it was to keep up with her. Occasionally she slowed her walk to a careful march, planting her feet sideways for traction, one hand finding the slick spring bushes. Her free hand dangled the lunch sack she was taking to Zeke. She had wrapped in the top of the bag a small piece of Italian bread, which she shredded for the birds that moved ahead of us in the trees.

Stopping, she ripped out small pearls of dough from inside the crust and threw them about randomly, not bothering to watch the birds come down.

"They'll find it," she told me. "They always do. That's their business. I never see it when I come back. They like the crust more."

"How do you know?"

"They fight over the crust. You ever see a bunch of chickens fight over a worm? It's like that."

We walked on. I stayed close to her, giving her my hand when it was especially slippery, although she walked every day without me. It felt good to touch her and even better to be in her company, walking the old path, listening to her talk about whatever interested her.

"You want to hear something?" she asked, still ripping the bread apart. We were at a steep portion of the path, and she had to walk slowly.

"What?"

"I think I saw a spirit here."

"Where? What kind?"

"I don't know. You believe me, first of all?"

"I guess. I have to hear first."

"Fair enough."

We worked our way around a long, subtle bend in the brook. The water moved faster here. White froth froze in long beards along the banks. A low mist netted the air above the stream bed, and now and then there were distant sounds of ice cracking and letting go.

"It was the summer your father left. I was walking home from the stable when I saw a light down there." She pointed. "It was a soft light, and at first I thought it was the sun hitting the water."

94

"And then?"

"I came closer, squinting to see, you know? Whatever it was didn't see me at first; I surprised it, I think. Anyway, I saw it was a woman, maybe three feet high."

"Seriously?"

"I swear. It wasn't frightening at all. It was like something wild—like a deer mostly—and it was way down, in that place where the trees grow together."

"You weren't afraid?"

"No, not at all. It didn't make me afraid. It was just like seeing something wild. It made you think maybe it had always been there, but you had just been too clumsy to see it. Know what I mean?"

"I think so."

She stopped and tore another piece of bread free. The remaining piece was too small to tear, so she grated it against the rough bark of the nearest tree.

"It had wings," she said when she finished.

"Honey . . ."

"It did. And when it saw me, it didn't panic. It moved off slowly, almost like it wanted me to follow. It was hot and misty, with bugs flittering and the fireflies already up, and I was tempted to try. I was. I don't know how I could have done it, but I had the feeling I could have done something. She moved off, she bent to go under the trees, I remember, and it looked like she was leading me down the stream. Then she disappeared."

"And that was it?"

"That's it. Do you believe me?"

"No, not really."

"Well, you're probably smart not to. I still don't know if I believe it, but I know it happened."

We stood for a second looking down the gully. Even now the trees were closely woven over the top and I could imagine an illusion looking real enough—the light slipping and gliding over the brook.

We climbed the last stretch to Trailside. A sign at the end of the path said the museum was closed, but I knew there would be a few animals around. A woodpecker beat on a tree near the hawk cage.

We went down the Braille Path and crested the rise to the stable. The horse smell came from farther away; it reached us in the chilly air quicker, more unmistakably than in summer. I heard a horse whinny just as a piece of ice broke free overhead and fell through a maple on its way down.

"I wish it would hurry up and get warm," said Honey.

"It was warm last week."

"Well, stay warm then," she said, then changed the subject. "How you getting along out there?"

"Fine."

"You're big friends with those boys, the Kellermans, your aunt said."

"They're good friends."

"You and Martin are the same age, aren't you?"

"Yes."

"And school?"

"Bs and Cs."

"You can do better, can't you?"

"Maybe. I guess so."

"Jack said you did pretty good on the SATs."

"I did okay."

"And you'll be applying to colleges?"

"Yes."

"I can't believe it's that time already."

She touched my shoulder and then let me go. She didn't look at me when she asked her next question.

"No word from your daddy?"

"No."

"I think about that man so much. I think about him every day."

"So do I."

"Of course you do—he's your father. I daydream about him sometimes. I wonder what he's doing now, where he is. After everything is said and done, what was he hurting? Who cared if he wanted to dig around in the dirt?"

"It wasn't your fault, Honey."

"You're nice to say so, but I worry about him. You don't know anything more than you told your Uncle Jack?"

"No."

She touched me again. We saw Cherry Stable spread out along

96

the small ridges of the Watchung Mountains. The white fence of the paddock was dripping slowly, the ice going over to water. A trace of smoke went up, curling and waving in quiet wind, and two or three horses, out for air and exercise, whinnied and snorted at our approach.

"Anyone riding these days?" I asked.

"Oh, some. Spring mud is harder on these horses than snow."

We arrived at the barn, and Honey pulled open the small door beside the larger entrance for horses. Over her shoulder I saw the glassy eyes of two horses look up, troubled by the cold. It was warm in the barn and smelled like summer.

"Zeke?"

"Here."

"Where?" Honey called. "I can't see yet. My eyes are changing."

We walked down the center aisle between the horses. My eyes adjusted, but things became visible one at a time, taking form out of the darkness.

"Just back here." Zeke guided us. "In the last stall."

Zeke was putting a saddle on a small pony. The pony's name, I knew, was Teddy, and Zeke treated him like a pet, feeding him apples from his pocket, stroking him more than was his custom with horses.

Zeke finished with Teddy, then climbed out of the stall. The pony shifted feet, and his saddle crunched, giving off the good leather sound I associated with Zeke.

"Hi, Zeke," I said.

"My God, Max, you've grown," said Zeke, squaring my shoulders to look at me. "You look twice the size of when I saw you last time. What are you now? Seventeen?"

"Sixteen."

"You look terrific. How've you been? Everything okay out there?"

"Fine."

"And how's your uncle and aunt? They doing okay?"

"Fine, too."

"Well, everything's fine then?"

"Zeke," Honey said, handing him the bag, "he hasn't heard from his dad if that's what you're digging after."

Zeke smiled and wiggled the bag. He walked back and sat at

97

his table. Honey sat beside him while I wandered up and down the aisle for a few minutes, greeting some of the horses, petting them between the eyes. It was sleepy in the barn, and the horses dozed, oblivious of the thaw outside, their heads drooping like cattails over the wooden gates of their stalls.

"So," Zeke said loud enough to reach me, "she told you that story about the river witch, huh? The one she saw on the path? You believe her, Max?"

"I don't know. Honey doesn't lie."

"No, she doesn't," he said, taking a curl of cheese off his knife, "but this time she might be off."

"Zeke . . ." started Honey.

"No, now I'm serious. You think that forest is haunted, and that's the truth."

"But in a good way."

"But haunted."

I came over and sat down as Zeke went on, taking a bite of cheese and bread together.

"I asked your father about it, you know that, Max? He said they used to believe in more things like that. He said there were jinns—little people that brought the town gossip to kitchen witches—and there were nymphs. These nymphs live in brooks, and you only ever hear about them on summer nights. But they come out and tiptoe along rivers, dancing up and down and playing in the brooks. Except, your dad said, they don't drink out of the brook; they drink dew from clover."

"What else did he say?"

"Oh, he knew a lot about it. He said it was in Shakespeare, all this about summer nights. After Honey told him, he sometimes came up through the path late at night and stayed out until two or three, sitting in that pretty field on an old tablecloth, watching the stream. I thought—well, I thought it was just another thing he went overboard about, but he never claimed to see anything. He just said he wanted to look."

"You done with all that?" asked Honey.

"I'm just telling Max."

Zeke brushed some crumbs off his pants. Honey leaned back against the wall and closed her eyes. She still hadn't taken off her hat and coat, and whenever she moved, her arms and chest gave

98

off a whistle of nylon. A wind picked up outside, and the barn seemed to lean into it, rocking and twisting, the wood and nails yawning softly.

"Some nights, when I'm walking down, I half believe him. Of course, there've been times when I've seen animals—a raccoon or skunk or opossum—and all I could really see was their eyes. Now it's a funny thing, but after your dad took it up, I began wondering if those animals were just animals. You know how things look in the dark. But I never saw the light Honey said was with them."

"Zeke." Honey interrupted.

He put his hand on her knee.

"There was one night, though, when I ran into your father. He was out in the field, sitting in the darkness. It was a fine night, dark and clear and hardly any moon, but it was heading toward fall. When I ran into him, he was on all fours, sometimes coming up like a bear to sniff around him."

"How did you see him?"

"I don't know. I mean, I don't know how I sensed he was there, but I did. Everything was a little wild. Anyway, I saw him out in the meadow, leaning up and straining to see into the brook."

"Did you go over to him?"

"Yes. But when I moved toward him, he lifted a hand and motioned for me to be quiet. He pointed to the brook, the place where Honey said she saw the nymph; then he put his finger to his lips. He was very excited—I remember that. His body was tense and swaying, almost hypnotized or something. I can't explain it, but he was on to something. He had seen something, I'm sure of it, and I had come and broken it all up."

"Was he angry?"

"No, he gradually let up. He slouched down on his tablecloth and rubbed his eyes. I had some cheese left over, a little bread, too, so we ate that out in the meadow, listening to the bugs and the sound of the brook. It was magical sitting out there like that. I felt the appeal, if you know what I mean."

"What did he say?"

"He said he saw a light coming toward him. He didn't see it completely, though. He just saw the beginning of the light."

"And he wasn't angry you showed up?"

"No, because he said he had a feeling the nymph recognized him or knew he had been there before. The nymph was letting him see her, you understand? He also said sometimes when he sat out there, he believed the heads of the different weeds were talking."

I sat back. Honey breathed deeply, and I wondered if she was really asleep. I came close to telling them about the room then, explaining the story of the boy chained up in the house, the stalking my father did at night, but I wanted first to think about the whole matter on my own.

Zeke took a bite of cheese and broke off a hunk of bread.

"Did she ever show herself to him again?" I asked.

"I don't know. Not that he ever told me. He left pretty soon after."

"Did Honey ever see it again?"

"No. She must have surprised it that one time. She walks pretty quiet in those sneakers."

"Oh, come on." I laughed.

"She does."

Zeke finished his lunch. We let Honey sleep, and I helped Zeke the rest of the afternoon. We swept out the stalls, forked down new hay, and groomed two of the horses. Now and then I had an image of my father in that meadow, the light coming slowly up the barrel of the brook.

We finished around five. Zeke led us out and locked up. It was colder now. The forest and the path leading to the zoo were already dark. The wind found a hollow in the barn and began to call.

We walked into the woods and back up the Braille Path. The horses whinnied as we left them, but after a while I couldn't hear them anymore.

❖❖ 17 ❖❖

SPRING settled on the rill behind the house and caused the skunk cabbage to send up its young leaves. The cabbage smelled rank, even while we still had nightly frosts, but Gertrude came out to see it anyway when I reported its appearance. It was the first green thing, the first true sign of winter's end, and she bent over it, squinting a little, making me imagine that if she could not see it, the season might reverse.

"It's up, isn't it?" was all she said.

Jack taped a five-dollar bill to the refrigerator that spring and stipulated it was to be awarded to the first person who saw a robin. He won his own bet but used the money to take us all out to a local Stewart's root beer stand. We sat in the car, the windows cranked low, the engine and heat running, drinking milk shakes and nibbling french fries.

"You can feel spring coming, can't you?" we said to one another, straws in our mouths, although it felt nothing like it.

Other signs proved things were on the move. Gertrude went out into the garden and spread manure, breaking up clods of earth with her bare hands. Jack, smelling like pipes and insect spray, made his annual pilgrimage to Wesqwemot Lake with a few friends. It was ice-out, and he fished for landlocked salmon, bringing their heads home to dice in the garden.

In school the season hung on one bee that made it through the window of Miss Sinclair's third-period Algebra II class. I watched the bee sweep through the class, its drone lazy and hinting of summer, while Miss Sinclair lifted her chalk and gazed up, her own season done, her hold over us disappearing in the gentle quiver. "Class," she said, but it was too late. The bee continued hitting the ceiling, flapping its hum across us, finally becoming a burr of noise behind the venetian blinds. "Class," she said once more, but we were gone from her, floating with the bee into open meadows.

It was during this season that Stu started his first company, Handy Dandies. He cut lawns, raked leaves, cleaned garages, and weeded gardens for people all around town, charging them next to nothing and showing up with a smiling face, schoolboy zeal, and evoking a trust the local homeowners could not place in the small Italian-American population that usually handled such work.

Stu tried to seduce Martin and me into working for him, but we would have none of it. Still, he had a manager's heart, a pimp's cunning, and he liked to come to the willow, thumbing a roll of dollar bills, wagging them in front of his face, saying, "Just say the word, and you've got a job. I'm not holding grudges."

"Hold my dick," Martin told him.

"Ahh, ahh, touchy, touchy, Martin."

"Screw off, Stu. We're Communists," Martin said from the hammock.

"Dad says a Communist is only a man without a job, so I guess you qualify."

With Stu's single-mindedness, his business began to flourish. The Italians, in their rickety green trucks that stank of lawn mower gas and deep-rooted grass stains, were no match for honest Stu. Stu played on the town's prejudices. Where before a home-owner could look forward to a summer of thick-gutted men in T-shirts lazing around his yard, drinking orange soda and eating submarine sandwiches, now he had Stu arriving on his bike, duti-fully towing a lawn mower behind him, a faggot of rake handles and gardening tools lashed across his handlebars. Stu gave lawn work a collegiate air.

102

His success was predictable, really, but maddening just the same, and Martin and I watched with horror as he conned Marcie into being a girl maid, sending her out to clean windows and silverware, to beat rugs and otherwise provide "spring cleaning" services for women who normally couldn't afford such luxuries. It was sickening to see Marcie duped, but even she had a certain greed, and she took pleasure in accumulating a cash reserve, which she knotted away in socks.

Stu was good—there's no denying that. He had an entrepreneurial eye, and he was soon looking for ways to expand his business, to improve his suburban conglomerate. In the first swell of profits he even bought a metal detector—a hand-held minesweeper—and this became the focus of his entire summer. Going to and from work, he stopped along various roads, parked his bike, and began his odd prospecting. He became, in a relatively short time, a municipal fixture. He was evident at any large gathering, an embarrassment to Martin and me, a raven picking carrion. He roamed behind crowds or drifted through local parks for hours, scything the grass with his minesweeper, bending every once in a while with his garden trowel to unearth his latest treasure.

In his first month Stu found roughly a hundred dollars' worth of metal—rings; necklaces; even a money clip with a twenty still in place. Stockton had never had a minesweeper before, so Stu worked virgin turf. His hundred dollars made him insufferable. In our teen-age world he was a millionaire, and he lavished gifts on himself as freely as a sailor, going to sporting goods stores for new bats and balls, picking up a belly television he could watch in bed, parading past us a constant flow of gum, jawbreakers, sodas, and seedy paperbacks with diluted sexual passages.

"What did I tell you?" he asked, demonstrating still another gadget—a cheap wristwatch, a fungo bat, a new medicine ball—rubbing in the fact of our laziness, our lack of judgment in not entering into partnership with him.

Martin and I avoided Stu when we could. We had no wish to work, no inkling of a desire to join him. We played wiffleball in the mornings against Martin's garage door, waving to Stu as he took his bike out.

We stayed under the willow through the hottest part of the day, but in the afternoon we went to the YMCA. We rode Martin's bike double, slowly wobbling down his lawn and across the small creek that separated our yards. At the front of my house he let me down on the sidewalk and waited while I ran up the steps. Each afternoon I checked the mail.

"Anything?" he asked when I came back.

"Nope."

And always he answered, "He'll write one day, don't worry."

"I hope so."

"He will. People don't just disappear."

But that was a lie, and we both knew it, because the fact was, my father had disappeared awfully well.

❖❖ 18 ❖❖

WE TRAVELED from my house directly to the Y. Only one of us rode up hills; the other ran beside, holding the handlebar like a Navaho. On downhill slopes I would jump up on the frame and we would teeter down the long grade, Martin's face near mine, his breathing close.

"Duck," he said, and we both leaned forward, streamlining our bodies. The tires hummed and the bike shivered, but if we squatted low, we sometimes had enough momentum to make it up Gallow's Hill. If we didn't, Martin stopped and angled the bike to one side, allowing me a chance to break free and begin again the dogtrot we used whenever we needed to make time.

We parked the bike, running it into a hedge and hoping it would stand, then sprinted up the old stone steps and banged open the front doors. We were greeted with a smell as rich as any kitchen. It was a familiar smell, a sweet smell of chlorine and sweat, a small-time hustle and con.

I was fond of Zong Kong, a slick red machine that featured a woman with flashing hand waves and a huge gorilla that was, at alternating times—and over a certain point total—friend or foe. Martin, beside me, played Zork, a space game with firing missiles and ray guns. We played until we lost or became bored, joined by the sexual thumping we did against the machine's front legs, by the slap and twang of the bumpers, by the frustration, built into the game, of knowing we would never win.

Our money didn't last long. Without the machines Martin and I were at loose ends, and we began our daily migration through the building. If no one was around, we normally spent ten minutes trying to gouge the pistachio nut machine with a knock hockey stick to rob it of a dime's worth of food.

There was a second room beyond the game room. This functioned as an adult sitting room for the ten or twelve lodgers the Y took in, and it was here our education took on an accelerated pace. A small contingent of caddies had moved into the Y, boarding upstairs and going out early in the morning to work at Echo Lake Golf Club, a posh country club in the middle of town. They returned to the Y in late afternoon, content with their small salary. They were hoboes, for the most part, and they trailed the weather, migratory as geese, coming up the coast in summer, slipping back down as the courses closed.

Martin and I envied them their freedom, their loose way of living, and we aped them as much as possible. We took on their ways, slinking around the sitting room, running errands for them, even taking Martin's bike out to Rosen's, the local liquor store, to fetch a pint or two once old Rosen had received the order by phone. We were paid liberally for anything we did. The caddies were paid in cash, and it never stuck. It was nothing for them to tip a dollar, to flip a quarter over their shoulders, lipping at us around a cigarette, "Here, kid, go get yourself something that won't bite."

It was an easier room to enter than to leave.

Deado, a two-fingered, snaggly-bearded man, was the king of the second room. He didn't caddie; he was a permanent guest. He had first squatter's rights, and it was though his welcome we were invited in, given a place, asked to sit and chat. Deado was always in the same position: halfway between two open windows, a hot plate and a can of Campbell's soup on the sill, a checkerboard open before him. This was his office, his schoolroom, and we came to him each day ready to take up the thread of his discourse, able, with little effort, to link it to the last lecture or project it forward to the next.

106

Another man, Small, was Deado's butler. He kept the cans of chicken soup boiling, ladling out mugs to me and Martin and Deado himself. Small was short and wore tight Levi's with wide belts and extravagant buckles. He rolled his shirt sleeves and sculpted his sideburns into lamb chops. He chain-smoked and could do wonderful passes with his cigarette, wonderful flips and twists, sometimes swallowing a lit cigarette with his lizard tongue, simply rolling it back, singeing his tonsils, then flicking it out once more like an iguana. He held to manual labor, believed it proved a sort of puritanical worthiness, so his conversations were full of fork-lifts, trucks, engines, diesel fuel, and tire irons.

Combined, the men gave off an aroma of failure. The room itself was filled with failure, and on the summer days we went there, it was something to play shuffleboard on a table near the door, carefully sliding the silver disks along the sawdust surface of the grid while each man held up his story for our examination, pointing out his errors, examining his life, extolling us to greater virtue, harder work, or, at the very least, bigger schemes.

"So," Deado might say, leaning back to take a sip of chicken soup, crossing his legs and nodding at us, "you don't want to do anything penny ante. If you're going to fuck up, you might as well fuck up in a big way. Am I right, Small?"

"I had a truck," Small would say, "and I was making some money until the refrigerator blew . . . you know, the refrigerator device—"

"But it has to be in a big way," Deado would interrupt. "You're talking now penny ante."

Then, while Martin and I listened, there would be a peculiar silence as they both thought through their schemes that went nowhere.

"I needed capital," Small said.

"What capital? Trenton? Des Moines?"

"No . . . I—"

"Women will do it. As God is my judge, you can't chase after women and money at the same time. It'll make you cross-eyed."

There was something splendid in their acceptance of fate. Not once in their litany of woes did I see them expose any real self-doubt, any personal failing that might have caused their ruin. No, it was always history, the tides, fate, the spinning wheel that kept

107

them from their true achievement. They had been there, had won, and I always gathered that if they desired it, they could still stalk out of the room and begin a slow roll toward wealth and profit.

In payment for the chicken soup, for the stories, we ran errands for Deado. He sent us to the corner store for cigarettes or down to the basement for two or three of the *National Geographics* he stored there. He had tentacles all over the building, and he could send or retrieve us in twenty different ways, playing the long corridors and sweaty locker rooms like a keyboard, exposing secrets about the way things were in any given portion of the building, monitoring the seasons by the height of his window, accurately judging the time the machines would be filled, and explaining he knew Harry, the man from Carnival Candy, who would give us five candy bars for fifty cents if we caught him while he stuffed the slots. We functioned as Deado's eyes and legs, giving him good service, pestering him only a little, and believing what we could of his stories.

Around four Jock came in. Jock was the only Jew in the Y. He had freckles all over his shiny, bare scalp, and he wore golf pants —bright green slacks or odd red pants with whales spouting up the legs. The pants were always too thin, and they revealed his boxer shorts underneath, his old man's butt, while his change rested like cellulite across his thigh.

"Who's running?" he asked as soon as he was in the room. "As if I didn't know, right? I know who's running. What I don't know is who'll be running when the race is over. I bet on a horse, it breaks its shinbone. Imagine! A big, healthy animal like that breaking a shinbone. I've seen women with skinnier legs, and they could run, let me tell you. But this horse goes down like an acrobat. He's trying to entertain us, for God's sake, and I'm betting my life savings."

He went to the reading table for a copy of the *Star Ledger*. Then, whisking Martin and me out of the way, he spread it out on the shuffleboard table.

"Coffee, black," he would tell one of us, pulling up a folding chair. "And see, now just see, and make sure you don't tell anyone I told you to ask—get around that, you understand me? Use your old cue ball there—you ask the manager, but don't ask him

108

straight out, whether he thinks the pipes will be giving another concert tonight. Tell him the Philadelphia Harmonica is living upstairs, will you? Tell that as sweet as you can. Now, you go try that, understand? See if something can be done—that's all I'm asking."

Somehow Martin usually got picked for these missions, and I was left to pull up close enough to listen. I sat near Jock's side and watched him work his pencil over the racing page. He had a round, heavy profile that in some way reminded me of fruit. His throat was red, and the heavy moles along his lower eyelids were bagged and black. They reminded me of some sort of glacial moraine, the product of tears or torment, and I watched, fascinated, when he squinted over the *Star Ledger*.

"What is this shit?" he asked us all. "These horses ought to be served to Frenchmen. Look at this one! Handicapped? I'll say he's handicapped—what's this, the three-legged race? And you see what they name him? Danny O'Dare. Now they know good and well any poor slob of a sentimental Irishman will put two dollars on him. It's a whiskey bet—they're counting on it."

When Martin came back, Jock stopped whatever he was doing and began stirring his coffee with the wooden oar Martin was sure to bring. He didn't tip, although he was big on giving the impression that he would tip someday, rolling around the Y the way a swank summer guest might put on his tab a season's charges.

"Bluebell in the fifth," he said to Martin, "that's the tip you need."

"The custodian says if you want better, you have to find better."

"He does, does he? Who does he think he is? What the fuck? It's like sleeping in a submarine. Not a breath of air and the whole place clanging—and can you believe the shit they have running today?"

At five Meat came to take Jock's bets. Meat was a slender Italian man, lean and slightly lethal, who wore his shirts unbuttoned to expose the ribbed whiteness of his T-shirts. On certain days he wore a gold-plated New York subway token on a chain dangling between his jutting collarbones. His shoes were fence climbers—sharp, pointy affairs, which always suggested switchblades and machete fights. His story went that he had once cad-

109

died for a leading money winner on the pro tour but left because the pro had been prone to tantrums, throwing clubs at Meat, berating him, once even calling him an Italian nigger in front of a camera. Meat was a celebrity of sorts as a result, and the loose migration of caddies that passed through mentioned his name whenever anyone needed something "done."

"Here he comes." Jock started as soon as Meat came in. "He's a remora. Anyone know what that is? How about you, Martin? You got any idea?"

"No."

"Of course you don't. You haven't been educated. Right now your teacher is still carrying around a big plastic shoe, giving you gold stars for tying your laces. You haven't begun to think yet; you're just doing mechanics."

"You want to lay something down?" Meat asked. "I haven't got all day."

"What do you have if you haven't got all day? Do you think of that?"

"Jock, what do you say?"

"No, no, wait a minute. See, a remora sucks onto a shark, you understand? He eats whatever flecks of fish are left after a shark bites the head off some other poor fish. It's called symbiosis—how's that for a word, you Christians? It takes an old Jew to know that one."

"How much and what?" Meat asked, taking out a notepad.

As much as he hated Meat, Jock still pulled him over and went head to head with him, whispering bets, giving him variations to play in case one of the horses was scratched.

After Meat left, Jock launched into a betting lesson. Deado's parlor became a casino, and Jock was the chief dealer, the house, the croupier. He played a thousand games—checkers, chess, pinochle, card tossing, gin, blackjack, stud, five-card draw, fantan, pitch. He was deft with cards yet not quite smooth enough to draw attention to himself, and I recall watching his neatly manicured hands work over the cards, cutting them easily, dealing with the lightest touch, skimming the cards in perfect lag shots to my position at the table. He was, for all that, entirely small-time, and Martin and I understood he was more than willing to take our money.

110

It was addicting. The day was evaluated clearly by the change in our pockets at the end of the afternoon. It was entertainment, summer camp. Besides which, Martin and I sometimes won, and Jock was not above complaining and pouting, cringing a little as he paid off his marker, his wheels working to find some way to put us off, to rob the jackals of their meat.

"Double or nothing," he tried. "Run this on tomorrow's tab, eh?"

He was crafty, a slick hustler who, like a old lion, was gone in the teeth and ready to feed on the easiest flesh available. The dollar or two he won from us weekly went to his cough drops, his occasional cigars, his coffee. I know for a fact he spent some of the money on the vibrating bed the Y had somehow received from an old motel that went under, because I caught him once upstairs, his door cracked open, his thin arms a clothesline for his T-shirt, his snore gargling at the shake of the bed.

❖❖ 19 ❖❖

AFTER DINNER most nights I went to my room to work on my dinosaurs and wait for Martin. I had exchanged the three models my father had given me—*Brontosaurus*, *Stegosaurus*, and *Tyrannosaurus rex*—for more sophisticated copies of the same creatures. They served as the foundation of my collection. It took me weeks to make them. They were extremely complicated, extremely exacting, since each bone had to be fitted together beneath a clear plastic skin.

Gertrude was my sponsor. She liked to see me working on the models, and during the first stages of my interest I returned from school one day to find a bookcase erected in my room. It was made of gray metal, and it was cold and hard and scientific. Gertrude had assembled it and placed the three dinosaurs on different shelves, pointing them toward a common center, where she had set out the tiny plastic ferns that had come with the kits. Two more models stood on the bottom shelf along with three resource books and a small magnifying glass.

Since then I had built ten additional dinosaurs. I had also constructed a small world on each shelf, improvising with real ferns, adding sand and potting soil, punctuated by rounded rocks that looked like boulders. I hung pterodactyls from thread above the flesh eaters and duck-billed water dwellers, and whenever the wind blew, the pterodactyls moved their heavy wings, their boned arms rowing gently.

For two nights running I had been gluing together *Allosaurus,* a thirty-five-foot meat eater. Twice the tail had come loose, and I was just in the process of putting it back in place when I heard Martin coming up the stairs. He didn't bother knocking.

"Max?" he asked, pushing through. "We're supposed to be going out, remember? Where were you?"

"Just a second."

"Back in the old lizard age, huh?"

He walked to the shelves and looked at them. He touched the pterodactyls to get them swinging, then made a low-throated monkey chatter. He picked up the magnifying glass and turned it on me.

"A Maxydactyl. Very rare, very rare indeed."

"Let me just glue this in."

"What is it? No, don't bother. I always forget as soon as you tell me. It's ugly, though, isn't it? What did this one do?"

He bent close and continued looking through the magnifying glass. He was just above my shoulder, and I smelled some sort of hair tonic and after-shave. His breath made an ocean sound in my ear.

"You have after-shave on?" I asked.

"Natch."

"What for?"

"For you, what'd you think?"

"No, seriously."

"I thought we might visit Chris and Marla after."

"Who said?"

"Max, no one has to say you can visit them. Chris loves you anyway."

"Bull."

"It's what Marla says."

He put his hand on my shoulder.

"What did it do?" asked Martin again.

"It ate brontosauruses."

"Is that right?" He straightened, not really interested. "Jock

113

says there are lots of balls in the fifteenth hole. He says he'll take as many as we can give him."

"Okay. I can stop here."

I finished with the *Allosaurus* and put it on the shelf. Martin bent past me and stared at it through the magnifying glass.

"Marcie likes this sort of stuff, too. You know that?"

"I thought she just liked taking care of animals. You didn't tell her about this, did you?"

"No. Don't worry—nobody knows you're Mr. Dinosaur but me. You ready?"

We went downstairs. Gertrude was in the basement, so I yelled to tell her I'd be back later, then ran outside with Martin.

His bike was in the driveway. Marcie had been using it all day —she had gone to a bike rodeo at a local playground—and it still had baseball cards clipped to the spokes. The bike made a motorcycle sound that Martin liked. He pretended to shift gears as we started.

We headed down Woodland Avenue, a deep, shady road. It had rained earlier in the day, and the air was heavy with mist. Trees dripped and the sewers ran full. A few late sprinklers were still on, forgotten in the rain, and the sun was just bright enough to give rainbows to their spray.

"Hot, huh?" Martin asked as I jogged beside him.

"Pretty hot. You really want to go to Chris's house?"

"Sure, why not?"

"I don't know. I'm just asking."

At Skinner's house, the last yard before the golf course, we parked the bike and chained it to an old wooden fence. Roses climbed along the fence, crawling and weaving over the planks, the dense buds dipping and hanging like a neighbor's hands draped loosely in gossip. I smelled the roses and heard bees moving in and out, their drone lazy at this time of night. In front of us Skinner's yard caught the first fireflies.

We vaulted Skinner's fence at a spot without roses. I landed on the edge of the small garden and felt my foot sink. I stopped, took off my sneakers, and threw them back toward the bike. Martin did the same thing.

We broke into a dogtrot. The golf course was long and green. A flock of starlings broke from the ivy climbing Skinner's house,

114

calling wildly and flying in formation over our heads. The grass was warm and moist, and each time I pushed off my toes squeaked a little.

The pond was at the bottom of a long hill. We sprinted down, stripping our shirts and tucking them over our heads to keep off the gnats. The pond came up too fast, and we skidded to a stop, our approach sending frogs and toads snapping into the water.

"You ever think there could be snakes?" asked Martin.

"Maybe. More likely rats."

"You think?"

"I don't know."

I balled up my T-shirt and threw it to one side, then stepped into the pond. I swept my feet in small circles, sensing the bottom with my toes and soles.

"How is it?" Martin asked.

"Terrible."

"Mucky?"

"Really mucky, but come on."

The water was tepid and smelled stale. Martin drew in his breath as he entered. "Shit," he said, but kept coming, wading too fast to feel anything.

"Go slow," I said.

"What the hell was that?"

"What?"

"It felt like a frog. Oh, Christ, they have grass clippings on the bottom. It feels like I'm walking through a woman's scalp. Come here and try it."

"No, thanks."

"It feels like a new hairdo. It's awful."

I found the first ball a couple of minutes later. It was about five feet from shore, and it must have been hit with some force since it had burrowed into the ground.

"Got one," I said.

"Got it?"

"Yep."

I bent close to the water and put my arm in up to my shoulder. The ball slipped away, but I found it again and managed to hold it. My ear filled with water, and all sound died for the time it took me to rinse the ball clean.

"Maxfli," I said.

"This pond is disgusting."

Mosquitoes buzzed around us. I slapped at them as I waded, intentionally going deeper to get away from them. The bottom of the pond was a little more sandy toward the center, and it was there we found most of the balls. They had rolled or drifted to the center, working their way down into a small nest.

It took us an hour to search the whole pond. Martin cursed most of the time. He didn't like the water, the bottom, or the thought of stepping on a frog. After each new find he asked how many we had.

"Ten, I guess, about ten."

"That's enough."

"A few more."

By the time we climbed out, it was completely dark. Frogs, back in the grass and weeds around the pond, sang and croaked, their drum necks stretching and releasing air.

We collected the balls from the fairway, where we had tossed them making a bag out of our T-shirts, knotting them into an egg sac.

"How much they worth?" Martin asked. He picked mud off the hair on his calves. I knew he was afraid of ticks and leeches.

"Around five bucks. I don't know."

"I don't know if it's worth wading through that shit for five bucks. Each of us gets what—two fifty? I can find two bucks in the sofa cushions at home. No one else looks there."

"Not even Stu?"

"Stu looks in closets. He brings the minesweeper through your shoes and things at the bottom of the closet; then he laughs like crazy if he finds a quarter. I think it's stealing personally."

"You ready to go?"

We headed off, Martin carrying the golf balls against his chest. The mosquitoes were thick, so we jogged easily, digging our toes into the soft grass, leaning forward a bit to climb the slope. The moon was ringed by fog and mist, and I felt the heat closing in, the air becoming thick and still.

We jogged to Skinner's and stopped. The sprinkler was on, flapping in soft loops against a patch of lily of the valley. Martin carried the balls to the bike while I crept to the sprinkler and

116

snared it. Martin came back and took the spray on his upper body, leaning forward to rinse his hands and face, cleaning himself like a sleek raccoon.

"Hot," he said after.

"You want to go see Chris?"

"You want to?"

"I asked you."

"She likes you, not me," Martin said.

"So? What's the difference? Besides, Marla could be there. You wouldn't mind seeing her, would you?"

Martin shrugged, then came over and held the sprinkler for me. I washed myself slowly, shaking every now and then when the bugs became too dense.

We hopped the fence, and I tied the balls under the bar in front of Martin's seat. Martin pedaled around them, his knees out, his feet touching the pedals only at the heels. The baseball cards were not as crisp as they had been, and as Martin pedaled, the sound was softer, more gentle.

"You want to go right up?" Martin asked. "I mean, ring the doorbell and everything?"

"Well, what do you want to do? Stand out in the bushes and make noises?"

I trotted beside Martin the length of Woodland Avenue and up Topping Hill Road. I jumped on the center bar as we coasted down, keeping my legs up, being careful not to jostle the golf balls. I squinted against the insects that snapped against us, their bodies stinging for a second before they rolled off.

"What do you think?" Martin asked as we banked around the turn and entered Chris's street. Her house was brightly lit. A small gas lamp on the front lawn had a ring of moths circling it, their bodies tapping into the glass, their ticks almost as loud as the gas jet. The front yard was spotted with dandelions, and the grass itself was too long.

"Here goes nothing," Martin said, picking up the pace.

We had some momentum going from the run down Topping Hill, so it wasn't difficult for him to keep it up. His legs whirred, and he strained with his arms to get us moving faster.

"Wait," I said.

"Too late."

117

"Hold it."

I tried to drag my foot. I wanted a few minutes to think about what I would say, how I would act, but Martin wouldn't stop. He pedaled as fast as he could up the narrow driveway, the baseball cards humming, the golf balls swinging.

"Whoooaa," Martin said, applying the brakes.

We almost slammed into the back of a Chevy parked in the driveway. Martin had to swerve to get past it, and we shot through a tiny gap between the car and some bushes, the leaves twanging in our spokes and chain.

Chris and her entire family were in the backyard. Janet, Chris's older sister, toasted marshmallows at the grill. Chris's mother was there, stacking dishes on a tray. Her father looked as if he'd just stepped off the commuter train. His tie was loose around his neck, and his white shirt glowed in the dark. His beard, even from where I stood, appeared dark and heavy. He looked like a marine, a foot soldier, and he jumped up when we crashed through the bushes, his hands coming up instinctively, his stance quartering to a boxing pose.

"What the hell?" he asked.

"Hello," Martin answered.

Chris melted back. She actually pulled away from the tables and the candles as if to retreat into darkness. Seeing her, I realized how wrong this was. I didn't know her well enough. I had seen her in school, of course, and also at her ballet class at the Y, but I had never talked with her for any length of time. I also knew we looked like savages: Martin hadn't bothered to put his shoes back on, and we both were without shirts. We were streaked with dirt and mud, and our hair was still damp from the sprinkler.

"What's this?" Chris's dad asked, turning to the girls. "Who are they? Have I met them before? Are you here to rape or plunder, or both?"

"Daddy," Janet said. She blew at her marshmallow. "They're some of Chris's queer friends."

"Oh? And I suppose your friends are all clean-cut? How about that boy who rides motorcycles—what's his name? Setto? Stiletto?"

"Steel. His name is Steel, for the hundredth time."

118

Chris's dad sank back on the bench. He was larger than I had first thought. He put his elbows on the table and spoke over his shoulder to Chris. "Why don't you see if they want something? They look like they might eat insects."

"Daddyyy," Chris whined.

"Well? Come in, come in," he said to us. "Do you have shirts, or is this some sort of initiation rite? Are you part of a tribe?"

Chris's mom finished with the dishes, shook her head, and carried the tray inside. The screen door ticked shut. Janet lifted her marshmallow a second time, but now it was burning, and she made a series of blowing noises, trying to get it out.

I was off the bike. Martin moved it back and let it rest on the bushes. He untied the bundle of golf balls and carried them toward the table.

"Wampum?" the father went on, expanding over the table, taking up an empty beer bottle.

"Golf balls," Martin said. "We found them at Echo Lake."

"Really? How many do you have?"

"I don't know. Max, how many?"

"Around twenty."

I came closer to the table. I looked at Chris mostly, although Janet stuck her skewer in front of me, the black marshmallow bobbing.

"You want it?" she asked. "I hate when they're burned."

"No, thanks."

"You sure? They're still good."

"No, really."

She turned, made a throwing motion, and the marshmallow catapulted off the skewer. It hit in the bushes and fell down through the branches until it was still.

In the meantime, Martin had spread the balls on the grass at the edge of the picnic table. Chris's father bent close and, examining each ball, separated the better ones and tossed back the rest.

"Hello," I said to Chris.

"Hi. Would you excuse me for a second? I'll be right back."

She stood, but before she could move, Janet said, "Don't forget to take in some dishes. Just because your dreamboat is here, it doesn't mean it isn't your night to clean up."

Janet smiled, her teeth white in the darkness. Chris loaded her arms with dishes, the whole time shaking her head at Janet. When she went off, I moved to where Martin talked to Chris's father. He smelled of beer and cologne. He had a bald spot at the back of his head, a soft glow of scalp ringed by hair.

"Maxfli, Spalding, another Spalding," Martin said.

"How much do you want for them?"

"I don't know."

"Give me a round figure. There are enough balls here to last me a season. What's a season's worth of golf balls cost? Any idea?"

"No, not really," Martin said.

"Oh, Dad, just give them something for it."

Janet was back toasting another marshmallow. She wore cutoff jeans with frayed edges. The cutoffs were extremely short, and I found myself looking at her legs, the wide, soft curve of her upper thighs.

"This is business," Chris's dad countered. "We're bartering."

The screen door clicked again, and Chris stepped out on the back stoop. She had changed her top, and her hair looked combed. Her cutoffs were as short as Janet's, and since she was barefoot, her steps were completely silent.

"Hi," I said again, idiotically.

"Hi."

"Bring me a beer, would you, Chrissy? That's a good girl."

Chris turned and went back inside. I saw her head in the kitchen window. She talked to her mother, both of them standing slightly hunched, apparently bent over the sink.

"So you boys went where? Up to the course? Did they know you were there?"

"No, sir," said Martin.

"They let dogs run on it, you know? Big, damn shepherds, too. You were lucky."

"Daddy, you don't have to curse," Janet said.

She winked at me. I winked back, and she burst out laughing.

"Oh, jeez," she said.

"That's cursing right there," her father said. " 'Oh, jeez' is the same as saying, 'Oh, Jesus.' In fact, it's worse. You're not even calling Him by His right name."

"It's not a curse; it's slang."

120

"Who says? I'm telling you, it's a curse. You think He doesn't know what you mean?" he asked, pointing toward the stars.

"Then it doesn't matter what you say, does it?" Martin asked. "I mean, if He knows everything and even does everything, then He knows what you're going to say or think before you even think it. Cursing then is destiny."

"Ahaaaaaa." Chris's father rocked back. "Where'd you get that? You think that up on your own? No, you've been having your head filled, that's what. Sit down here. Come here for a second. Chris? Chris, is there a beer left in New Jersey?"

"You're in for it now," Janet said. She finished with her marshmallow and picked it off the skewer. Her lips were speckled with white. "You're in for it. Here comes the old 'I was trained by the Jesuits' routine. Right, Dad? When the talk turns to philosophy, he calls up the ghost of Brother Aquinas, his teacher in senior ethics. Wait, you'll hear."

Martin took a seat on the picnic bench. He liked a good argument. Chris came out before they started. She carried a beer for her father and two sodas for us.

"That's a girl," her dad said, taking the beer. He dug in his pocket, produced a cigarette, and struck a wooden match against the edge of his wristwatch.

"Now," he said, "go ahead, what's your name?"

"Martin."

"Martin, huh? Well, call me Mr. Row, I guess. I always feel funny being called that, but that's another topic. Now, what's this you were saying?"

Chris sat across the table. Janet held a marshmallow up to her mouth and began speaking softly into it, pretending it was a microphone, exaggerating her facial expressions.

Martin was serious, and he cocked his head to think, finally coming up with a collected sentence. "I guess what I'm saying is that, given the definition of God, it's impossible to offend Him. I guess that's it."

"One point, Martin," said Janet.

"Now, now, not so fast. No, no, you have to define a few things first. You have to define God, for one thing."

"That's simple enough," Janet said.

"What happened while I was gone?" Chris asked.

121

"Daddy is turning into a Jesuit before our eyes," said Janet. "In a minute he'll be talking about the great mystical continuance of the Catholic Church."

Mr. Row ignored them. He frowned, then said, "Then there's no free will?"

"None."

"Why do you stay alive then?"

"To see what God has in store. I stay awake all day long on my birthday to see what my parents bought me, and I have no control over that either."

"That's hardly an analogy—"

"It is, too, Dad," Janet said. "It's a perfectly good analogy. God put it in Martin's head."

I looked over at Chris, who was arranging the empty glasses and bottles in small squadrons on the table. I had a feeling she had experienced this type of thing before.

While I was thinking, there was a noise in the driveway and three girls appeared. I recognized two of them immediately from school. One was Marla, the girl Martin had his eye on. The other was Alice, a fat girl who seemed to hang out wherever Chris and Marla happened to be. The third girl I didn't know at all.

"Hi," they said as they came into light. "Hello, everyone."

"Imagine," Janet said. "All of you just taking it into your heads to come over at the same time. Isn't it a wonder? *Quelle* coincidence."

"Janet . . ." Chris said.

Mrs. Row stepped out on the back stoop, and a large dog barreled past her, his mouth already opening to bark.

"Oh, Christ," Mr. Row said. "This is some place for a conversation. Why don't you hire a goddamned band to march through on the hour? Is the beer all gone?"

The girls approached the table shyly. They all looked freshly washed, and their hair fell in soft swishes against their shoulders. Martin bent to pick up his T-shirt and straightened to throw me mine. I pulled it on quickly and watched Chris get up. She threw a short wave to the girls, then ran past them into the kitchen.

"Reinforcements, huh?" Mr. Row said. "Well, sit, sit. What's better than to be young and all sexed up on a night like this?"

"Dad . . ." said Janet.

"Dad, stop it," Chris yelled from inside.

"Sorry, everyone. I'm just being a Jesuit."

"A what?" Alice asked. "What did you say you were?"

"A Jessy," Janet said.

"What's that?" Marla asked. "A Jezebel?"

"More or less," Mr. Row said. He rubbed his eyes and took a long swig of beer. He flicked his cigarette toward the grill, then reached down to pet the dog, who snorted like a pig around our feet, searching for scraps.

The girls sat at the table. Marla managed to sit near Martin. Alice and the third girl moved in tandem, closer than dates could have been, and propped themselves on the smaller bench at the end. Chris reappeared with a tray of iced tea.

"You know what I always wondered?" Janet asked, moving to the head of the table and picking up another marshmallow. "I always wondered what age you are in heaven. Are you a kid soul or a grown-up soul? And if you're given a choice, what if I choose to be a grown-up soul and Dad chooses to be a kid soul? Then do I get to send him to bed when I like?"

"Is she serious?" Alice asked, making a short, barking laugh.

"Janet, don't you start, too. Don't get him going again," Chris said.

"It's a good question," Mr. Row said. "The second part isn't so sound, but asking what age you are in heaven—that's a damn good question."

A breeze moved over the table, taking a couple of balled-up napkins with it. The napkins spilled onto the ground and tumbled across the grass, skimming lightly. Chris began putting glasses on the remaining napkins, pinning them down. Martin rolled a golf ball back and forth on the table, letting it run in the crack between the slats, bouncing it on his hand and sending it back.

"So, what now?" asked Janet. "Is everyone having a great time?"

"Janet . . ." Chris said.

"Okay, okay. Who wants a marshmallow? Anyone? How about you, Clark, old dog? You want a marshmallow?"

She held a fresh marshmallow at waist level, jerked her hand up, then dropped it a few inches as Clark jumped up, his jaws clicking, his body twisting. "Ho, boy," Alice said, and Janet did the trick again, this time pretending to throw the marshmallow first. Clark turned his head toward the darkness beyond the table but then caught on and began whining, his ears cocked like a movie dog.

"Oh, the poor thing," the third girl said.

"Suffer," Janet said. "Suffer, you fat dog."

Mrs. Row stepped out, smiled quickly, then called to Mr. Row. "Jeff, can I see you?"

"Uh-oh, you're in trouble now, Pop," Janet said.

"Right there, darling. Hold on a second."

Mr. Row stood, his hand tapping his pockets to check for cigarettes. He was a bit tipsy, and I saw the notions for his movements come into his head a second before he executed them. There was something sad about his gathering himself so, collecting his beer bottle, picking up his matches, shuffling his loafers on the grass to get his heels inside. Now and then, in the slow process, he looked at Martin and me and shook his head. He pulled his tie and opened his collar wider, straining to get his neck free.

"Go on, go on," he said. "Don't let me stop you. The voice of reason has sounded once more."

"Daddy, you're drunk," said Janet.

"Drunk? Maybe a little. Do you know it was a hundred and twelve on the train tonight?"

"So?"

"So? A man could keel over and die in heat like that. We had the window open, but that only made it hotter. The conductors didn't even collect the tickets."

"Oh, God, imagine," Alice said.

Then Mr. Row was out of it. It happened just like that. First he was part of our group, his age unimportant, and in the next instant he was alone, ten paces from the table, walking slowly toward the back door. A wedge of sweat ran down his back. I wanted to tell Martin we should give him the golf balls for nothing, but Martin was already warming up his tricks, pretending to make a pack of matches disappear behind his head. The girls watched him, somewhat out of politeness, although Marla was more attentive than the others.

Chris looked up at Janet and asked, "How many marshmallows you going to eat?"

124

"Is that a hint?"

"Duh."

Janet, in a last frenzy, pretended to take the skewer and run it through her head. It was plenty realistic in the dim light. She took one end and pretended to stab it in her ear. With a little yelp she made her head fly to one side as if from the force of the insertion; then she began feeding the metal through, at times tapping it with her hand to get it past imaginary bone tissue.

"Oh, oh, oh, oh," she said, knocking it with her fist.

"Janet, I can't believe you're going to college," Alice said.

"Oh, oh, oh."

"You are so disgusting," Marla told her. "You are. You have a warped sense of humor."

"What? I can't hear you. I have a skewer through my brains."

"I can't look. I really can't," the third girl said.

On she went. She was a natural ham, and she carried the whole thing off. Never once did she stop and say it wasn't real. She made the show into a small torture, ramming the skewer in, her eyes rolling, her tongue coming out, her eyebrows dancing.

"Owwwwwww, owwwwwwwwww." She changed her sound and hopped on one leg to shake the skewer loose. "Here it comes, here it comes."

"You know, it almost looks real," said Marla.

"Through the eardrum, bing, boom, there it goes."

She made the skewer stick in her hair and now, at the crucial point, took her hands away and left the metal suspended there. It looked real, and it gave me a moment's pause even though I knew it couldn't be.

"It doesn't even hurt. It doesn't. The brain doesn't have any sensations."

"Okay, Janet," Marla said. "Whatever you say."

"Do you know Stu?" Martin asked her. "If you don't, you should."

"Stu who?"

"Stu, my brother. He's your age."

"I don't think so. What's he like?"

"Never mind."

"No, tell me."

"It's not worth it, believe me."

125

Janet pulled the skewer free, making the appropriate grinding noises. When she finished, she made a small bow and headed for the back door.

"I know you want me to stay, but I really must be off," she said in a high, British accent.

"You're off all right," Alice said.

Marla poured herself some iced tea. Chris drew a face on the cold glass, giving it curly hair and a bland smile.

"Who's that?" Martin asked.

"I don't know."

"It looks like—who does it look like?"

"We're heading off," Alice said. "We're supposed to meet Jane Royal over at the Lytes'. She's baby-sitting."

"Are you sure?" Chris asked.

"I'm sure," Alice said. "Aren't we?"

"Sure," the fat girl said, hurrying to stand.

I knew it had all been planned, but I didn't care. I was sure Chris had called on her first trip inside and they had been rounded up. Now they were superfluous and willing to be shed.

"You sure you have to?" Marla asked, covering herself.

"Positive."

We said good-bye all the way around, then watched them turn the corner of the garage, Alice's hand lifting in a final wave. Clark trotted out to the front yard with them, and we heard his collar jingle as he returned, his tail going, his nose close to the ground. At the same time I heard a shout from inside the house. It was Mr. Row.

"You want to walk?" Chris asked.

"I'll walk. You want to walk?" Martin asked me.

"Okay."

We stood and moved away from the table. We were awkward at first. I didn't know where to stand, although it was obvious we were walking in order to be closer to one another. Chris was taller than I remembered.

"Where do you want to go?" Marla asked. "Anyplace special?"

"I don't care," Chris told her. "Why don't we walk toward Wilson?" she said, naming the old elementary school. "I normally walk Clark up that way."

Once we were out on the sidewalk, we paired off. Chris and I fell behind, while Marla and Martin took off at a quicker pace, Martin hopping a little in his bare feet.

"I'm sorry about how we came in tonight," I said.

"Mom's the only one who minds."

"I'm sorry."

"It doesn't matter."

We walked down her street and took a right. Clark ran somewhere in front of us, sniffing through the neighbors' yards, stopping every once in a while to wait for us. His eyes were bright.

"Am I walking too fast?" I asked.

"No, not at all."

"I've seen you at the Y. At your ballet lessons."

"I saw you once."

"Why didn't you come over?"

"Why didn't you?"

"I don't know. It's funny at the Y. For some reason you always feel guilty for seeing anyone you know there. Do you know what I mean?"

"Exactly."

"I like it, though. There are some nice guys there. You ever meet Deado or Jock or Small?"

"No, who are they?"

"Just some guys."

Our hands brushed together and sometimes we bumped shoulders. I was aware of everything she did, her slightest movement. I smelled her perfume; under it was the scent of some powder that I had smelled before but couldn't name. Under the streetlights I saw the pale print of her blouse and the gentle flex of her thighs. Her hair, soft and shoulder-length, had two darker stains along the temples where her perspiration had matted it.

We didn't talk again until we reached the school. Chris whistled Clark nearer, slapping her thigh, and bent to nuzzle him when he ran to her. She patted his sides, her hand making a hollow thump on his ribs.

"Where did they go?" I asked.

"Marla probably asked him to walk her home."

"Is it late?"

"It's getting there. I should go in pretty soon."

"Your dad was nice."

"You think so? I always think he acts stupid around my friends. I guess he's all right. He's better than most."

"No, he was nice. He really was."

"What did you think of Janet?"

"I liked her. She doesn't seem like your sister."

"What do you mean?"

"She seems wilder or something. She's more like your dad."

"Maybe so."

She straightened up, leaning a little back and forth to stretch her leg muscles. We stood looking at Clark, taking an interest in him neither of us felt, watching him drift off again into the shadow of the school building.

"Want to swing?" I asked.

"Sure, if you do."

"Come on, I'll push you."

It was something I had seen in the movies, but it seemed romantic. I wasn't sure how she would take it. We walked to the swing set, and I waited while she took her seat, her legs stretching out in front of her. I moved behind and pushed, my hands spread wide on her back, my thumbs feeling just the smallest ridge of her bra.

"I haven't been pushed in years. Sometimes I come up here alone and swing. It's cooler."

I didn't talk. Pushing her was simply an excuse to touch her. I concentrated on my hands, on the strange sensation I felt each time she came back into them, her legs going up on the other side.

"Higher," she said.

I pushed harder. She didn't turn to look at me, yet I knew she was as aware as I was of my hands touching her back. Her shoulder blades were very slender.

"You swing, too," she said once, but I didn't listen. I knew at some point the swinging would end in a kiss, but I wasn't good with girls, and I wasn't sure how to go about it. I was nervous when she began dragging her feet, slowing herself down, her back coming up straight.

"We used to jump when we wanted to stop. We called it parachuting," she said.

"Did you?"

"Yes. But Janet never jumped. I don't know why."

128

I no longer pushed. Her feet made a steady beat on the ground. Small puffs of dirt came up each time, coating her legs. Her swing twisted a little, and she soon had it going around, the chain above her knotting and creaking.

"We used to do this, too," she said.

"Did you ever get sick when you went around too much? Or on those spinning things they had on some playgrounds?"

"The little carousels?"

"Yes."

"Sometimes. I used to get headaches on them. Why do they put them on playgrounds? I never figured that out. Kids always get sick."

I moved and took the chains in my hands. She hardly spun any longer. I held the chains still, then bent quickly to kiss her. She looked up, prepared to kiss me, but the chains uncoiled a notch, and I ended up kissing her cheekbone. I felt her eyelashes against my lips.

"Sorry," I said.

She laughed and stood. I leaned forward again and kissed her. This time our lips met and I brought my arms around her. I wanted to say something, but anything I thought of seemed silly, unimportant, and so I concentrated on kissing her, feeling her body slowly fit to mine, the sound of a mosquito so close to both of us that we lifted a hand together.

❖❖ 20 ❖❖

A FEW DAYS later I went to the YMCA alone. It was after dinner. Martin was out with Marla, and he was supposed to meet me later. Stu was off cutting grass.

I found Deado sitting in his parlor alone. The evening was warm but overcast. He had both windows open, the chicken broth on low behind him. It was dim in the room, quiet and calm, and Deado was in a near doze when I entered.

"Deado?" I asked.

"Who's that? Max?"

"Yep. You okay? You mind if I come in?"

"I'm fine. Come in, come in."

I moved to a chair across the card table from him. I could tell Jock had just been there. A cigar still smoked in an ashtray.

"Where's Small?" I asked.

"Where's Martin? You think they're necking in a closet somewhere?"

"Martin's out with a girl."

"Small's just out for smokes."

I fanned a deck of cards on the table, then practiced cutting them with one hand. Deado leaned back in his chair, took a mug from a windowsill, and poured me a cup of soup, reaching in with a fork to herd the noodles out.

He looked older in the dimness. His profile was sharply cut, and I noticed for the first time that he was handsome. It was an old-style handsome, like last season's coat, the line no longer in fashion.

"So?" Deado said. He put a cup in front of me. He was framed by the bare windows, the soft, shaggy heat of the evening.

"Hot, huh?" I said.

"You telling or asking? If you're telling me, I already know. If you're asking, it means you got here without going outside to see for yourself."

He took a sip of soup, then said, "Don't talk about the weather. You can only sound dumb when you talk about the weather. Unless you're a farmer or maybe an astronaut, what does it matter?"

"Still."

"You want pepper in that?"

"No, it's all right."

A truck went past the window, and we listened to it for a while. Deado rolled one of his *National Geographics* into a tube and pretended it was a gearshift. He worked the truck up until it slipped from our hearing.

"You know those ballerinas?" I asked. "The ones that practice in the gym with Mrs. Minifie?"

"You should."

"I started dating this one—"

"You should," he said, looking at me over his cup. "Anything you're going to ask about them—you should."

"But I was going to ask about taking one out."

"You name it, you should. It's sort of like a rule with women. You want to ask one out, you should. You want to kiss one, and she's willing, you should."

"So you think so?"

"What's the opposite of *should?*"

"*Shouldn't.*"

"So what am I going to tell you? You shouldn't ask her out? You shouldn't see anyone? What kind of life would that be? You're a young man, so you should. Almost everything should be

131

a 'should' right now. You give it some time, you'll get to 'maybe.' After that it's 'when I can.'"

He laughed at his own joke and sprinkled some pepper into his plain white cup. He reached behind him and turned down the temperature gauge on the hot plate. It was getting dark.

"Seriously," he said, turning back to me. "You're a young man; it's a sweet time of life. Both of you—the young girls and you, I mean—you're both waiting for something to happen. Don't be shy about it. There's nothing to be shy about. Everyone wants someone to talk to them. Tell Martin he should do the same thing. Only Stu shouldn't—he might reproduce."

"I'll tell him."

I worked on the cards for a while. I expected Jock or Small to enter at any time, but the halls outside remained empty. Once we heard the custodian pass below, his keys lifting and jingling in time to his stride, but otherwise the Y was quiet.

"You know," said Deado eventually, "my dad left me, too."

"Who told you?" I asked. My face flushed, and I couldn't think for a moment.

"Oh, people talk. No one means anything by talking; it's just all there is to do in life. You'll see what I mean someday. People know everything if you're around them long enough. There's no point in keeping secrets."

"Did Martin tell you?"

"Like I said, there's no point."

"Did Martin tell you that?"

"No, I really don't think he did. Maybe he did, but I'm not sure. It could have been Stu."

"So what did they say—whoever it was?"

"They said your father took off and that no one knows where he is. Is that right?"

I tapped the cards into a neat stack and nodded. Part of me pulled to get up, but another part wanted to stay and hear what Deado had to say. He had said that his father had left with such calmness, such casualness that I wondered if I could ever feel the same way.

"You're from a different class, of course. You're supposed to be middle or upper middle, and this sort of stuff isn't supposed to happen to you. But it does, it does sometimes."

132

"Why did your father leave?"

"I don't know."

"Didn't you try to find out?"

"Oh, sure, but mostly I knew why. I saw things around me; I saw how it was. I had friends whose fathers left. I mean, they weren't the kind of fathers who played catch out in the backyard with their kids, you understand me? There was a lot of drinking and a lot of roughness. Sometimes kids were glad to see them go."

"Were you?"

Deado looked at me. He went to sip his chicken soup, but the cup never reached his lips.

"I wasn't glad, no," he said. "I kept thinking he was going to come back and that we'd have all this phony father and son stuff that you saw on TV. I even asked for a fishing pole one Christmas because I thought that's what we'd do—go fishing out on the old Schuylkill River in Philadelphia. I didn't know the river was so polluted that any decent fish would have died in about a minute and a half in there. The bad part was that I knew it would never happen, I knew the whole thing was just a dream on my part, but I went along with it anyway. Then I felt embarrassed about it. The whole thing was a big mess. I finally threw the pole out."

"But you actually got the pole? You bought one?"

"My mother bought it for me. She knew what I was doing and offered to take me out fishing, but you know, there was no sense to that. When I think back . . . Christ, we would have had to take a subway out there. You can't go fishing on a fucking subway, can you? You can go to a ball game, but you can't go fishing."

I wanted to ask him to go on, to talk more about his father, but just then Small came into the room. He stopped in the doorway, fumbling for the switch. Deado and I blinked when the light finally came on.

"You two," Small said by way of greeting.

He had some packages, and he put them down on the shuffle-board table, arranging them in a neat row. The largest bag was filled with cans of chicken soup, and he began unloading them, stacking them in the far corner of the table. Most of the items were food—crackers, cold cuts, mustard, hot dogs.

When Small finished, he went back to his last package. He

133

turned it upside down and dumped the contents onto the table.
The bag was crammed with yo-yos.

"What the hell?" Deado said.

"Wait a second," Small said.

"We can't waste money, Small. What's the fucking idea?"

"Wait a second. Wait, don't jump all over me. Wait until you
see it."

He picked up two yo-yos and went out into the hallway. He
disappeared from sight; then we heard, faintly, his voice coming
to us through his pinched nostrils. He tried to make himself sound
like a PA system. He announced his own name, calling out the
syllables, pretending to fight an echo. Finally his hand came
around the wall and flicked off the light.

Small jumped into the room without further explanation. He
had two yo-yos going, and they both glowed. The yo-yos flew
like fluorescent bats, whizzing in tiny orbits around Small's head,
then back and away, disappearing for a second before they came
flying out at us again.

"Christ," Deado said.

But Small was on. He began zinging the yo-yos faster, whipping
them in erratic loops, his dark hands touching the strings. He
gained his rhythm slowly, but when he did, he began skipping and
humming lightly, switching from foot to foot, causing the lamps
to shake, Deado's cup to chatter. He looked like a fighter, a pug,
as he whizzed around the room, sparring with the darkness.

"What do you think?" he asked, running through some new
tricks. He stopped one yo-yo long enough to use his other hand
for Rock-the-Baby.

"You're something," Deado said.

"Where'd you learn that?" I asked.

"Just picked it up. Jack-of-all-trades, you know. We used to
play with them when we were kids."

He moved to the wall and turned the light back on. I took a
closer look at the yo-yos on the shuffleboard table. There was a
wide assortment: butterflies with wide, winged spreads; imperials,
which were glassy and clear; hummers; whistlers; even one that
could double as a top.

"Some beauties," Small said. "They didn't have all this stuff

134

when I was a kid. They had a monster yo-yo, though; it must have been a foot across, but it was too expensive."

"Who paid for this stuff? You or me?" asked Deado.

"You did—on loan. I'll make it back."

"Sure you will."

"I'm telling you."

"You got a job?" Deado asked. Small sometimes repaired cars for friends. Once or twice he filled in for a mechanic at Larry's Service.

"No, but I'm going to put on a show. There was a guy in our town named Yo-Yo Yancey used to make a bundle on kids' shows."

"If he made so much, how come he didn't fork up the dough to change his name?"

"I'm telling you."

Small went back to twirling the yo-yos. He nodded toward the table.

"Go ahead, Max, give it a try."

"Can't you work one with your pickle there? You could lasso your dink and jump up and down."

Deado bent back and poured himself more soup. Just for a moment our eyes met, and I knew the conversation was over. If Small had left immediately, if he had just delivered the groceries and gone, we might have continued talking. But Small had stayed, and now Deado looked at me, his head nodding slightly.

I picked up a plain brown-twirl yo-yo. It fitted nicely in my palm. I flipped it down and felt it climb back up, then suddenly go into a sleep.

"Too much sleep," Small said before I could correct it. "You've got to wind it tighter."

"I will."

"Max, you listen to Yo-Yo Yancey now," Deado said.

I got the yo-yo going gradually. I could do only two tricks—Walk-the-Dog and Over-the-Falls—but I showed them both to Small.

"Good, good," he said.

Meanwhile, Small went through a sequence of tricks. He was an expert. He did another Rock-the-Baby, a Loop-the-Loop, then a Shoot-the-Moon. He kept his left hand going full time, looping

135

his yo-yo in a yellow orbit while his right hand occasionally came in with a new demonstration, a new trick that stole the limelight from the left.

He finished, saying, "Ta-daaaaa," and made a strange little stage curtsy.

"Fucking-a," Deado said.

"It'll be money," Small said. "Wait and see."

❖❖ 21 ❖❖

I DATED Chris through the rest of the summer, although
she went to camp for most of July and our romance
was reduced to letters. The months passed quickly for the first
time since my father had left. Cold weather finally set in, warning
first in blue nights and short afternoons, then easing up the boles
of trees and entering the branches. Night by night the temperature dropped, and one afternoon afghans and comforters appeared
at the ends of our beds.

Autumn was Gertrude's season. She let it be known that this
was a time of storage and harvest, and she rose early each day to
prove it, her waking an alarm to us all, her vigor a silent rebuke.

Most days she went outside to work in the garden. As I lapped
my breakfast cereal, I saw her winding the fat, frost-glittered
hose, bending over the mysterious clay pots she brought up from
the darkness of the basement, and pruning the hedges with violent
jerks of her thin arms. Later she went to the vegetable garden and
inspected it like a gull, her eye darting, her head cocking, her
fingers moving nimbly to pick late squash, beans, cukes, and a
few stray tomatoes. She was fierce at this time, done as she was
with the lethargy of summer, and she bent down old stalks, broke

them away, and threw them to rot on the lawn, saying to me if I was near, "Rake these with the leaves."

At the end of each day there was a pile of vegetables on the lawn, and it was my job to bring them inside. Gertrude guided me in the work, supplying me with wicker baskets for the job, elbowing aside the screen door as she backed into the kitchen.

"There, there you go," she said, at the same time stripping off her old leather flying jacket with its fine fur collar. "Just set it on the newspapers."

Newspapers lined the floor, and it was here Gertrude knelt to pick over the produce. She could have been a craps player or street shill for the attention she lavished on the vegetables, and it was a wonder to watch her separate the basket loads into various piles, the colors combining to form a palette, her mind working at some internal filing system, the clear, boiled Mason jars glinting to one side of the newspaper island.

This is what I remember of her: Gertrude, her biceps shaking softly as she turned the flames to orange on the range, her hair trailing down, her heavy pots, stored in inconvenient places, clanking and banging as she pulled them out. A broom remained propped against the refrigerator now, and she used it two or three times a day to sweep out the chaff and stalks, the thin skins of onions, and green stems from tomatoes. The broom bristles left black streaks where the newsprint and moisture had dampened the floor, and the rough brown welcome mat appeared combed at the end of each day. The door was left open, and the breeze would find us there, passing the odor of her chili sauce, her relish, and piccalilli, the stern scent of onions and peppers, while now and then she bent over a meat grinder, or perhaps gave the job to me, and I fed the grinder herbs and spices, raw hunks of stew meat, bread, scallions, turning it steadily and watching the spew of it fall into a thick mixing bowl. The kitchen turned into a laboratory, and all night things cooked, the flames lowered to a simmer, the long, even heat fighting the frost outside.

Once started, she could not get enough of cooking. It was during this spree that Uncle Jack and I carved the pumpkin into a jack-o'-lantern, lifting the tangled pulp out onto the kitchen table, cupping it in newspaper, then giving this also to Gertrude.

138

"Just set it there." She instructed us with her elbow, her hands deep in the sink.

We put it between the scattered jars and lids, pushing away spoons so she would have a clear work space. This done, we went to work on the apples, spinning their skins off with our penknives and slipping the slices into a large colander she'd put out for us.

"Thin . . . thinner," she chided, though she never made us recut them. The shavings were dumped into a burlap bag and given to a pig on a nearby farm.

Once everything was diced and prepared, Tilly pitched in, occasionally bringing Marcie with her. Tilly dressed in Gil's cross-country letter sweater, a large R hanging at her pocket.

These days marked a strange period for both Tilly and Gertrude. Once, at dusk, Tilly took Gertrude out onto the back step and taught her an old cheer. They made an odd pair: Tilly, young and pretty, her hair hanging in tendrils, her legs shapely; Gertrude, large and serious, her hands worked to twice their age, bending along with Tilly, kicking up, shouting tentatively at first, then louder:

> Gilly, Gilly,
> he's our man.
> If he can't do it,
> Jacky can.

On weekends Uncle Jack took part. This also seemed to be his one season of domesticity, and besides gutting the pumpkin, he worked with me to clear the yard. It was hard work and cold, but we cleaned all the beds, raked the yard, did some final pruning, and put insulation over the cellar window wells. We raked toward the creek, at first for safety reasons since we intended to burn the leaves, but later it became a neighborhood tradition to bring the leaves to the Kellermans' lower yard and burn them all together on the evening of the first full moon.

Gertrude, as a result, gauged the moon to determine her final day of canning. It was late in the afternoon, toward evening, when she came out on the porch and sat on the steps. Over the years this had become a signal, and what had once been an informal gathering now took on the aspect of ritual. Jack, standing near the doorway, set out the bar on the kitchen table. Neighbors slowly began to collect.

It was a party, the only kind Gertrude threw, and soon the yard was crowded with adults carrying Halloween masks, folded lawn chairs at their sides. Often the small children wore their costumes—small clowns with red noses, witches in black crepe, devils with shiny horns and triangular tails—and milled nervously near their parents' chairs, turning on command or pouting when attention was directed at them. Gertrude made over the children lavishly, occasionally winning one to her lap.

Later, when full darkness arrived, Martin and Stu and I ran off to rake the leaves to their final height. Earlier in the day we had crumpled newspapers and buried them in the pile, and now we uncovered them partially so that we'd be able to find them when it was time to light the fire. Stu howled, but it was in the spirit of the night, and he eventually darted off to become a demon in the bushes, a snarling, slavering animal that shook the trees and frightened the children just to the edge of panic.

After a time the adults rose and moved quietly toward the brook, where they lined up single file for the plank. Martin went to the end of the plank and helped the ladies across, extending his hand and leading them up to Stu. I took charge of the children and made them stand back. Marcie served as guard, her arms outstretched, her hair moving in the wind.

"Ready?" someone would finally shout.

"Who's not here?" another called.

"Someone's missing—who is it?"

Families generally stood together for the lighting, and I searched out Jack and Gertrude. I was now taller than them, and as I stood on one side of Gertrude, her arm around my back, I felt her frailness, her thin bones. Jack, on the other hand, seldom looked at either of us. He smelled heavily of scotch, and on these occasions he became sentimental, afraid to talk for fear of faltering.

Gil set the flame. He moved around the pile clockwise, "to the sun," he said, touching each newspaper with the end of his candle, cupping his hand over the small flame. He recited a Druid ballad in a mixture of German and Gaelic, his hands lifting toward the sky. Whether his chant was real or not, I never knew.

140

In the end he hurried back to be with Tilly and his family. There followed a quick clap, a low murmur, then silence. The children would watch and I would watch until the leaves burned away to a shimmering bed of coals, which blinked and glowed at each press of wind.

❖❖ 22 ❖❖

THAT FALL Stu worked to get his driver's license. His epilepsy had caused some legal skirmishes. The doctors, however, assured the officials, and Tilly and Gil as well, that Stu was fit to drive, that his petit seizures were very predictable and well under control, and that he would probably end up being a superior driver because of his tentative position with the law.

Martin and I already had our licenses, but we went along with Stu when Tilly gave him his lessons. Tilly made us swear each time that we would be silent and not kibbitz.

"Swear? Do you promise?" Tilly asked as we climbed into the back seat to wait for Stu. "I don't want you two getting Stu all wild."

"I promise," Martin said.

"Crossies don't count. No tricks, you understand, you two?" asked Tilly again, bending to look at our faces.

"Okay," I said.

Stu came out of the house, eating a sandwich. He had a ravenous appetite now, working out as he did twice a day. Raising his hands in the signal of a champion, he stood by the hood, a peanut butter sandwich dangling on his chin, his crazy look more insane than ever.

"Come on, Stu," Tilly would say. "I don't have all day."

"What do you have if not all day?" Martin asked from the back, mimicking Jock. "Do you ever think of that?"

"Stop it, Martin," Tilly snapped.

Martin turned to me and made a face while Stu climbed in, his sandwich wedged in his cheek like a chaw of tobacco. Eventually he sat straight, his meaty bicep bulging on the door.

"Ready?" Tilly asked. "Concentrate now."

"There is someone in the audience whose aunt is sick," Stu would say, putting his hand to his head. "The aunt lives in Ottawa."

"Be serious or I'll get out right now."

Stu winked at her, his eye stretched to a swollen line from the sandwich wadded in his cheek. Then, wildly, he would start the car and begin ramming gears, bucking us down the street, swooping around turns. Tilly, her head jagging back and forth, her hand always outstretched to the dash, would say, "Easy now, Stu. Easy."

But he had no natural rhythm and, worse, no caution, and he liked to rely on the gas to overcome any troubles he had in shifting. As a result, we lurched wherever we went, Martin breaking his vow of silence to shout, "Ride em, bronco!," while Stu fought for control of the car, winking at us in the rearview mirror to show how silly he thought Tilly's constant shouts of guidance. Occasionally he reached forward to adjust the radio, and Tilly would grab his wrist and wrestle it back to the steering wheel.

"We don't need music, too. Not now," she said, her voice broken.

Then, a moment later but no more collected, she might say, "Oh, Stu, maybe you should just wait until we can get an automatic. That's just steering. Don't you think that would be better? You have trouble with your hands and feet. Look out!"

But Stu was immune. He claimed driving as his right, and he often reached up and rapped on the roof as Tilly talked, then stuck his head out as if to see who could be up there.

"Come in, who's there?" he called in a singsong voice.

"It's Zorro," Martin screamed. "It's Godzilla!"

"Stop it, Martin," Tilly warned.

This was Martin, of course, and he couldn't stop. Following Stu's lead, he stuck his head up to look, then pretended to be

143

caught by something. Stu began trying to scrape him off, swerving the car intentionally to pass close to bordering trees, sometimes reaching back to roll up the window on him.

"Would you both stop that? Stop it!"

For a month Stu had a Cinderella license, good for daytime driving only. It kept him in check at night, but he used the car regularly for his lawn business. His license came just in time because he had spread himself too thin and was barely able to keep up with the work. To help him out, Martin and I went along on the afternoon jobs. We were his yard boys, and we worked under his direction, always lackadaisically so that he wouldn't take our contribution as an indication we wanted more hours.

"Wind that hose," Stu would shout, and Martin would reply: "Tote that bale," forcing Stu to come over and take the hose away, shaking his head in disgust.

"You're a retard, Martin. You should be on a telethon."

"Okwayy, Stuueey."

We went with Stu, too, as he traveled to each customer's home to present the final bill. Stopping a block away, he shamelessly padded anything he could think of, making up new charges on the spot and writing them down on his triplicate billing paper, using the sun visor as a desk. He counted on the homeowners' trust and their mistaken belief that he would be too innocent to try such a thing. Moreover, he finagled tips from most of them by standing with perfect ease in their doorways, shooting the breeze, shouting to us to tend to some last task he had deliberately left undone, his posture clearly stating he would hang on until the homeowner was forced to reach into his pocket as if he had forgotten to tip in the first place.

"For being so dependable," more than one said, handing him a ten or a twenty, just wanting to get rid of him.

Back in the car, Stu laughed and tapped the steering wheel. He pulled over to count his money, laughing even harder as he did it, pretending to shave with the edge of the bills as Martin shook his head.

"You're disgusting," Martin told him.

"Thank you."

"You are."

144

"I'll send them Christmas cards, too. I will. Who wants to look like a piker around Christmas? Figure it out. They're all worried I'll tell the other customers what stiffs they are."

"You sick thing."

"Thank you."

On the first night he was permitted to drive alone, Stu took Martin and me trick-or-treating with Chris, Marla, and Janet. Marla arranged everything. She said Janet was home from college because she was having trouble there. The date was intended to pick up Janet's spirits.

"Does she have big bongos?" Stu asked, climbing into the car and settling himself behind the wheel. He wore a Latin night-club singer's shirt with wide, frilly sleeves. He also wore a matador's hat, which gave the impression of mouse ears.

Martin, dressed as a pirate in long johns and a scarf over his head, snapped his eye patch at Stu's question.

"Don't start," he said.

"Does she?"

"You saw her around school last year. You tell me."

"Someone said she's a nympho."

"Someone said you're a weenie."

I stood next to the car when Gil came out. I was dressed like a hobo. I wore a suit jacket that was too large, sneakers also too large, and a red polka-dot tie. I had corked my face dark, smudging it around my eyes to make me look older.

Gil raised his hand. The keys spun on his finger, then snapped into his palm. He cupped them once or twice quickly, making a castanet sound as he came down the steps. His smile was tight.

"Here comes the sermon," Martin muttered.

Gil heard him.

"Okay, wise guy. Yeah, it's a sermon. A car's a dangerous thing."

"So's cliff diving."

"Don't get smart, Martin."

"Then why send us to school?"

Stu elbowed Martin. Gil stood beside the window on the driver's side and tapped the keys on the roof.

"You can get in, Max. I want you to hear this, too."

I climbed in. The front seat was almost too small for all of us,

145

and Martin had to sit with his feet up on the console hump, his knees near his chin.

"I don't know if you all should sit up front," Gil said.

"I'll get in back," I said.

"Oh, Dad." Martin sighed.

"There isn't much room for Stu."

"If he wasn't wearing a leg of lamb on each arm, he'd have plenty of room."

Gil lifted one finger and put it to his lips. He stared at Martin for a long time. Martin stared back but finally shook his head and looked down at his lap.

"No drinking," Gil continued. "No grab assing, no screwing around with other cars . . . by that I mean, no racing, no chicken matches—"

"Dad, that went out in the fifties," said Stu.

"No riding across fields or whatever they do these days."

"No parallel parking," Martin said, and began to laugh, his shoulder rubbing against mine.

"Damn it, when will you learn?" Gil asked.

Just then a light flashed, and I looked to see Marcie standing at the edge of the driveway, holding a camera.

"Mom said I should. She said you all looked so cute."

"Oh, screw it," Gil exploded, stepping back and throwing the keys at us. "What's the use? How can anyone be serious in this house?"

"I was just doing what Mom said," Marcie whined.

Stu hit the horn when he put the key in the ignition, and they both jumped. Stu waved at them, then started the car. He gave it too much gas, and it roared. Gil grabbed Marcie and pulled her back.

"We have lift-off," Stu said. He leaned forward at the waist, his attention focused on his feet. Tilly stood on the porch, her hand raised to send us off, a large book weighting the pocket of her sweater.

We started to move. Marcie ran alongside and tried to get another snapshot. The flash went off, and Stu blinked, suddenly blind.

"Holy Christ," he shouted, putting his hand to his eyes. He jammed on the brake, and we stalled.

146

"God damn it. Leave them alone!" Gil screamed.

"I'm sorrrry." Marcie started to cry, breaking into her flabby trot and heading for the garage.

"Oh, sweet Mother of Jesus, what do I care? Go ahead, wreck the car, what do I care?"

Gil walked away, storming up toward the house. Tilly backed through the screen.

"Let's get the fuck out of here," Martin whispered.

Stu started the car again. It was still in first gear, so we took a couple of hops down the driveway. He pushed the clutch in, turned the ignition once more, and we finally eased into a smooth motion.

As soon as we were away from the house, Martin pulled out a cigar and lit it. He puffed at me, then at Stu, and finally made an elaborate process of flicking the ashes. He didn't use the ashtray for fear he'd leave a trail, so he leaned across me and hung his hand out, his pirate's bandanna flapping against my cheek.

"So what's this Janet like?" Stu asked again. "Is she really a nympho?"

"You nervous or what?" Martin said.

"Just tell me, you little jerk."

"She's all right."

"What do you think, Max? Is this the kennel corps or something?"

"No, she's nice."

"That's it? That's all you can say? Think she'll try to get fresh with me?"

"She's kind of nutty. She can stick a skewer through her head," I said.

"Come on."

"You asked."

It took ten minutes to get to Marla's house. She lived in a split-level. The foundation of the house was covered with fake field-stone siding, and above it, the siding was aluminum with an intricate swirl pattern that was supposed to look like wood. The house and the neighborhood were new; all the trees and bushes were thin and short.

"What time is it?" Martin asked. He was nervous about meeting Marla's parents.

"Nighttime," Stu said.

"Oh, Christ. Max?"

"Eight."

"It's time. You got a Life Saver, Max?"

I climbed out. Martin came out after me, and I gave him a Life Saver. He took two and pushed them under his upper lip. He sloshed saliva around in his cheeks.

"I hate this shit," he said. I climbed back in with Stu.

We watched Martin ring the bell. It was like watching a movie to see him standing there, his hands held carefully at his sides. He checked his fly just before the door opened. Marla's father reached out and pulled Martin inside.

"Hope he remembers to trick-or-treat them," Stu said. "I'm starved."

"He can't trick-or-treat them."

"Why not? What are they, Arabs?"

Martin appeared on the front step and waved to us.

"What's he want?" I asked.

"I don't know."

Martin waved again, then finally came down the steps and stuck his head in my window.

"He wants to meet us all," Martin said. "Come on. Wait until you get a load of this guy."

"What for? I'm not dating his daughter," Stu said.

"But you're driving her. He won't let her go if you don't come in. He was really sly about it, but he's an old cornball. He has his wife sitting up to see the whole thing."

"Sitting up?" I asked.

"She's got some sort of bad back. She's in a wheelchair half the time. Who knows? Marla says she's a hypochondriac."

Martin was in a full sweat. When he pulled back from the window, one of the Life Savers fell out of his mouth.

We followed him up the walk. I was in the middle when he pushed open the door. We crowded into the main foyer. The lamp above us was dimmed by an orange crepe paper pumpkin that someone had propped on top of it.

I didn't see Mr. Babcock at first, but I heard him from just in front of Martin.

148

"Come in, come in, boys. Warm yourself by the fire. Go ahead, that's what it's there for," he almost shouted.

I caught a glimpse of him past Martin and Stu. He was wide and green. He had dark red skin, swarthy from booze, and his sharply creased trousers, his knife-edged shirt collar made him seem very powerful. He was a man I instantly suspected of owning guns, and I let my imagination run over the possibility that there was a glistening cabinet in the house filled with shotguns, pellet rifles, and German Lugers. It was easy to imagine him setting his drink aside, perhaps deliberately making a ring on an armchair so that someone would have to go at it with lemon and steel wool, while he lifted a gun free, tossing it in his hands as lightly as a pool cue.

"Come on," Stu said next to me. I stepped across the threshold of the living room and saw Mrs. Babcock. She sat in a brown easy chair, dressed in a flannel nightgown, her feet up on a piano bench. She wore a witch's cap and held the fireplace broom very near her. Her fingers toyed with a bowl of candy corn, which was balanced on the arm of the chair.

"This is my brother," Martin said, "and this is Max, a friend of mine."

Mr. Babcock hopped across the room to greet us. No doubt he had been in his chair a minute ago because now he moved with a slight limp as if trying to get the blood working again in his toes. The limp gave him a martial air, and I waited for him to say his leg had been blown off by a land mine in a distant war. Instead, he grabbed my hand and pumped it once or twice, his pulse rising and churning as his fingers closed over my knuckles.

"Babs, is it?" he asked me. "I didn't quite catch your name, young man."

"Max."

"Oh, Max. Like Max . . . what was his name? The kraut that beat Joe Louis? Darn, I remember listening to that fight on the radio . . . what was his name?"

He crouched and tried a few lefts on me, pawing the air between us with wide bear swats, his eyes level with mine, his jab coming far too close for playfulness.

"Come in, boys. Marla will be ready," Mrs. Babcock said. "Fred, why don't you call her?"

We hadn't really moved from the doorway. Martin took another step forward out of politeness. Mr. Babcock angled through us, turning his shoulder and knifing along, but Marla was already coming down.

"Hello, everyone," she said.

She was dressed like a fairy princess. She had on some sort of long white gown, a white conical hat, and small white slippers. She carried a wand at her side. It was made from a twirling baton with a small star stapled to the rubber end. Two tin-foil wings bobbed and flapped behind her, their movement directly opposite to hers so that when she took a step down, the wings sprang up.

I said, "Hello, Marla. You look great."

"What are you, Max? A bum?"

"Yes."

Mr. Babcock stepped between us before Stu or Martin could say anything.

"Let your mother see you, darling. Go ahead."

Marla turned bright red. Her throat flushed. Her bra straps kept slipping out from under the smaller straps of the gown, and she had to switch the wand from one hand to the other to put them right.

"Oh, don't you look wonderful! Those wings turned out, didn't they?" Mrs. Babcock said. "And the wand! Oh, don't cast a spell on me, fairy princess."

"Oh, God, Mom," Marla said, her hand coming up to hide her face. "You are so queer sometimes."

"Amen," Stu whispered to me.

"We should be going," Martin said, making an elaborate show of looking at the clock over the mirror.

"Right," said Marla.

She kissed her mother, then came back toward us.

"My jacket's right here. We all set? Stu . . . you're Stu, aren't you? You're driving?" she asked nervously.

"I'm Stu."

"But you'll be careful now, won't you?" Mr. Babcock said, his hand coming up to my shoulder. He slid his hand across my shoulders once or twice, then squeezed my neck. I didn't know if he thought I was Stu, the driver, or what, but I tightened my neck and moved from under his hand.

150

"Very careful," he repeated. "You have our princess, remember."

"Dad, you'll kill me if you keep talking like that."

"A princess," Mrs. Babcock called.

"You are, honey. You are to us."

Martin helped Marla with her sweater. She couldn't put it over her wings, so she simply draped it over her shoulders.

"Good night," Mrs. Babcock called. "Be good. Nice to have met you all."

"Good night," I said. Stu nodded. Martin turned and waved.

Marla went out the door first. Her dad stepped out to send us off. He rocked a bit on his feet, moving back and forth gradually. He sniffed at the wind and raised his scotch glass slightly, as if toasting the moon.

"Almost deer season," he said. "You boys hunt?"

"No," Martin said. "Good night."

Marla was already halfway down the walk. Martin hustled after her. When Stu and I got to the car, Martin was helping Marla get her wings through the door. He had to hold them as she crawled through; then he reached in and made sure they didn't bend as she squared herself on the seat. She sat on the edge, her wings just nipping the back upholstery. Her wand rested on the seat beside her.

"I feel so stupid," she kept saying, and Stu, next to me, said, "Not half as stupid as you look."

Martin climbed in behind Stu.

"Everybody ready?" Stu asked. "If I don't start the car right, will your father come running after me?"

"Stu . . ." Martin said, but laughed.

"I know, I know," said Marla.

"Come on," Martin said, "let's go."

"I feel so stupid."

"Don't have a cow. It's a good costume."

Stu started the car and pulled away smoothly. Mr. Babcock waved and shut the door. I saw a bunch of kids coming down the sidewalk. A father in a white raincoat trailed them. He had a Chesapeake Bay retriever on a long silver chain.

"Stu, what are you?" Marla asked after a few minutes.

"Good question." Martin snorted. "What are you, Stuuey?"

Stu shot a quick punch behind him, his leg-of-lamb arm firing out like a horse kick. Martin caught Stu's arm and managed to hold it for a second. Stu rose off the seat, then almost yanked Martin up front with one giant heave. Martin's shoulder crushed one of Marla's wings.

"Sorry," Martin said when Stu let him go.

"I just meant, what was his costume?" Marla said.

She tried to remold her wing as Stu parked across the street from Chris's house. The small cul-de-sac was lined with cars. Marla explained that Chris's parents were having people in before the whole group went dancing at the country club.

It took a few minutes to get Marla out of the back seat. Martin maneuvered behind her, giving her directions, carefully guiding the wings. In the meantime, Stu and I straightened our costumes. Stu went to the trunk and took out a tambourine.

"Marcie gave it to me," he said. "You think it's too much?"

"No, not at all," I told him.

"You sure? I hated this stuff in music class. You ever have to play the scrape box? I always did. That and the triangles . . . which I got to hit about once every three periods. Mr. Modica always put me on percussion instruments."

"I wonder why," Martin said.

Marla took a last look at herself in the side mirror. Stu slammed the trunk and rattled the tambourine. He did a quick gypsy jig, a sort of awkward leap, thwacking the tambourine the length of the car. Martin pretended to take up the dance, and he began hopping around, hitting himself all over. With amazing speed, Stu clamped Martin in a headlock and began tapping a new rhythm on Martin's head.

"Do they always act like this?" Marla asked me.

"Almost. This is mild."

"You look insane," Martin whispered to Stu, his voice strangled. "You look like you should be shot out of a cannon."

"Yank me."

Just then Clark came barking across the front lawn. Stu let Martin go, giving him a last pat with the tambourine, then threw it onto the front seat. We heard noise from the party as we crossed the lawn. The grass was cold, nearly frosted, and I saw Clark's breath whenever he brought his muzzle near the ground.

Marla rang the bell. I heard a Glenn Miller record playing,

152

soft and sentimental. A man passed by the picture window, holding his hands up to a make-believe trumpet. He riffled the finger keys, saw us, then called to someone deeper in the house.

Finally the door opened. Mr. Row stood squarely in the center, a glass in his hand, a cigarette somehow notched between the glass and his finger.

"What the hell?" he asked. "Aren't you going to say, 'Trick or treat'? Aren't you a little big for going to people's houses?"

"It's me, Marla."

"And who else? Who goes there? Halt."

"Hello, Mr. Row," I said, stepping forward. Clark shot between us and dodged through Mr. Row's legs.

"Damn, I didn't want the dog inside. That's okay. What's it matter? It's a night for dogs and animals, wolves, I should say."

"This is Stu. And you already know Martin."

"Martin I know. Swearing is destiny, wasn't it? Isn't that what you said? The suburban philosopher. How are you, Martin? And this is Stu. Stu," he said, putting his arm around Stu's shoulders, lifting his glass as though he were going to force-feed Stu, "Stu, you are a legend. Did you know? You are an absolute legend in this town, in this house, and probably in the entire state."

"I know," Stu said.

"You know?" Mr. Row said, slapping him on the back. "You know, do you? My, such confidence. Did you kill any bulls on your way over? Of course, even though that's a matador's hat—that's a matador's outfit, isn't it?—I wouldn't expect you to kill with a sword. Oh, no. You're more the Herculean type. You'd rip their heads right off, wouldn't you? I can picture you turning the heads right up into the Mediterranean sun."

"Are you serious?" Stu asked. "I mean, are you always like this?"

"Direct question, good, good. Now come in. I've kept you outside too long as it is. Marla, you must be frozen. You noticed, didn't you," he continued as we passed by him, entering the hallway between the living room and dining room, "that I am not wearing a costume? Let me say that I am indeed wearing a costume, but I've chosen to wear it on the inside this year. I'm a drunk, you see, so this is all I need. *Comprendez?*"

Mr. Row grinned. The house was very warm. There were people everywhere.

153

Mr. Row spun Marla around, examining her wings.

"What happened? What kind of angel is this? Fighting with the devil, eh? Are you a fallen angel? Back seats will do it to any angel."

"Oh, Mr. Row." Marla giggled and broke away. "I'm going to run up and get Chris and Janet. I'll just be a minute."

"Chris and Janet—Janet and Chris. I show no favoritism, but the fact is most people say it 'Chris and Janet.' Why is that, do you suppose? That can establish a pattern. A whole life can be influenced, even arranged, by something like that. What should you feel like if you always have to go second? Now, how is it with you two? Is it Stu and Martin or Martin and Stu?"

He led us slowly to the bar. Bottles were set up on a small card table covered by a white tablecloth. Small lemon moons were scattered across a wooden cheese board.

"Stu and Martin," said Stu.

"Is that right, Martin? I would have thought it was Martin and Stu."

"It is," Martin told him.

"Well, as long as you both think you're first. That's what counts. Now, what can I get you? Help yourself to some of this food, too."

The faces of the people around us were vaguely familiar. Some I had seen at Echo Lake Country Club; others I had seen around town. A bark of laughter snapped out of one corner, but I turned too late to see who had made the sound. Glenn Miller was finished, and someone had put on a Charleston.

"Well," Mr. Row asked again, "what will it be? Don't be shy."

"Whiskey straight up," Martin said.

"I'd rather you were a little more shy than that. You are a philosopher, remember. I'll tell you what. Why don't I give you three beers? Do you drink beer? Stu, can you handle one and still drive?"

"Certainly."

"Certainly, is it? Well, don't forget the food," he said, handing us three beers from an ice chest under the table. He raised his glass in a toast.

"To God," he said.

A couple of people laughed behind him, but Mr. Row carried

154

it off with perfect seriousness. Perhaps he was serious—I couldn't tell.

He drank. We drank. Stu drained off half his bottle. He drank too long and slugged at the end with great, greedy gulps, sucking a little as he cocked the bottle farther and farther back. Finally he stopped and wiped his mouth with the broad saw of his bushy sleeve.

"And you're driving," said Mr. Row. He made a quick cross and took an ice cube from the open bucket. "I've got to mingle."

A small roar went up then. A man near the dining room shouted that the Browns were doing the black bottom. This started a move in that direction, with Mr. Row leading. Martin and Stu and I stood stiffly near the bar, now and then glancing at the disappearing crowd.

Stu started eating as soon as we were alone. He began cramming pumpkin-colored cupcakes into his mouth, wadding up the cupcake papers and rattling them off Martin's head. "Quit it, asshole," Martin said each time, but Stu was too busy moving around the table. He drank the dregs of several glasses, lapping at the ice, announcing after each, "Scotch, bourbon, vodka, I think." At odd intervals he slapped his stomach, said, "Aaaaah," then moved even more rapidly around the table. The candlelight turned his sleeves wild colors, and he looked like a hulking maître d', a mandrill ape, a homosexual conga player.

"You eat like a lizard," Martin told him.

"Fuck . . . you." Stu burped. He shaped the words perfectly but was careful to keep the volume low.

"You eat like a carp . . . like a—a what? Like an animal."

"Fuck . . . you." Stu burped.

"Stuff a little more in your face. Go ahead."

Stu nodded and shrugged. His cheeks were jammed. When he finally swallowed, he looked to see if there was anyone around.

"Mar-tin." He burped.

Martin shook his head and took a swig of beer. Clark made another appearance, and we played with him awhile, tossing pieces of cheese on the floor and watching him snuffle them up. We stopped feeding him when we ran out of cheese. He sniffed at the table, his tail flicking the tablecloth.

155

"Clark," Martin said, "how nice of you to go out with Stuart here."

Stu, his beer bottle dangling from one finger, bent and took the dog's head in his lap.

"Nice Martin," he said. "Good Martin."

Someone turned up the music. A few shouts came from the kitchen. One man hooted and made loud, kissing sounds. The house shook lightly.

I bent to pet Clark again but straightened as Marla came down. She was excited, almost out of breath, and she swept in with great speed, her wand hitting the wall.

"They're all set. They'll be right down. Don't those cupcakes look delicious? They make them instead of giving out candy. Sweet, isn't it?"

"Stu ate about twenty," Martin said.

"Oh? Well, it doesn't matter. Chris said they don't get many kids here. There's one big batch . . . you know, the group she baby-sits, but they all come at once; then it's quiet for the rest of the night."

She stood near the table, flustered, looking over the food. Twice she started to eat something, then pulled her hand back. Clark stood next to her, his head moving whenever she reached forward.

Finally Chris and Janet came down. Janet was dressed like a clown. She wore wide trousers with red suspenders, a pair of high black sneakers, and a crinkled hat pushed back on her head. She had a large white mouth painted in a smile, red lips, and exaggerated eye sockets. She was self-conscious and kept her thumbs crooked in her suspenders as she came down the stairs.

Chris was dressed like a ballerina. It wasn't really fair since she dressed that way often, but it still had the effect of a costume. It made her seem lighter somehow, and I watched as the tutu flexed whenever it touched anything. Her hand smoothed the edge of the ruffle constantly. She looked very beautiful.

"Janet, Chris, I'd like you to meet Stu," I said too formally.

"Hello," said Chris.

"Hello," Janet said. "New in town?"

"No, I'm your date," Stu said. "I'm Martin's brother."

"It was a joke. I was kidding. I know who you are."

Marla giggled. Clark snorted softly. The snort seemed to remind Chris of something.

"We forgot Clark's costume," she said, moving to the bookcase.

"Come here, Clark," Janet said. "Come here, darling."

She grabbed Clark and held him between her legs, petting his body in long strokes. Chris lowered a paper party hat onto Clark's head, snapping the elastic under his chin.

"He wears it to all celebrations," Chris explained.

"And he keeps it on. He likes it, I think," Janet said, then bent to rub Clark harder. "You like it, don't you? You good dog, you good, good dog."

"Well," Marla said.

"We didn't say hello to your mom," I said to Chris. "Should we say hello or anything?"

"No," Janet said, letting Clark go. Clark walked in a small circle. He looked idiotic, but he didn't seem to mind the hat.

"Who takes the hat off?" Stu asked.

"His butler," Martin said. "Either that or he tosses it into the hatrack after we've left."

"Should we go?" I asked.

Chris went to the hall closet for her coat. Janet was dressed warmly; she showed us the sleeves of her thermal T-shirt. Marla had to run back upstairs to get her sweater, and we all listened to her heavy steps pounding up and down the length of the second story.

She came down as I was helping Chris on with her coat. By this time some of the adults had filtered back into the living room, and Chris whispered to me, "Let's go. Let's get out of here before I have to say hello to everyone."

She turned to Janet and said, "Come on, Jan, we better get going."

I opened the door and held it while everyone passed through. Stu had to punch me lightly in the stomach, bending close enough to whisper, "She loves me already." His breath smelled of cupcakes and beer.

Clark held his nose to the crack as I closed the door. He watched us off, his eyes catching the lamplight, his party hat cocked at a rakish angle.

157

❖❖ 23 ❖❖

UNCLE JACK was waiting up for me at the kitchen table, a glass of scotch in front of him. I remember being conscious of the details around him: the wall clock, its face turning yellow from age, the tip of its hand disappearing for three minutes each hour in its own fog of dirt; the silver flecks of the linoleum; the shift of the refrigerator; the soft beat of the draw cord attached to the fluorescent light over the sink.

"What are you doing up?" I asked him.

He didn't answer. Instead, he said, "How was the costume party?"

"It was okay. Not great. Stu and Janet didn't really hit it off. I don't think they even liked each other. They're too much alike."

"You look beat."

"I'm tired."

He took a sip of scotch, then nodded at the chair across from him.

"Sit down for a second," he said.

"What is it?"

"Sit down, I just want to talk with you."

I sat down and looked at him. His face was lined, and he

looked very tired. The whites of his eyes had tiny cracks of yellow, tributaries of age building into cataracts.

"Do you want anything?" he asked. "A beer? Do you drink beer?"

"No, not really."

"I wouldn't mind. I'd rather you drank around here, where I can watch out for you . . . well, you understand. Sure you don't want something?"

"No, I'm sure."

He crossed his legs and took more scotch. The ice cubes were gone in his glass, but the scotch still looked dark.

"Well, I have a thing that—it's given us a hell of a night, I'll tell you that. Your aunt is against bringing it up, and me—I suppose I think you have the right to know. To have it, anyway."

"Have what? It's about Dad, isn't it?" I asked.

Jack sighed and took another sip, let it linger in his mouth. He set the glass down too heavily.

"What is it? You're making it worse, Uncle Jack," I said.

He opened his fingers once or twice, fanning the rings the drink had made into large fields of beaded water. Afterward he tapped his fingers on the table, then stood, suddenly resolved. He opened the hall closet just behind him and bent inside.

He pulled himself slowly out of the closet and slid a box across to me as he sat. The box was covered with odd stamps, postal marks, and a frayed band of twine. It was as large as a record album, as thick as a folded newspaper.

"It's from your dad," Jack said simply. "The police sent it."

"Is he dead?"

"No. He was taken in on vagrancy."

"Where?"

"In Colorado. The police couldn't hold him. They didn't have any real charges. He left without taking this package, and the police sent it to us because it was the only address your father gave."

Jack's voice broke on the last word. He shook his head and put his hand to his eyes. I almost started crying watching him, yet there was a stillness that entered me, a calm that somehow grew as Jack went on.

PART TWO

"I called them this evening. They don't know where he went,
or what his means of support was, or anything else about him.
He had no car and no luggage. He said he was a prospector. A
prospector! He gave them the name of a mountain as his place of
employment."

Jack began to laugh; then his mouth suddenly wrenched to one
side, and his eyes began to tear. He took another drink. His hands
trembled. His tobacco pouch was on the table, and he picked it
up, stuffed his pipe, and lit it. I watched his movements with
great concentration. I couldn't think at all.

"At least he's alive," Jack said finally, and began to smile out of
relief, out of frustration, out of impotence. "Thank God for that."

It was my father's journal. I knew that in the first instant Jack
pushed the box toward me, even before I glimpsed the green
leather cover resting inside the brown wrapping paper. I held it
against my chest and put my forehead against the edge. The
calmness was still with me, and I felt it, hard and solid, as solid
as the journal, as quiet as the house beyond the buzzing lights of
the kitchen.

"It's his journal—the journal of the dig," I said.

"I thought it was something like that. I remember the ledger he
was writing in—that's it?"

"Yes."

"I love him, but he's not right. Max, we can't think of him the
same way; we can't expect the same things of him. It's unfair to
him. I'm not angry at him anymore. I was. I thought he could
just snap out of its somehow, but now I know differently."

It was a long time before either of us moved. Finally Uncle
Jack followed me up to my bedroom. It was an awkward moment.
"Cold up here" was all Jack said, and bent to shut the window
over the cedar chest. I waited, the journal clamped to my side,
my fingers squeezing until I felt the binding start to go.

"Are you okay?" Jack asked, straightening, his body passing
close enough to me so that I smelled his scotch and tobacco.

"I'm fine."

"We could stay up awhile. Tomorrow's Sunday."   .

"No, I'm fine, really. I guess I have to think about this."

"All right. Maybe we can talk tomorrow. Maybe once you know
what's inside and everything . . . maybe we can talk things over."

160

He moved toward me. In the dimness he looked like my father.

"I've always wanted you here," he said.

"I know."

He rested his arm for a moment on my shoulder, touched the back of my neck, then let me go. He paused at the door to their bedroom, his ear close to the white wood, his hand on the doorknob.

"Good night," I said.

He nodded, twisted the doorknob, then went inside.

❖❖ 24 ❖❖

IT WAS still almost completely dark when my ride dropped me off a half mile from my house. Dull, quiet, in a trance, I stood at the side of Route 22 and watched the car pull away. A pain worked in from my skin like the rot on fruit or vegetables, and I tried to force myself to feel something. It was impossible to push my thoughts away from my father. I imagined him being locked up, the officer leading him down the hallway of a prison, eyes coming up to see who had entered, who was new. Why hadn't he called? Why hadn't he asked for help if he needed it? Why wouldn't he have contacted us if he intended ever to come home?

And of course, that was it; that was what moved in me, choked me. In the wind of the road, the tired flash of lights out on the highway, I realized he had no intention of returning to us, to me. He would not be back, not ever, and that I could not accept.

I started up the long hill toward my house. It was nearing daylight. Far away I heard a power saw start, then stop, then begin again. A paperboy pedaled past, a baseball cap pulled down over his ears. He lofted a paper at the front step of the house on the right, not stopping but tossing with perfect ease in a backhand motion.

The houses were more familiar now. A small convenience store, where I used to go with Honey for bread and milk, was on my left. I leaned against the front window, put my hand to my eyes to shield them, and read the clock. It was only five. When I looked away, a blue jay shot over me, calling a warning, then landed on a phone wire, swinging gently.

I pushed away and headed home. The house came in sight as I rounded the last turn. The bushes, I saw at once, had grown. They were spread and untended; they covered most of the windows. The lawn was shaggy, and there were leaves scattered through it. A small Japanese maple had withered and died, its red arrow leaves banked around its trunk like a scarf. On the small steps leading up to the front walk a piece of brick had splintered off and lay, too orange, against the black driveway.

My breath shortened. I was attentive to every detail, to every motion and step. I looked to the windows, expecting at any moment to see Honey or Zeke, even my father, yet nothing moved. There was no motion at all inside, no chair scraped back, no water turning off in the sink, and no wet, soggy toss of a dishtowel as someone came to greet me.

I circled the house to the backyard. I knew where I was going, and I didn't stop until I had the plot in view. The land still was not even. I saw the topsoil had been quilted on top of the dig, patched, reminding me of a scalp, a graft of skin. Here, too, was the old baseball field, and I walked to it, standing for a second where the clothesline used to be. I took a swing, then moved off, walking the length of the yard until I stood in the center of the dig. I knew it was the center only from old landmarks. Still, I understood I had lost him in this soil, in the sweaty summer nights years before, lost him to the constant digging, the hazy bugs that rode him deeper and deeper, wild moths that followed his flashlight, reeling with him like sparks set free from the land itself.

With my hands I scraped a shallow hole in the earth. The soil was nearly frozen, but I managed anyway. When the hole was deep enough, I took the journal out of my backpack and buried it.

After that I am unclear about what happened. I broke into my house by smashing a window near the back door. I know for certain that it was not planned, not premeditated on my part.

Neither was it planned to open all the windows as I did; it was simply a reaction, a cleansing. I remember, however, standing in the center of the living room, listening to the wind find each new entry, the curtains and shades snapping in the fresh air. It was cold, very cold. And I recall climbing the steps to my father's room, lifting the mirror down off the bathroom wall, and crawling into the small cave with its rusted shackle. I did not seal the room after me, a fact that comforted me later. It was not suicide I was after, although Honey, who found me, thought it was. No, it was not that at all, even though it was difficult to convince Jack and Gertrude. What they could not see was that it was the only way for me to begin to mend. With the shackle, with the heat of day just starting on the roof, the cold, stale air in the wood all around, I closed off a room deep inside me, one my father could no longer enter. Looking for me, he would find nothing but the reflection of the medicine cabinet, his own exclusion of me mirrored back to him.

PART
❖❖ 3 ❖❖

❖❖ 25 ❖❖

I WAS PUT in bed for a week after that. Dr. Cohen came
and examined me, shone a light in my eyes, asked me
questions about my attitude toward my father, then left. He remained downstairs a long time. After I heard his car pull away,
Jack came up to see me. He knocked softly, then came in, his pipe
smoking.

"Dr. Cohen just left," he said, sitting at the end of my bed. "He
recommends putting you in a hospital for observation."

I nodded. Jack stared at me for a long time. Finally he turned
and faced the window.

"I told him we didn't have to . . . Was I right to do that?" he
asked.

"Yes."

"You frightened us, Max."

"I didn't mean to."

"I was wrong about your father. I don't want to be wrong about
you. Are you all right?"

"Yes."

"Will you promise to talk to me the next time you feel—what's
the word?—desperate?"

"I wasn't desperate."

"Maybe you weren't. I don't know what's in your mind. I just don't want you to be hurt."

"I'm okay, honest."

He looked at me again, then patted my knee. He told me dinner would be ready soon.

That was how we left it. Gertrude doted on me for a week, keeping me fed and quiet. I did not try to persuade her that I hadn't attempted suicide. I knew she wouldn't believe it deep in her heart, so I left it alone and took her remedies and remained quiet.

It snowed the last day of my confinement. By evening the snow was deep and still coming. Martin came up to visit. He was very tentative when he entered the room, and I knew, as I knew with Gertrude, that it would make no sense to deny whatever version Martin had heard. Watching him move around the room, touch the dinosaurs, I understood what my father might have been up against. I knew that I would never be believed and that my own knowledge of the event would be stretched across the frame of other people's conjectures until my memory of it would match their own.

Martin and I were uncomfortable for a time, but gradually the awkwardness disappeared. He sat at the edge of my bed and told me about school and Marla. Later Gertrude brought in hot chocolate on snack trays and asked Martin to help her wheel in the portable TV she kept in her room. Martin sat in a chair next to the bed, and we watched *All Quiet on the Western Front*.

As he was about to leave, we heard another car door slam. Nobody rang our bell, so Martin went to the window and looked out. He squinted for a long time into the darkness, then turned back to me and shook his head.

"Come here," he said. "You won't believe this."

"What?"

"Just come here."

I went to the window. There, down on the lawn, I saw two yellow globes spinning and shooting out like giant fireflies.

"It's Small," Martin said. "Old Small's down there."

In the middle of the lawn, the snow up to his ankles, Small did his yo-yo dance. He did a series of Loop-the-Loops, Over-the-Waterfalls, and Around-the-Worlds. Neither Martin nor I said a word. We watched until he tried one last trick. A string broke, or he let it go, and his right-hand yo-yo shot up, drifting almost to our height, descending directly on top of Small. He caught it, bowed, then ran to the car. It was the last I saw of him.

Jock moved away around Thanksgiving, heading off to Florida for the winter caddie and horse circuit. We helped him pack his car, an old Chevy that was badly rusted on the sides. The car was square, with a standard shift. The upholstery was durable plastic with small marks like a nubbled bedspread. A Christmas tree-shaped, pine-scented deodorant hung from the stem of the rear-view mirror, but it couldn't begin to cover the scent of old cigar smoke, coffee, newspapers. Dead flies caked the dashboard, baked and fossilized into varying stages of rigor mortis, and I had the sensation of witnessing a miniature desert, the death of pilgrims.

"A hundred and fifty thousand miles on it," Jock said, climbing in behind the wheel. He hunched over comfortably, read the odometer, and marked down the number in a small ledger. He winked at me, then said, "Taxes. Got to keep a record, you understand? Distance is as good as money to me."

He drove off a moment later without any long good-bye. We waved to him from the steps of the Y. He didn't wave back.

Deado followed Small after Christmas. I don't think either Martin or I believed he would actually go until we saw him rolling the thick black wire around his hot plate. He had been called by Small, who had landed as a fleet mechanic for the public works department in a town in Oregon. There was also some talk of a sister in Olympia, Washington, yet knowing Deado, I didn't think it likely he would ever see her. I could not imagine him traveling, making social calls, looking up old family connections. He was too solitary for that, too rigid in his ways.

Early in January, Stu, Martin, and I drove Deado to the bus stop. We sat up front, Deado in back, surrounded by his few possessions—his suitcase, a paper bag for his hot plate, two or three cans of chicken soup, an old fedora he felt silly wearing. He rustled when he moved, rocking back to see a last glimpse of the Y, raising his hand to no one in particular.

"Here I go," he said a few times as we went through town. "This is it. Always hate to leave a place."

"Always will, though, right?" Stu asked. "Isn't that life?"

169

"For a messenger pigeon," Deado said.

We drove to the bus stop. We hadn't left ourselves enough time for a slow farewell, so we were forced to hurry to grab his things and carry them to the platform. We should have slowed down, asked him to catch the next bus, but I think we were unconsciously pushing to be done, to let him go without trouble.

"Okay, okay, okay," Deado continued to say, accepting the packages back from us. His three-fingered hand tilted the fedora on his head, and he tried to look nonchalant as he struggled up the steps of the bus. "I'll just put this on," he said over the hissing. The driver punched his ticket, and we walked beside the bus to watch him choose a seat, the packages falling into an empty place beside him as soon as he tilted in that direction.

He could have made it back, but he didn't. The door closed, yet even then he might have asked the driver for one more minute. Perhaps it was better, though, to see him disappear this way. He was gone faster than I would have thought possible, covered, even as the bus backed up, by the shiny reflection of neon lights. He was gone in white, gone to reflection, and I had only the barest glimpse of him as the bus rocked away, his fedora on, a *National Geographic* pressed to the window to show us the better life ahead of him.

❖❖ 26 ❖❖

THE Y was dead for us after that. Stu still went there
to lift weights, but there was nothing left to draw
Martin and me. We had our licenses but no car to drive. We
applied to colleges and sat back to wait. The weather was very
cold, and the days were extremely short.

With nothing else to do, we hung around the pet infirmary
Marcie had built in the garage. The infirmary had begun very
slowly, then expanded. Marcie had first taken in only a few animals: hamsters from neighbors; rabbits; a kitten or two. People
heard about her, and soon they were bringing her every sort of
unwanted or sick animal. She cared for wild birds and mice,
gerbils and snakes, asking only a small stipend for each animal.

By the time Martin and I began hanging out there, the dispensary was fully established. In the first turn of weather Marcie
had asked Gil for a woodstove. It was a major purchase, a considerable hunk of money, and Gil balked. But Marcie produced
the money at once, saying at the same time that she wasn't asking
him to buy it, simply to install it.

"Where'd you get the money?" he asked her.

"Working. I'm charging for some of the animals now."

"Enough?"

"Enough to buy their food and get them a woodstove."

Gil bought the stove and installed it the next weekend. It was Tilly, however, who provided the finishing touch. She disappeared one Saturday and returned later with three chairs, a small desk, and a black colonial floor lamp.

"Here, give me a hand," she called. "Garage sale stuff, but it's good just the same. We used to have a set like this when we were first married."

Marcie arranged the furniture around the small woodstove. She took special care to arrange the animals, too, measuring their distance from the warmth according to their needs and habitats so that her pet iguana was closer than the lame raccoon. She bought four or five thermometers and hung them around the room, the mercury turning the sunlight to prism rainbows. She checked the temperatures regularly, adding wood as needed. She even went so far as to chalk pale yellow relief lines on the cement floor, giving it the look of a weather map.

"Tahiti," Martin called, watching her. "Now Bayonne, now Vancouver, now . . . what the hell? Anything over there has to be dead. That's Antarctica."

"This corner is for hibernation."

The dispensary made a perfect hangout in the short days of winter. This was where we went each day after school, sometimes beating Marcie, other days coming in to find her already puttering around the cages, the soft squeak and scratch of animals following in her wake.

"Hello, Madame Curie," Martin said, going over to Antarctica to retrieve the half gallon of milk we kept stashed there. "Any breakthroughs in the world of science?"

"Nothing."

"Are you sure? Nothing? No new habits examined?"

Marcie ignored him and went about her feedings while Martin filled an aluminum saucepan with milk. It was my job to add hot chocolate mix to three cups. Lounging in the chairs, we watched the pan heat, heard drops of moisture hit the stove, smelled the soft odor of chocolate and cooking milk. Martin always took the rocking chair for himself, and it was from there he directed traffic, directed the cooking, ladled out scoops of milk, his right leg dangling over the arm of his chair.

"Hot chocolate, Marcie?" he called.

172

"In a second."

"You must eat to keep up your strength, Madame Curie."

"Let me just get this."

Marcie was clinical in her attitude, firm and curious, lifting the sick creatures with sure hands, prodding them with the nub of a pencil, the dull end of a letter opener.

"Well," she said under her breath, then retreated to the bookcase along the wall, searching quickly through the reference books, her index finger touching the binding of each one before finally selecting. She reminded me of an alchemist, a female Merlin.

"Find it?" Martin asked.

"Not exactly, but close."

Eventually Marcie would carry the book to the chair, would huddle over it, loosening the knots of the sweater she had tied around her neck.

"Here," Martin would say, giving her a cup. "Just for you."

She would take the cup, saying at the same time, "I don't know what it is. There are some bald spots."

"On what? The squirrel?"

"Yep. The one the Taigens brought over. The one they trapped."

"Have-A-Heart-Traps," Martin said. "I love that name."

"They trapped it because it looked sick, but now I don't know what's wrong with it."

"Maybe it's old," I said. "Maybe he's just, you know, going bald."

"I doubt it."

We would sit quietly. Marcie regulated the light, and she turned it on only when the afternoon grew too pale, too gray, the windows black squares on a smooth wall. The stove turned red, the sides warming to a blush, while all around us the animals made noise. The noise was comforting. I could look in any direction to see animals burrowing in sawdust or wood chips, field mice curled in heavy balls beneath the surface of their patch of soil.

Around five Stu came in, announcing his arrival by skidding his gym bag across the cement floor. The bag would slide on its metal cleats, its sound rising before it slammed into Marcie's worktable. It disturbed the animals and set them chattering, and Stu would begin making sounds back at them, mimicking their cries.

"Cold as a witch's toenail," he would say a second later.

"Hello, Stu," called Marcie.

"Cold as a Martin Burger. Cold as a Maxy Boy. How's the Stu Club today? How's Mr. Won Ton?"

He brought air with him, carried in the outside world. He liked to come over and give me a small knuckle bop on the head.

"How are you doing, Stu?" I asked.

"I'm doing fine, Max. Nice of you to ask. I appreciate you taking an interest in my welfare, I really do. It shows a great human spirit."

"Any word from schools?"

"No, I imagine they're writing to each other, trying to see who has the best facilities to educate a mind like mine. It's very important for the future of our nation. I've got to find out what college is good enough for me."

"What are you doing, applying to weight rooms?" I asked.

"Funny. Max, you're a card. It's hanging around with Mr. Won Ton that does it. Things rub off. Martin's a comic jackass—I mean, genius."

He gave me another knuckle bop. It normally took him this long to remember the hot chocolate. After stepping over our legs, he poured milk in the pan and put the chocolate mix in Martin's cup.

"What's for dinner, Marcie?" he asked. "Did Mom say?"

"Caviar."

"Is that right? Is everybody a joker around here? Is this the kind of behavior we want from members of the Stu Club? You'd better be nice, Marcie, or you'll come out here someday and find all the cages open. I'll be the Moses of the animal kingdom, leading the animals from the land of Marcie, the evil pharaoh."

"Stu . . ."

"Like Moses. I'll find the Covenant written on stone—or maybe just on Martin's head."

By this time the milk was ready. Spinning, Stu asked, "Anybody want some?"

"I do," I said.

"You do? How's it feel to want?"

"Either give me a cup or not. I don't care."

"Oh, you care. Everyone cares. Unfortunately there is just

174

enough for one good-looking guy, one large, muscled hunk of a man. One big, red-headed guy, with bulging biceps, leaping lats, trembling triceps—one man among weenies, you might say. One rock, one slab of granite."

"Be quiet," Marcie told him. "Just shut up if you can't be still. How can you be like this every day?"

"It's wonderful, isn't it? To be like me every day? Look at how dull life would be without me? What would you all do? Play checkers with Martin Won Ton? Make pencil marks on chipmunks? Come off it."

Then, turning to me, he said, "Do you want to get out of that chair, Max, or should I twist your head off?"

"You're an asshole."

"But a comfortable one. I'll be sitting down at the count of three or you'll be in the one and only anaconda vise."

"That's fair."

"One, two . . ."

I moved. There were no options with Stu.

Finally he settled in his chair, hot chocolate on his lap. As soon as he was comfortable, he started in on Marcie. He was after her to put in mesh cages around the garage—dog runs—in the hope of attracting the kennel trade. He had boarding fees all worked out.

"Listen," he said, "you house one dog for a weekend, you know, for some family that goes away. They're afraid to have the neighborhood kid come over because kids always forget and then the dog hangs around the kitchen and the family comes back to find their dog spent his weekend in a concentration camp. Do you see it? Anyway, you charge what? Twenty dollars? Even thirty? We can call some kennels and undercut whatever price they give. No matter what, it has to be near twenty dollars. So for twenty dollars you can take care of a dog. But think what you get, right? You can get three or four dogs pretty soon. You'll be making around sixty or seventy a weekend. That will keep some of these rabbits in food pellets. Hell, you're doing the same sort of thing right now with all these pets, right? You are, aren't you?"

"This isn't a business, Stu. I don't do this for money. I'm not like you."

"I'll say."

175

"Besides, I don't have time to organize it."

"I'll organize it. The Stu Kellerman Handy Dandies, general lawn work and dog school. You say yes, and I'll start it up."

"I want to ask Dad."

"Sure, put it through the zoning board, why don't you? Ask Congress for permission."

The conversation went like this most evenings until six, when Tilly whistled from the house. Marcie held the door for us. Afterward, stepping backward, she went into the middle of the yard in order to see the roof. This was a fire check Gil insisted on, and she was conscientious about doing it every day.

Most nights I walked with her. Stu and Martin would disappear into the house, leaving Marcie and me to examine the shingles, to watch for any sparks. The smoke would rise, and Marcie stood beside me, still too fat, too saggy, yet always quiet and kind. We seldom spoke, but when we did, Marcie discussed her work, talking about animals, sometimes pointing out significant changes in the season around us. She liked birds best, and she told about the different species that came to the feeder she had nailed to the garage wall. Above all, she talked about the blue jay she had cared for when she first started with the animals.

"I banded him," she told me one night. "I didn't know what I was doing. I thought I was being scientific, and I wanted to mark him. I didn't have a real band, so I used a pipe cleaner instead. It was a stupid thing to do, but what did I know? Anyway, I'd give anything to see that bird again. I'd give anything to be able to take the pipe cleaner off. I feel like I sent it to its death."

Saying this, she moved closer to the feeder. We stood in the near darkness, the ground white around us, watching the dark shapes of birds flutter to the feeder. Sometimes the birds were barely visible, and we were left with their sound, the snap of wings, the soft, scratching pull they made at the seeds. Marcie stayed even after Stu had appeared at the back door, his head coming out into the cold only long enough to say, "Here, Spot. Here, pooch. Dinner's ready."

She stayed until he called a second time, moving closer and closer to the feeder, making herself still and quiet, examining each dark silhouette, waiting for the raucous cry of the jay, the return of her only unkindness.

176

❖❖ 27 ❖❖

I N THE middle of January Stu started the kennel. A delivery truck came on Friday afternoon from Spoer Hardware, its flatbed filled with tightly wound bales of chicken wire. I was in Marcie's dispensary with Martin, and we watched Stu help the driver lift down the wire and stack it against the garage.

Marcie was at the dentist. Stu, I was sure, had counted on it, planning to have the kennel runs begun before she came back.

Martin and I went outside as the man drove away. It was late afternoon and cold. The sky was gray, and I smelled snow coming. It was quiet except for the engine of the delivery truck as it backed away. Stu adjusted the bales of chicken wire, slapping them into a neater pile.

"Did he give you money off for helping him?" Martin asked.

"He said he'd take off twenty if I promised you'd sleep with him."

"Did he give you money off or not?"

"It's business, Mr. Won Ton. No tickee, no washee."

"Did Marcie agree to it?"

"Of course she did. She's a money grubber just like me. Only you are too stupid—I mean, too pure to make a buck."

"How about Mom and Dad?"

"They think I'm doing Marcie a favor. They think it will be one or two dogs. Don't ask me why they think I couldn't use a leash, but yeah, they know."

Stu grinned. His grin was sly but friendly, too. He made you want to go along with him, to bend rules, to giggle as you made a profit.

He bent to the wire and counted the bales. There were five all together. One, the largest, was wrapped around a set of metallic green fence posts. Stu counted these, too, then looked up at us.

"You guys want to make some money? I want to get started."

"You're going to turn me into a Communist, swear to God," Martin said.

"Who are you kidding? Who uses the dispensary at night to boff old Marla? At least I'm giving Marcie a piece of the action. You use the place and tell her to keep out."

I looked at Martin. I didn't know about his arrangement, but it didn't surprise me. He shrugged and toed the metal wire.

"How much?" I asked.

"Twenty bucks each."

"I'll do it," I said.

Martin turned his collar up but didn't say anything. He didn't leave either, so I knew he'd eventually work. Stu understood it also and nodded at the top bale.

"Bring it around, would you? Mr. Won Ton, you in or out?"

"In."

Martin and I lifted the top bale. The mesh dug into my hand, and I could lift it only to waist level. We waddled with it to the rear of the garage, then tossed it onto the cold grass. Stu disappeared and came back in a few minutes with a pick and a fence-post digger.

"We'll make one pen to begin with, all right? Max, you want to use the pick?"

"Not really."

"You want your twenty bucks, you'll use it."

He handed me the pick. Martin slouched beside me. Stu hadn't drawn any plans. We went free-form, setting up the first pen by eye.

The wind was cold, and I smelled snow again. A puff of wood-

smoke disappeared before I really knew it was there. From inside
the garage I heard the occasional clank of a cage. It was late
afternoon, the animals' feeding time.

"You dig here," Stu told me. He produced a ball of twine from
somewhere and began laying out the pen. He couldn't put sticks
in the soil to lay out a proper bed, so he laid the string on the
ground, framing a long rectangle at right angles to the garage.

I started to work. The first strike with the pick at the frozen
ground was hard and jarring, but after a time I liked the steady
weight of it, the satisfying chug each time it hit. A few inches
below the frost line the soil softened.

Stu talked as he laid out the rest of the run. "I'm going to put
in one of those . . . what do you call them? A doggy hatch, you
know? I want to put in one of those doors that dogs can squeeze
through. That way we don't have to bother with letting them in
and out. Mr. Won Ton can come in, too, can't you, Marty Ton?"

"Sure, Stwewwy, whatever you say."

"No, seriously. I figure to have three runs, maybe four. I'll make
different size doggy hatches so we can accommodate different
size dogs."

"Brilliant," I said, finishing. "You want another fence post dug?"

"Yeah, come over here. Dig right here. We'll make this the
corner, so dig it deep enough. We want this post to be real tight."

"Yes, sir."

I heard a car door slam in the driveway. We all stopped to listen.
Tilly's heels sounded on the walk. A moment later I heard them on
the gray wood of the back steps.

"Now you're in for it," Martin said.

"Bull," Stu said quietly. "Marcie just needs to get used to the
idea. She'll go along with it."

"I was thinking of Mom," said Martin. "Does Marcie even know
about this?"

"*Oui, oui*, Wonny."

"Oh, Jesus, what's the use? Stu, sometimes I really think you're
insane. Do you know that? Are you really listening to me? I think
you might be crazy."

"Coming from you, that carries a lot of weight. Gee, I really
appreciate you leveling with me this way, Martin. I think I'm
going to change as a result of what you just said."

179

Just then Tilly called from the back porch, "Stuuuu?" Marcie must have been close by, because I heard Tilly ask her to go out and get us. Marcie came down the steps.

"Back here," Martin said. "We're burying treasure."

Stu flicked a clod of dirt at Martin. It hit him in the chest and rolled to the ground just as Marcie appeared around the corner.

"Oh, no," she started. "No, you don't, Stu. I didn't give my permission."

"Shhhh," Stu whispered.

Marcie wasn't dressed for the outdoors. Her shoes were small and dainty. She wore white tights that bagged at the knees. Now, her glasses reflecting light, she turned this way and that, her toe coming out to nose the twine and fence posts.

"Damn it, Stu, I told you I hadn't decided."

"But I did, you see? I'm going to make a kennel for me. You don't own the yard."

"That isn't the point."

"Oh, come on, Marcie. It'll make us both money. We'll get Mr. Won Ton to shovel out the pens. What's the big deal?"

"Stuuu?" Tilly called from the porch.

"In a minute," Stu yelled back.

Marcie leaned close to whisper. Her right hand went to the back of her dress and smoothed it unconsciously.

"I don't want to be responsible for a lot of dogs. I won't even be able to leave the house."

"Why not? You ever hear of a leash? Besides, you going to give one mouth-to-mouth if it keels over? If you're going away, you just don't take any dogs that weekend."

"And what if . . . oh, forget it."

"What, what? What if some man invites you off to Acapulco? You go, that's all. Jeez, Marcie . . ."

Stu stopped. Tilly rounded the corner. She wore low heels that twisted a little on the uneven soil. Her hair was up, and she smelled of perfume.

"All right, what's going on?" she asked calmly.

"Nothing," Stu said.

"Am I blind?" Tilly asked. She put one hand on the corner of the garage. Below us I heard some ice slip free on the creek.

180

"We're building a cage for Stu," said Martin.

"We're building kennels," Stu told her.

"Kennels? Why? Marcie, did you take in a dog?"

"No."

"Are you sure? I asked you please to let me know what sort of animals you take in."

"It's Stu's idea."

Tilly nodded. She raised her hand and rubbed her forehead. She didn't look angry for some reason. She listened a few more minutes to Marcie and Stu, then held up her hand. A long strand of hair came loose and flapped just above her right ear.

"Listen," she said, interrupting. "Listen, just stop. I don't want anything else built around here until we have a family conference."

"Oh, not one of those," Martin said. "I hate sitting around the kitchen table like that. It's one of the corniest things you ever invented, Mom."

"I don't care, Martin. It goes to a family conference, and that's that, understand? They aren't your onions to cook anyway."

Martin turned to me and made a face. Stu, taking a cue, crossed his eyes and spoke directly to his mother. "Okay, Mom, we'll have a family conference."

"Uncross your eyes, Stu, and stop it."

Tilly reached inside the pocket of her coat and pulled out a letter. She held it up, then ceremoniously took a step toward Stu.

"Here," she said. "I think you'll want to read this, won't you?"

Stu crossed his eyes again at us but stepped forward to take the letter. He tripped a little on the twine, which was still anchored by Martin's foot. Marcie moved to look through the back window at her animals. She shivered once and wrapped her arms over her chest.

"It's cold," she said.

"It's snowing."

It was snowing, although the flakes were barely visible. Listening closely, I could hear them on the dead leaves around the trees. It was a slight, quiet fizz, like the slow movement of a snake through dried grass.

Looking for the snow, I forgot Stu for a moment. I didn't see him take the letter. He opened it quickly, and when I turned back, I saw him look up from the page just once. His eyes met Tilly's. She started to cry.

"What's going on?" Marcie asked. "What's in that letter?"

Stu and Tilly hugged each other. Stu, too, was close to crying. Tilly, so much smaller than Stu, patted him on the back, consoling him. I felt embarrassed. Marcie and Martin took a step forward, but at that moment Tilly and Stu separated, both of them laughing and wiping their noses at the same time.

"What is it?" Marcie asked again. "I hate when people do that."

Stu smiled. He put the opened letter on his head, stood very straight, then began humming "Pomp and Circumstance."

"You're drafted," Martin said.

"College!" Marcie squealed. "Is that it? That's it, isn't it? You're accepted. Early acceptance, isn't it? Where? Where did you get in?"

Stu marched in place. Marcie tried to snatch the letter off his head. She tripped on a fence hole and slammed into him.

"Jesus, are you that happy?" Stu asked.

Marcie hugged Stu. She kissed his cheek. Over it all, Tilly said, "We probably should have waited for your father, but I couldn't. I couldn't wait. I can't believe I have a son old enough to be going to college . . . Rutgers, too. That's a fine school, Stu."

Martin held out his hand to Stu. Stu took it, then jerked him forward. He caught Martin up in his arms.

"I love you," he said to Martin.

This started Marcie and Tilly crying. They both came close, and Stu did his best to kiss all three. Martin didn't try to pull away.

I stood on the outside, feeling a little sorry for myself, until Tilly broke off and brought me into the circle. I was not one of them, not family, but Tilly put her arm around me and herded me closer. She passed me on to Stu, who, in turn, put his arm around me, too. He held me close, his arm and expression sincere, the warmth of our bodies holding off the cold, holding off the quiet tick of snow falling through the leaves.

❖❖ 28 ❖❖

IT WAS still snowing later that night, when I arrived at Chris's house. I went up the front walk and rang the doorbell. Janet pulled open the door a moment later. She leaned against the doorframe, thrusting out one hip like a debutante, and said, "So glad you could make it, Isaac. Do come in for tea on this horrid, horrid night."

She spoke with her jaw locked. She shook back her hair, then looked over her shoulder.

"Mummy, Isaac is here."

"Hi, Janet, what are you doing here?"

She broke then.

"I'm here because I hate my roommate and I hate school. How's that?"

"Sorry."

"Don't be so sorry. It isn't the end of the world to not like college, you know?"

"Okay."

"Do you believe this snow?" she asked. "I keep thinking it's going to stop, but it doesn't."

She stepped past me. I smelled her perfume and her freshly washed hair. She held my arm and leaned over the railing of the porch. She scooped a handful of snow from a cedar bush and held it to her mouth. Her tongue was pink as she ate it, using my arm to pull herself back up. Watching her, feeling her hand on my arm, all I could think of was her reputation.

"Come in," she said. "You ever put honey or maple syrup on snow? It tastes like a snow cone. Come in."

The house was too warm. A fire burned in the living room, although nobody was near it. There was a newspaper spread out on the floor.

"I saw Clark as I came up the street."

"Imagine that," Janet said, shaking her fingers free of snow. A few small crystals remained on her top lip. "Daddyo is already at the pond. He's shoveling it for all of us. He always does that."

"Is Chris here?"

"No, she's in Aruba."

In the same breath she leaned on the banister and yelled up the stairs, "Chris, there's a Royal Canadian Mountie here for you."

Janet looked at me and grinned. Then she led me inside, her socks slipping on the floor. She raised one arm and pointed to a chair. She flopped down in front of the paper.

"You know, I've been trying to read something besides the social pages. You ever do that? I made myself a promise I'd begin following world news, but to tell the truth, I don't care about it. I can't even look at the pictures. Look . . . two zillion starving people blown away in a hurricane, another hundred crushed by an avalanche, and what am I supposed to do? Am I supposed to drop everything and fly to New Delhi? I get hungry every time I read something like that, so I go out and eat about fifty cookies, then I feel guilty, then I feel sick, and what's changed?"

"Are you always like this?"

"No, it's just because Dad and I had a big fight over it. He says even if you can't do anything, you can at least pray. He says that's the real value of prayer. It doesn't help hopelessness; it helps the people with the responsibility."

She ripped off a shred of newspaper, balled it into a wad, then threw it in the fire. The flames jumped for a second, and I saw the black shadow of the balled-up newspaper slowly turn white.

"Do you pray?" she asked.

184

"No, not really. My aunt Gertrude prays. She treats the saints like a secretarial pool."

"I think it would be the best thing in the world to be able to pray. To pray and really mean it—that's something. If you could really convince yourself you're doing something good by it, it would take a lot of pressure off."

Chris came down then. She was dressed in a heavy sweater and her father's old parka. She wore a soft white ski cap and heavy wool pants. Her socks came to the tops of her shins.

"Is Janet arguing about world prayer again?" Chris asked. "You should have heard her a little while ago."

"Oh, Chris, just because you're only interested in looking utterly Doris Day."

Chris turned and began digging in the hall closet.

"Max, you take size tens?" she asked.

"I think so. I haven't skated in a long time."

"It will come back."

I went to look over Chris's shoulder. The bottom of the closet was covered with old skates. Chris looked up and smiled.

"Everyone gives us old skates—when kids leave and stuff. Mom and Dad used to have skating parties."

She looked for a few more minutes. Once she reached over and put her hand on my ankle.

"It's awfully quiet over there," Janet said.

Chris ignored her.

"Do we have any tens, ten and a halves?" she asked.

"I don't know."

"Can you wear an eleven, Max?"

"I guess."

She handed me a pair of black figure skates, then pulled out her own. Hers were white, and they had a pair of large furry balls at the ends of the laces. Chris stood, and we kissed once in the shadow of the open door. Janet started making loud, smacking sounds by kissing her wrist.

"Let's go," Chris said. "Janet's having a seizure."

"Want me to come as a chaperone?"

"No, thanks."

Outside I put the skates over my shoulders. Three or four inches

185

had already fallen, and the flakes were still large. The wind had died to nothing, and the flakes came straight down through the trees.

We walked a block and a half, then turned down a lane. Mr. Row must have dragged the shovel as he walked because there was a wide swath down the center of the lane, a trail that led directly into a small wood. The bushes on either side of the lane were already white. The branches bent to the ground, leaving small tunnels and hollows.

We heard Mr. Row before we saw him, his shovel scraping across the ice. We cut toward the sound, bushwhacking between the trees and saplings. Chris came close and touched my sleeve. She pointed ahead, and I saw Mr. Row skating easily, moving effortlessly across the ice. Straining, I heard the quick scrape of his skates as he circled. He was dressed in an old hockey uniform that made him look wide and bulky: The pants were short, but padded, and the jersey was wide and extra long. He wielded the shovel like a stick, moving it from side to side, dribbling an imaginary puck across the woodland pond. He had the smooth, powerful gait of someone used to being on skates, and I saw him speed up, then stop, his skates coming together, a silver spray of ice chips flying up beside him.

"You look great!" Chris called. Her voice startled him. As soon as he looked up, he grabbed the shovel like a farmer, the game gone, the puck lost.

"It's beautiful, huh?" he said quietly, his voice carrying. He tapped the shovel a few times on the ice. "Hi, Max, how are you?"

"Hello, Mr. Row."

"This is the kind of night," he said, turning a little to wave his arm at the woods, "that comes pretty close to meeting your hopes for it. It doesn't happen very often in life. I was just thinking about it when you came up."

"You were not. You were thinking about hockey," Chris said. She sat on a log near the edge of the pond. "Dad used to play for Boston University. The Terriers, right dad?"

"Right. The bowwow Terriers. Of course, nobody played hockey in those days. All the decent players came from Canada. Still, I got a letter. I played."

As he spoke, he drifted backward. His skates moved in a slow

186

zigzag, weaving him away from us. The pond was almost completely shoveled. The ice looked gray and smooth, and even in the darkness I saw a faint shadow marking the reflection of the woods. A three-quarter moon was already up, and I slowly realized I could see for a good thirty feet into the woods, picking out shapes and deeper darkness under the trees.

I handed Chris her skates and squatted in front of her. I had some idea I was supposed to help her on with them, but Chris pulled her foot away.

"Max, get up. I can put on my own skate."

"Of course you can," Mr. Row said, "but this is a politeness, it's a forgotten custom. Let him do it."

Chris put her mittens to her eyes, but she left her foot in front of her. My own cheeks were flushed; I felt embarrassed and silly, yet there was no way out of it. I was thankful to hear Mr. Row shoveling again.

When I finished, she thanked me, then stood. She was not at all wobbly. She moved to the edge of the pond.

"I'll wait for you," she said.

"No, go ahead. I'll be a few minutes."

"You sure?"

"Yes. Go ahead."

With a single, graceful movement she glided onto the ice. Her steps were lighter than her father's. I barely heard her skates hit, although each stride pushed her along faster. Near the center of the ice she gave a small shout and lifted her hands higher, her motion becoming more certain.

Mr. Row skated to meet her. He skidded the shovel in my direction, then held out his arms. Chris skated to him, and I had the sense I was watching something that had been practiced into ritual. Chris folded one arm behind her, slowly taking up her father's rhythm.

"You don't mind, do you, Max?" Mr. Row called to me.

I waved for them to go ahead. Their legs moved together. Their stride was the same, and their knees flexed at the same instant. They moved like an old couple, graceful and quiet, the snow whirling around them, the night behind them dark and still.

They circled twice before Mr. Row began to pick up speed. He raised his hand, and Chris skated on one leg. She leaned forward, her body turning into a beautfiul arc, while Mr. Row maintained their momentum. He reminded me of a circus horse skating dutifully while the beautiful woman performed tricks on his back.

"Were we good?" Chris asked when they had circled near and Mr. Row let her go.

"Wonderful. You were both great."

Mr. Row looped up beside her. "You should have seen her when she was small. I used to play crack the whip with her, and I flung her so hard sometimes I worried I'd hurt her, but she always kept her balance."

"I loved it."

Mr. Row took out a flask from somewhere near his belt. He was sweating. One of his hockey socks had fallen free of his knickers, and I saw his shin, the white flesh incongruous with the bulky uniform.

"Down the hatch," he said, and took a drink.

"Dad, you're steaming, look at you."

"It's cold, I'm hot."

"Max, you ready?"

"In a second. You keep skating if you like. I can't skate that well."

"I'll teach you. I taught Janet to skate, believe it or not. Janet is the worst athlete I've ever seen."

I was still seated on the log. I held my foot in the air while I straightened the tongue of my skate.

Mr. Row went to finish clearing the ice, his hands digging at his belt to put the flask back in place. He skated across half the pond while Chris led me onto the ice, her mitten tight under my elbow.

The toe of my skate caught, and I nearly tripped.

"I'd rather you just skated," I said, embarrassed at having her so close. "Go ahead. You don't have to stay with me."

"No, I like it."

"You can't have much fun this way, though. Go ahead, really. I'll be all right. It will just take me awhile to get the hang of it."

"Positive?"

"Yes, honest."

She let go of me, and I almost fell. My ankles were weak, and the skates felt too big. Chris's hand had been a brace, and now,

188

with it gone, I was powerless to skate. The speed I had built carried me a few feet more, but I was left near the edge of the pond, perhaps twenty yards from Mr. Row.

"How you doing, Max?" he called.

"Great."

"Think of it as moving from side to side. Relax. Just try to be smooth."

"It isn't easy."

"Max, I have to say you skate like a cow," he said.

"I know."

"Come on, one circle, huh? One with me."

"Oh, I don't know . . ."

"And why not? Humor an old hockey player."

Chris whistled. Mr. Row came toward me. He thumped over a small bump, then hit the ice on the run, an old hockey player changing lines. He glided within a foot, then held out his arms.

"Come on, loosen up," he said.

His breath smelled like whiskey. His beard was dark and heavy. It was impossible to be this close to him, to be this close to an older man, without feeling strange. Still, there was something oddly pleasing about it as well, and I found myself trying to pick up speed, my awkward steps weak and childlike.

"That's it, go ahead, that's it."

His arm came around my back. His free hand held me under my forearm. Somehow he did not press his weight on mine. He was not a constant support, yet he was there, ready, his weight and strength timed to my movements.

"Better, better," he said in a whisper.

Chris skated behind us. Mr. Row was directly to my left, although I didn't glance at him. Both of us stared straight ahead, but we went fast. The trees whizzed by, and I was conscious of the ice passing beneath me, the snow banked around the pond, the scrape of skate cuts in the ice. I felt Mr. Row's breath, heard him gasp a little as he stayed with me. His hand on my back beat softly in time to my strides, and I knew I was moving better, actually on the verge of skating.

Finally we broke apart. Mr. Row took two strides and glided back to his shovel. I had to scramble with my arms out now that he was gone, although I felt a hint of rhythm coming into my

189

skating. Chris moved around in front of me, her hips and heels moving to keep her going even in reverse.

"You're doing fine," she said.

"Thanks to your father."

"It's the best way to learn."

"That's it then." Mr. Row interrupted. "I'm going. I bequeath the pond and all its beauty to you both."

"You don't have to go because of us," I said.

"Don't I? You're nice to say so. No, to tell you the truth, I've had enough. I'm cold. It's going to get colder, believe me."

"Tell Janet if she's thinking of coming out that we're not going to be here very long, okay? She might as well stay in tonight."

"Will do. Good night, Max. Maybe I'll see you later. Bye, sweetheart."

Mr. Row walked off, a cigarette in his mouth. He hadn't changed shoes. He wore his skates through the snow. I imagined he would walk across backyards, bushwhacking as we had done, skating across ice-covered lawns, gliding quietly past windows.

Chris skated for a while, but I became tired after a few shaky laps and went back to put on my boots. She skated close to the edge of the pond, moving effortlessly.

"You know, Dad doesn't always drink like that," she said.

"He was just letting loose a little," I said, taking my skates off one at a time. "Why? Does he normally drink too much?"

"Sometimes he does. He drinks to erase my mother. That's his phrase, not mine."

"Don't they get along?"

"No."

"Is it bad?"

"If they weren't Catholic, they would have been divorced years ago. Religion, you see, holds them together so they can hate each other."

Chris was breathing rapidly. She sprinted once to the middle of the ice, then swept back in, rearing into a stop with a spray of ice.

"I'm sorry," I said. "It must have been hard on you."

"I feel like a baby when I think about . . . you know, your dad and everything."

We had never talked about my father before. I had assumed

190

she knew, but it hadn't come up. I finished putting on my boots without saying anything. Chris moved quietly on the ice.

Finally I said, "It hasn't been so bad."

"I can't believe that. I know most of the story. Martin told Marla, and Marla told me."

"I figured that much. I mean, I thought you probably knew."

"Did you ever feel responsible? I guess I should ask if you still do. That's always been it with me. I've always wondered if my father and mother wouldn't have been happier without me. Kids aren't always a blessing like everyone says. Maybe they would have done something else if it hadn't been for me and Janet."

Her scarf fell and curled on the ice. She picked it up and wrapped it around her neck.

"I don't know if I feel responsible," I said. "I always think if I knew enough, I'd know his reasons for leaving. But you don't figure something like that out."

"But with my parents it's different. They're right here. Dad is so bitter, and Mom is weepy all the time. Sometimes I feel like I actually hurt her in birth. Sometimes I think my body going through hers actually injured her in some way. I wonder if I didn't drag something out of her. Doesn't that sound crazy? Sometimes I feel like I stole her soul."

Suddenly Chris's jacket exploded. Her parka hissed and then gave off a solid thud. It took me a second to realize it was a snowball.

"Here's a soul for you," someone shouted.

Another snowball flew through the air. It landed on the ice and skidded across the pond, its momentum breaking it apart.

"God damn you!" Chris screamed. "How dare you make fun!"

She was sobbing. It still wasn't clear to me what was going on. For a dreadful instant I thought it could be Chris's mother. I imagined her knee-deep in snow, lunging from tree to tree, rolling snowballs in her bare hands, her hair wild and frosted. The image was reinforced by a wild laugh.

"Quit making it so dramatic," Janet yelled, coming onto the ice. "They fight like fucking boxers . . . so what?"

Janet clumped through the snow and hit the ice running. She wore only a heavy white wool sweater with a gray scarf draped over her shoulders. Her ears were covered by bright orange ear-muffs.

"You bitch," Chris said. "I hate you."

"Don't hate me. Hate Mumsy and Popsy. I'm just their gifted daughter."

Chris wouldn't look at Janet. Janet was stationary. I walked off to go to the bathroom and to get away from them. I didn't listen intentionally, although I heard them begin to argue. I walked to the fartherest end of the pond where it was very dark. Once I thought I heard a dog nearby, but it never came into view. I whistled softly, but the sound passed.

When I finished, I went back around the pond. I didn't see Chris at all. Janet skated quietly in a circle, humming something very solemn.

"Where's Chris?" I asked.

"Who knows? She's gone off dramatically. She always retreated; I always stayed. That's the way we do things."

"You acted shitty."

"It wasn't an act."

"You know what I mean."

"Oh, you don't live with her. I can get sick of her, too, you know. It isn't all me. Besides, I don't like her making the whole thing worse than it is. If you haven't noticed it before, Chris likes everything to be slightly exaggerated."

"Forget it."

Janet shrugged. She skated beside me on the ice while I stayed on the bank. Halfway around, I saw Chris's tracks in the snow. I took a few steps into the woods and called her name. This time Clark came running up. He stopped fifteen feet away, his eyes glowing in the moonlight.

"Come here, boy," I said. "Come here."

Clark snorted and ran off. I listened to him work through the trees, his chain jangling. As soon as I stepped back near the pond, Janet swooped down, her face red from the cold, her hands held out a little at her sides. She wasn't the skater Chris was.

"Chris go home?" she asked.

"I think so."

"See? You never know with her. She likes to keep it all mys-

terious. Who knows where she is? Maybe she disappeared forever. Maybe she's home, already tucked in bed. Maybe she's
wandering through the woods."

"There are houses all around here."

"So? Don't you get it, Max? That's the way she likes it. She
wants you to come running after her. Or, better still, she wants
you to search unsuccessfully for her. That's the real thing, see?
She'd like it if you could come close to freezing to death following
her false trail into the suburban woods, which at no place get
deeper than a hundred yards."

Janet skated to the edge of the pond, exactly where Chris's
footsteps began, and shouted into the woods, "Chris, you little
actress! Come back here, little Nell! Come out, come out, wherever you are."

We both listened. It was very silent. A slight breeze moved over
the pond behind us, and I turned to watch the snow skid.

"Yoo-hooo," Janet yelled again.

"I saw Clark."

"What fun."

"Do you think she really went back?"

"Of course. That way she can seem tortured. It's very important
to Chris that she look tortured at all times."

Janet wobbled on her skates. She held out her hand. I took it
and walked her in a small circle. She kept her weight back, her
hand light in mine, but I could not be so close to her without
thinking of her reputation. Once she nearly slipped, and her
shoulder moved against mine. Her sweater was soft, and I felt the
outline of her body, like a weighted pocket watch covered in a
silk cloth.

I waited for her joke, her quip, but instead, she moved more
surely against me, her hand tight on my elbow, her breath a
white cloud in front of us.

"I'm not a good skater," she said, and listening to her, I realized
her voice had gone lower.

"That's all right. Neither am I."

I walked her in a circle for five or ten minutes, each of us
adjusting to the other's weight and balance. "Oh," she murmured
once. Her earmuff knocked against my cheek when she stumbled,

193

and I saw it was crooked on her head. I tried to lift my hand to fix it, but her arms clamped on mine, as if she would lose all balance if I were to leave.

"Are you warm enough?" I asked.

"Yes, are you?"

"I'm fine. You think Chris went in then?"

"I guess so. Probably."

"You want to walk back with me?" I asked.

"All right."

"I don't feel like going right in, though."

"Maybe we could go somewhere—I don't know. Do something."

"Maybe so."

I'm sure Janet knew we were both lying.

"Come on," Janet said.

She skated across the ice to retrieve the boots she had left at the edge of the woods. I walked after her, feeling awkward on the ice.

"Ready?" she asked me once she had her boots on.

"Ready."

We didn't move at first. We stood looking at each other. It was a terrible thing to do, to betray Chris, but we both knew we were going to do it. And there was something unpleasant in seeing it in each other, in watching ourselves let go of decency so easily. We waited quietly, listening to the storm settle over the wood. The air was very cold.

194

❖❖ 29 ❖❖

IT SNOWED through the night, but the next morning the sun came out. The day was incredibly bright. The snow had already taken on a thin crust, and it made a loud, breaking sound as I jumped the creek bed and climbed the back slope to the dispensary. When I looked around back, I saw two more posts had been put in for the kennel. The wire was still on the ground, only the topmost bundle entirely free of snow.

Someone knocked on the window. Martin stood with his index finger curled to rap again, a long cigar dangling from his mouth. I knew he wouldn't be smoking unless his parents were gone for the day.

I ran around and went inside. Cigar smoke hung thick in the air. It hung near the rafters and passed in deep folds through the small rays of sun that worked to the center of the cement floor. Martin was alone.

"What's up?" I asked.

"Nothing."

"You work on the kennel this morning?"

"Some. Stu's got a new plan. He disappeared about an hour ago. He said he wants us in on it. It's for money."

"With the kennels?"

"No, something else he's dreamed up. He says it can't miss if he can swing it."

I took off my coat. The milk was already on for hot chocolate. I added more and scooped a couple of spoonfuls of chocolate into my cup. Martin blew smoke in the face of a chipmunk Marcie had saved from some neighborhood cats.

"I want him to think it's a forest fire," Martin said.

"Where are your parents?"

"Up in New Haven."

"They traveled all the way up there in this snow?"

"My aunt Paula's house caved in. I mean, a tree or something crashed in a screened porch, and it left a big hole in their living room. I didn't listen to it all. You know how Dad loves an emergency. He was up at four this morning, loading the car with all his tools. They called him especially because he can do carpentry work."

"When will they be back?"

"Tomorrow. Stu's in charge."

"Oh, Jesus."

"You aren't kidding."

"Where's Marcie?"

"I don't know. Last time I saw her she was in her robe, curled up in front of the tube. She watches Saturday morning cartoons, you know? Dad won't let her do it past nine when he's here."

"Didn't she feed the animals?"

"She said she'd be out. She's trying to turn herself into a hassock first."

Martin blew another puff at the chipmunk. I moved next to him and watched. The animals barely reacted. The chipmunk was slow and lethargic. It should have been hibernating, but the heat kept some of the animals awake.

Martin flicked an ash on the floor. "You see Chris last night?"

"Yep. We went skating."

"She called Marla. Marla called here. Did you screw Janet or not?"

"Who said I screwed anyone?"

"I did, just now. Did you?"

196

"What's it to you?"

"Nothing, but old Chris's heart is broken. I'm supposed to tell you that . . . from Marla, you know."

The milk started to boil. The pan rattled. I went to the stove and used my sweat shirt as a potholder.

"She didn't tell you?" Martin asked.

"Who?"

"Chris."

"No. Tell me what?"

"Tell you that the flow has stopped."

"What flow? What are you talking about? Here, come and get this. Leave the animals alone."

Martin didn't move. He took a few puffs on his cigar.

"Marla is pregs," he said.

"Pregnant?"

"We think so. She thinks so. I don't know."

"Are you serious?"

"We're about as serious as you can get."

"You're kidding me. If you're kidding me, I'll . . ."

"You'll do what?"

Martin grinned. He leaned on his free hand, propping himself up against the worktable.

"Don't believe me, do you?" he asked.

"I don't know. Did Chris know?"

"She knew. With Marla, are you kidding? You think she could keep it a secret?"

I still held the pot in front of me. A piece of ice slipped away from the roof and skidded in a slow glide above us. I waited for it to fall, but it twanged on the metal gutter and stopped. I sat down and picked up my hot chocolate.

"Bull," I said finally. "I don't believe you."

"And"—he waved his cigar—"we've already planned the child's future. Or, you might say, we've planned its lack of future."

"Martin, you'd better get serious."

"I told you before, you can't get much more serious than fatherhood. It's a big step, bigger than going steady."

"Sit down," I said, taking my old place by the woodstove. "It's freezing in here."

"It's not that cold. What are you getting pissed about?"

197

"Are you telling me the truth or not?"

"I'm telling you the truth."

"Marla is pregnant. You're the father. That's what you're telling me?"

"Exactly."

"Well then, what are you so fucking calm about? I hate you for being calm right now."

"What am I supposed to do?"

"Do something."

"What?"

"How'd it happen?"

"She went swimming at the Y. It was Deado's sperm. How do you think it happened?"

"Damn it, you're a jerk, Martin."

"We've been screwing, all right? Is that what you want to hear? What's the big deal? Just because Chris is the blessed virgin, it doesn't mean Marla and I can't fuck."

"Oh, shut up."

"You jumped on Janet fast enough."

"Just shut up."

Martin sat down. Somehow he was enjoying this, enjoying my discomfort. He seemed, even now, confident everything would work out. He twirled the ash off his cigar, his fingers rolling it neatly into a shaving, which dropped on the floor.

"You swear?" I asked after a few minutes.

"Swear."

"And what are you going to do?"

"Go to New York. We're going to slip away from the class trip."

"Jesus, you've got to be kidding me."

"I'm serious. Marla's supposed to arrange it. She knows some-place or something. I'm going to give her the money. I might have to borrow some. Can you do it?"

"I don't have much, but I'll give it to you."

"Thanks."

"But on the class trip?"

"How else? I thought of asking Stu to take us in, but you met Marla's father. He'd want to know where we were going, what we were going to do, the whole thing. Besides, I don't want Stu to know."

198

"Then why not just take a bus? Just make up something to tell Mr. Babcock."

Martin shook his head. He leaned forward and took down the cup of hot chocolate.

"It's the perfect cover, that's why. No special trips, no big plans, no chance of anyone seeing us over there that shouldn't. No, we're going over and then slip off. The whole thing doesn't take very long."

"Martin, don't do this. It's all crazy."

"What else should I do?"

"I don't know, but there must be a better way."

"There is. I drown Marla."

He grinned at me. It was more a smirk than a grin. He reached to his side and brought up a bottle of blackberry brandy.

"A celebration," he said, "cigars and brandy."

"On a class trip?" I said, ignoring him. He took my cup and poured me a brandy. "We're going to the Museum of Modern Art, and you're going to slip off for an abortion—just like that?"

"Just like that."

"How much?"

"Around four hundred."

"How are you going to come up with four hundred?"

"Steal it from Stu . . . I don't know. You going to drink any of that?"

"I feel sick."

"You feel sick? How about me?"

"You can feel sick, too."

We drank a little. The animals were more lively now. Two gerbils spun their exercise wheel. A guinea pig let off a long series of squeaks, and when I looked up, I saw a garter snake, asleep for days, suddenly lift its head and dart its tongue forward.

"Will you help me then? Marla wants Chris to come. I want you."

"Are you really serious?"

"I'm really serious, and I want you to come. Will you?"

"Sure, of course I will."

"Well then, here, have a cigar."

It was a lame gesture, but I took the cigar and allowed him to light it. I sipped the chocolate and brandy.

"I don't feel good about it, if that's what you're thinking," he said.

"I know."

"I don't like it at all."

"Okay."

"Neither does Marla."

"Okay."

Marcie slammed out of the house and appeared a second later, stamping her feet.

"Bugs Bunny must be over," Martin said.

"As a matter of fact, it is," Marcie said. "Hi, Max. You two better stop with the cigars."

"Forget it, toots. We're going to do whatever we feel like today, so you better get used to it."

"You're a jerk."

Marcie went to the workbench and started to feed the animals. She tapped the glass of the gerbil cage and made kiss sounds in the air.

"Isn't Stu back?" she asked. "He's supposed to get some food for me?"

"Stu went to Botswanaland. He's decided to become a nun."

"Max, has Martin been drinking?"

"No. Maybe just a little."

"Martin, you better stop."

"Yes, Grandma."

"I mean it, I'll call Mom and Dad."

"You will not, so why are you even saying it? Besides, what do you care? If I want to drink, it's my business, isn't it? Isn't it? Do I tell you that taking care of these animals is removing all the skin from your hands?"

This was a touchy subject. Marcie had some sort of allergy; her hands peeled when she came in contact with alcohol. When she doctored the animals, her hands puffed up and peeled.

She shook her head and changed the subject.

"It's started snowing again."

"Do I?" insisted Martin.

"It's supposed to snow all night. It's going to be a blizzard before it's over."

"We just had a blizzard. Blizzards don't come in pairs."

200

"Martin . . ." I said.

He looked at me and winked. He seemed tired. He put his head back on the chair and moved it slowly from side to side. I stood and watched Marcie feed the animals. I heard the wind pick up outside. The day was no longer bright.

Someone honked a horn, and a second later I heard the rush of a large engine. A loud scraping sound pulled Martin out of his seat. We went to the door and looked out.

A pickup nuzzled up the driveway. A plow attached to the front funneled snow to one side, pushing it sedately into a large mound at the border of the drive. Stu, of course, was behind the wheel. When he saw us, he switched on the rotating orange light.

"Look at him," Martin said.

Stu ran the truck in three swipes across the driveway. He looked more natural behind the wheel of a truck than he ever did driving a car. He backed up smoothly, then threw the truck into low, his head out the window, his large forearm flattened against the door.

"Ask him if he's got the food, would you?" asked Marcie behind us.

"Stu, do you have the food?" Martin whispered. He turned to Marcie. "He didn't hear me, Marcie."

"I mean, go and ask him."

"Did you? I thought I was supposed to use telepathy."

Martin went back and sat down. He added more brandy to his hot chocolate. I went to watch Marcie finish feeding the animals.

Five minutes later Stu came in. He was dressed in a flannel shirt and corduroys. His legs whistled when he walked. On his head he wore a bright blue ski cap with yellow lettering across the front. The lettering said "Bailey Dodge."

"Did you get the food?" Marcie asked.

"Did I get your food? Your food?" Stu yelled. He jumped across the room and grabbed Marcie in a bear hug. He started kissing her while Marcie tried to push him away. He kissed her again and again, saying the whole time, "Oh, Sister, Sister, I've returned from the war. Oh, Marcie-Parcie, my little bambino, I'm back from the front where our retarded brother, Mr. Won Ton, has been captured by the First Alligator Brigade. But I'm back. Your memory was the only thing that kept me alive."

Marcie laughed. Stu grabbed me.

"You are on the verge of becoming a millionaire, Maxy One Ball."

He slipped off my shoulders and gently took my head in a headlock, though he applied no pressure.

"You have money and riches ahead of you, but first you must help me rescue Mr. Won Ton from the Alligator Brigade. It's a dangerous mission."

"Where did you get the truck?" Martin asked.

"Where? Why, Bailey Dodge. Oh, I forgot. You can't read, can you Mr. Wonny Tonny?"

"I mean how."

"Now he's speaking Mohican to me. He's a linguist. Well, first I told the Bailey boys they could use your likeness for a hood ornament, but then they only agreed if the famed Mr. Won Ton would come and give them a karate lesson."

"Seriously," Marcie said.

"I made a deal," Stu said, letting my head go. "You guys want to be in on it?"

"What's the deal?" I asked.

"We pay overhead, plus ten percent. They put me on my honor, which was their first mistake, the puds. I need two sidewalk shovelers, though. I need two brave, strapping north woodsmen."

"How much?" Martin asked.

"For you, Mr. Won Ton, all the soy sauce you can eat."

"How much?"

"I don't know exactly. We can split three ways."

"When do we start?"

"June first. When do you think? Right now."

"It's still snowing," I said.

"Duh. People still need their driveways done. We can plow store driveways, anything. This is the land of opportunity. It's not every day that money falls from the sky."

"Can we make snow horses?" Martin asked.

"Sure. Let's just get going."

We put our coats on and followed Stu outside. It had become very dark, even though it was still early afternoon. Martin carried his brandy with him. He checked the flatbed of the truck for a rope, didn't find one, went back inside to get one.

202

"We used to do this with Dad. Mom made us stop, but Martin was always after him to let us try it again," Stu said.

"What is it?"

"You'll see. Let me turn the truck around."

Stu hopped into the cab and began backing into position. Martin came out with two long stretches of rope. When Stu stopped, Martin tied a rope to each side of the truck's flatbed. Afterward he took two snow shovels from the garage and tied the ropes to the handles.

"Here," Martin said, and pointed to the shovel on the left. "Try it."

"Try what?"

"You'll see. You'll get it in a second. Now, take off your scarf, and tie it to the handle of the shovel. See, like I'm doing."

"Are we going to ride these things? Is that it?"

"Way to go, Max. It only took you about fifteen minutes to figure it out."

I tied the scarf tightly to the handle. Stu revved the engine and yelled for us to hurry. Martin stepped into the scoop of his shovel, wrapping the end of his scarf over his hand and wrist.

"You ever see the old chariot movies? The ones with races?" he asked.

"Sure."

"That's what this reminds me of. I always think of chariots. That's why we call them snow horses."

I copied Martin's position. The scarf worked as a rein.

"Ready?" Stu shouted.

"You got it?" Martin asked. When I nodded, he yelled back that we were ready.

Stu gave the truck some gas. The engine chugged, and the necks of our shovels rose from the ground, straining against the rope. They didn't stay at a steady angle. They rose and nodded, their heads dipping like those of horses, the scarf pulling tight on my hand. An instant later the shovel began to glide. I looked at Martin and saw him lift one hand behind his head like a rodeo rider. A spray of snow from the tires struck him at the knees.

"Okay?" Stu shouted as we coasted down the driveway and out onto the street.

"Okay," Martin yelled back.

I wasn't steady. The shovel glided from side to side, and I had to lean over the scarf, then tilt back like a water skier. Stu revved the engine to get up speed for Topping Hill Road. The force of the acceleration made me lean harder into the scarf.

"What did I tell you?" shouted Martin.

"It's fantastic."

And it was. The hill rocked me back until I had the sensation of riding into the sky, tilting higher and higher, while the ground became nothing more than a smooth hiss beneath my feet. Stu, out of character, didn't speed up or try to kill us. I kept a constant pressure on the scarf, and by the time we were three-quarters of the way up the hill, I was able to stand without effort, riding smoothly, drifting behind the truck.

As we crested the top, Martin turned to me and said, "I don't believe I'm a father. I am a father."

But then things were moving too fast. Stu had to go faster to keep us from sliding into the rear. The shovel rocked. Its head dipped more from the uneven speed, and I had the impression of a horse pulling at its bit. I concentrated on the shovel, on staying balanced, but when we neared the bottom, I began to look around me. The snow swirled. Stu shut off the lights and I could see the pale field running up Doblinger Hill, the trees a dark rim, the stubbled brown grass thick with snow. There was silence all around me, and I did not even want to look at Martin. I was alone, gliding, and I thought of my father, of Janet, of Honey and Gertrude and Jack. I thought of everyone and no one, letting the earth spin under me, my friction with it removed. I closed my eyes, sinking into the motion while the snow flew up and held onto my eyelashes.

204

❖❖ 30 ❖❖

A COLD snap came in during the next week, freezing
   the snow to a brittle glaze. The bushes were glazed
and the trees were glazed. The street was coated thick with
patches of ice, and the few cars that passed crackled and popped.

It was below zero on the day Martin and I planned to go into
New York with Marla and Chris. My hair froze while I waited
for Stu to pick me up for school. I stamped my feet to bring the
blood back into them. I was about to go inside when Stu pulled
into view. He honked continuously, and his hand was up over the
roof, waving just from the wrist. The car was hot and smelled of
cologne.

"You going to New York with Martin?" Stu asked as soon as I
was in. "You going to the strip shows?"

I tried to see Martin's face, but he stared straight ahead. Stu
inspected me in the rearview mirror.

"Are you?" he asked again.

"What do you care?" I asked, stalling.

"Jesus, you guys get a little money, and you're ready to blow
it all at once. Mr. Won Ton here has all his money from shoveling
the other night. He's like a little fortune cookie."

"Eat me," said Martin.

"I'm trying to give you some financial advice," Stu said, pulling the car away from the curb. "I'm trying to teach you something. You don't work just to spend."

"Oh, no? What do you work for? To hoard?"

"No, security."

Martin snorted and wiped at the side window with his knuckle. The tires broke the ice that had formed near the gutter.

"Just don't spend it all," Stu said.

Stu drove us to the station. Despite the heat in the car, the cold came through the floor. I lifted my feet up onto the seat and listened to the chunks of ice hit against the chassis. Everything on either side of the road was frozen. The telephone wires were milky and slick. Several streetlights were entirely covered with ice. They looked like dead stars.

"Do either of you retards know the train schedule?" Stu asked.

"No," Martin said.

"They're probably running late anyway," I told him.

"What I don't get is how you guys dreamed this up. Is this a lifelong ambition or something? To skip school and go to New York for a strip show?"

"What do you care?" Martin asked, his color rising. "It's just money, isn't it? It's our money, isn't it? Is this a free country?"

"That's a logical argument, Martin."

"It is, Stueewwy."

"You're arguing like an airport Christian."

"That's Dad's line."

"I don't care. It's true. You want to go to New York, go to New York. I'm just trying to help you retire sometime before you turn ninety-seven."

"Who wants to retire? Just because you want to retire at thirty, you think everyone else does, too. You know, you get an idea, and you expect everyone to want the same thing."

"Who is this? Are we getting Karl Marx on strip shows? Is that what this is? Trotsky goes to a peep show?"

"Forget it. You take one course, and now you're an economist, right? Just forget it."

Traffic slowed near the train station. A long line of cars moved slowly ahead. Men in raincoats climbed out of the cars and made

206

their way to the station, their briefcases held away from their bodies for balance.

Martin jumped out as soon as we stopped. Stu watched him go, then turned in his seat and looked at me.

"Here you go," he said, "Mr. Marx and Mr. Lenin off to New York for a peep show."

"Can we leave this stuff here? Our books and everything?"

"What if my mom needs the car?"

"Tell her we went to the Y. She won't need it until after school, will she?"

"No, I guess not. Okay, leave it. And, Max? Make sure Mr. Won Ton doesn't do anything stupid, okay? He's got a lot of money on him."

"Okay."

I closed the door. Stu worked his way back into traffic, his exhaust turning pure white in the cold air.

A wind moved over the station. I heard a thick, booming sound, and when I turned, I spotted a small boy leaning against a mailbox. He had his back to the box and every now and then lifted his boot and pounded the heel on the flat blue flank.

"They aren't here," Martin said as I entered. "Glad we didn't do this thing on the stupid class trip."

"I told you. But don't worry, it's early."

"You'd think she'd be here. I mean, what the hell?"

"She'll be here. Should we get the tickets?"

"Why don't we wait? Maybe they won't show."

Martin took a few steps to one side and leaned against the wall. I crossed to the newspaper stand. An old man was busy counting change behind the counter, a bunch of quarters spread across the *Star-Ledger*.

"Yeah?" he asked, not looking up.

"A paper and a pack of mints."

"Which paper, which mints?"

"The *Ledger* and some Wintogreens."

The man slipped the paper out from underneath the pile of quarters. He nodded at the Wintogreens, and I took a roll.

"Seventy-five," he said.

I paid him, put the paper under my arm, and went back to Martin. He was still leaning against the wall, although every now

207

and then he pushed away and looked out the window. Commuters came across the icy sidewalk. A number of men pooled at the far door, their raincoats open.

"I don't believe this whole thing," Martin said. "You know, I understand it's happening, but it doesn't really make sense. It hasn't really sunk in, if you know what I mean."

"I think so."

"You do one little thing and everything blows up. Suddenly I'm a father, for Christ's sake."

"You knew that could happen."

"Of course I knew. You know you can die, but a lot of good that does you. I'm starting to think you can't know even the simplest thing until you go through it. How's that for a philosophy?"

He pushed off again and looked out the window. He put his forehead against the cold glass and rocked his head back and forth. He looked tired.

"See them?" I asked.

"Nope, not yet."

He kept his head on the window. I took out the paper and stared at it. I couldn't concentrate, and eventually I was distracted by a pigeon fluttering against the roof. It had some sort of nest on one of the high beams in the ceiling, and I could just make out a corner of straw extending over the rafter. The pigeon walked sideways on the beam, at times jumping high enough to tap its wings on the corrugated steel. A second pigeon floated down and began picking at a cellophane wrapper.

I looked back at Martin. His forehead was still against the window, but now he brought his mouth close enough to let his tongue touch the cold glass. He did it delicately, moving far enough ahead to touch just the tip of his tongue to the glass, then pulling it inches away. He finally adjusted himself to an exact distance, and nothing moved except his tongue. It flexed in and out, moving very slowly, almost painfully, while the rest of his body remained at a rigid angle to the wall.

"Martin?"

"This is the kind of thing," he said softly, "that your parents always told you you shouldn't do when you were growing up. Remember? But you can do it and nothing happens."

"You okay?"

208

He swiveled his head to face me.

"I'm okay," he said, then quickly went to the door. "They're here."

Chris came in first.

Marla had been crying, but she smiled when she walked into the lobby. She said, "Well . . ." yet couldn't finish the sentence. She stayed close to Chris and made no move toward Martin.

"Do you have the tickets?" Chris asked.

"Not yet," I said, realizing that we would act as spokesman for our different parties. "We didn't know if you would come or what . . ."

"Well, we should get them. There's a train due any minute."

"We'll get them," said Martin.

I went with him to the ticket window. We bought four round trips. I gave Martin one and held the other three. As we walked back to join them, a pigeon took off in front of us.

"We should get ready," Chris said.

"Do we have to change in Newark?" Marla asked.

"I think so," I said. "I don't really know. I've always taken the bus."

We moved slowly toward the door. A train blew its horn in the distance, and a few men folded their newspapers. A few more stepped outside and threw away their cigarettes. One man turned his pipe upside down but kept it clamped in his mouth.

"Is that it?" Martin asked.

"I guess so," I told him.

The train grew louder as it came into the station. The floors quivered. A voice came over the PA system announcing the stops. Marla put her hands over her eyes.

Someone propped open the door, the men began filing out, and we shuffled along with them.

"Move along now, move along," a conductor said, climbing down. "Boarrrd."

Marla went up first, then Chris. Martin went next, and I climbed in last. We stopped between cars.

Marla called back to us, "Which way should we go? Does anyone know?"

"Smoking on your left," the conductor said behind me. He pulled up the stairs and closed the door.

PART THREE

"Which way?"

"Off the platform, please. Smoking on your left."

We finally pushed through to the right. The car was not full. We found two facing seats. Marla and Chris squeezed into one, and Martin and I took the other side. We rode almost in silence to Newark, then switched trains. Out on the platform, before the second train arrived, I watched the ice glint on the tracks. Martin stood a few steps off and lit a cigar. Marla said nothing but stayed near the wall, watching old ticket stubs hop slowly over the wooden ties. Chris, gone from me, read quietly, her long gray coat flapping against a cigarette billboard.

❖❖ 31 ❖❖

"THIS IS IT," Martin said. "This is the address."

We stood in front of a brownstone that looked no different from the other buildings on the block. A short flight of steps led up to the front door, a small patch of dead grass on either side. A few bushes grew just beneath the first-floor windows. Some of the tenants had apparently tried to root houseplants, because I saw several cracked potting jars near the lip of a window well.

"This is it," repeated Martin.

"I don't see a plaque," Chris said. "If it's a doctor's office, it should have a plaque."

"Let's just go up," Marla whispered. "Let's just get it over with."

"You don't have to," Chris said. "No one says you have to."

"I know."

"Come on, it's cold," Martin said. "Max, you and Chris want to go back to that restaurant we saw?"

"Whatever's best."

"Go ahead," Marla said. "There's nothing for you to do here. Later, maybe, but not now."

"Are you sure?"

"Yes. Maybe you should go to that movie we passed. It might take a while."

Marla started to cry. Chris put an arm around her shoulders.

"Okay," said Marla. "I'm all set now. I'm okay. Come on, Martin. Let's go up."

Martin walked ahead of her up the stairs. I wanted to shout at him, to tell him to stay near her, but there seemed to be no point to it. He pulled open the door, held it for Marla, then bent to inspect the names by the buzzer. He pushed a bell, then leaned out to tell us it was the right place.

"Go ahead," he said.

Chris and I waited until they were buzzed in. We heard the buzzer even on the street. Marla pushed through, but the buzzer kept ringing long after the door had shut.

"I don't believe this," Chris said. "I don't believe this is happening."

"Neither do I."

"It's all so strange. You hear about it, but here it is, happening to a friend of mine."

"When did you know?"

"A while ago. I don't know exactly. Marla was so stupid, and Martin was worse. It was like they both let it happen."

"Martin's like that."

"I know he is. I told her."

We walked back toward the restaurant we had passed earlier.

"We could go to a museum," Chris said.

"I couldn't concentrate. Besides, Martin wouldn't know where to find us."

"We can't drink coffee for three or four hours."

"Do you want to go to the movie?"

"I don't care. Do you?"

" I don't care."

"Well? Do you?"

"I guess so. It doesn't seem right, does it?"

"The whole thing seems wrong, so I don't know why a movie would matter. The whole thing is awful."

It was two more blocks to the movie theater. When we arrived, I didn't recognize the name of the picture. It was something in

French, and even the title had accents over the letters. The first show wouldn't begin for forty-five minutes, but no one objected to our going in.

"You want anything to eat?" I asked.

"No, no, thanks. I'm not hungry at all."

We went into the theater. The floor was covered in blue carpeting. The screen was hidden behind a curtain. No music played, and in the quiet I heard some people talking in the projection booth. They went on about a bulb that had blown and apparently ruined one of the reels.

We moved toward the middle of the theater without a word. Chris went in and I followed. She sat when we were exactly in the center. I shrugged off my coat and sat beside her.

"I could sleep," she said. "I could just fall asleep and wake up when the whole thing is over. Marla could be killed. She could be sterile after this."

"No. Shhh."

"She could, though."

"No, it will be okay."

She shivered. I slouched down and put my jacket over me. I held up one end.

"Would you like to get under?"

"No."

"Are you sure?"

"Yes."

I sat up. People were still talking in the booth. Once, like a camera flash, a beam of light shot at the screen and turned it white behind the curtain.

"Are we going to see each other anymore?" I asked.

"No."

"Why not?"

"You know why. It's Marla and Martin . . . the whole thing. It's a lot of things, really. I don't want to be like them. I don't want to end up like that."

"Is that it?"

"And Janet."

She held up her hand before I could say anything. She didn't look at me. She stared straight ahead and drew in her breath. I heard her shiver at the same time and knew she was crying.

213

"Sometimes . . . I . . . breathe . . . too fast," she said, her hand going to her neck.

"Are you okay?"

She shook her head and put her hands on her knees. She leaned forward and put her forehead flat against her kneecaps. I put one arm around her shoulders, but she pushed it off. She slapped at it again even though it was gone.

"Should I get someone? Call someone?"

"I'm all . . . right."

"Would you like my coat?"

"No."

I was sweating. I saw a dull reflection from the movie screen on Chris's tortoise-shell barrette.

"Janet's done it before," Chris said finally, her voice more in control. "She's a nymphomaniac."

"She isn't. Shhhh."

"But she is. She is. She really is."

"Well, it doesn't matter. It doesn't matter right now. Can you sit up? Are you okay?"

"You don't believe me, do you? Everybody wants to believe it was just him. That's what you're thinking, isn't it?"

"Here, just take my coat. Go ahead. I'm going to go out and get some napkins. Stay here, all right?"

I put the coat over her shoulders and stood before she could say anything. I felt as if the floor were rising to meet me. I was barely through the door to the lobby when I saw Martin standing outside the theater, his hands folded behind his back, smoking a cigar.

I walked through the lobby and knocked on the door. Martin turned and waved me out. He flicked his cigar several times.

"What are you doing?" I asked. "Why didn't you come in?"

"You can't smoke inside."

"But what are you doing here?"

"I need some money. How much do you have? I'll pay you."

"Why? I thought you had enough. How long have you been out here?"

Martin snorted. I smelled liquor on him. He puffed quickly on the cigar, and the ash grew pale white.

"The whole thing is crazy," Martin said. He sounded as if he

214

might cry at any moment. "They took one look at her and said they wanted more money because the case is so advanced. They say it's more complicated."

"Oh, Christ."

"Marla almost started screaming that it moved. She's a mess. I need a hundred more, or they won't do it."

"I think we should get her out of there."

"Good answer, asshole. It isn't your fucking future, is it? What am I supposed to do? I might as well chuck everything. If she doesn't go through with this, what then? We'll get married? Am I supposed to marry Marla? Is that it? Is that what everyone wants?"

"I don't know, Martin."

"You don't know, do you? Then you ought to shut your fucking mouth and not tell me to get her out of it."

"Martin—"

"Oh, fuck it all. Will you give me the hundred or not? Will you? If you won't, just say it? I know Chris won't. She thinks the whole thing is a mortal sin. She thinks the pope will drop dead if we go through with it."

"I'll give you the money. I just want you to stop and think what you're doing."

Martin shook his head. It was a short convulsion, a nervous reaction. He pulled a flask out of his coat pocket and took a short nip. His hair blew all over, and his jacket was too big for him. He looked wild standing there; he looked old.

"Can I have the money?" he whispered. "Max, I need the money."

"Okay."

"I don't care if it's right or wrong; it's efficient. That's what Stu always says."

"Okay. All right."

I reached for my wallet. A wind suddenly snapped against the building, and I heard the streetlights begin to swing. A letter from the marquee above us flew off and fell on the sidewalk. It was a B, and it skidded on the walk, its edge gouging the rough texture as it went. Martin took a step closer. He blocked the wind with his body, and his cigar was very close.

Someone said, "Martin?"

I turned to look for Chris, and Martin turned with me. Chris wasn't there, and I leaned past Martin to look down the street. There, standing between two parked cars, was Marla. She didn't have her coat or hat or gloves. Her skin was red, and I saw a liquid glint under her nose. Even as I saw it, she reached up her arm and used her sleeve.

"I want to go home," she said.

"Where's your hat and coat?" Martin asked. He took a step toward her. "Where are they? Did you leave them up there?"

"It's all wrong, Martin. It's too late. I tried to tell you. The whole thing is wrong."

"It's not wrong. Come on. Max, would you give me the fucking money? Hurry up, come on. Hold on, Marla. We'll go back up."

"I'm not going back up there."

"You'll go."

Martin snatched the wallet from my hand. He put it in his coat pocket, then ran at Marla. Marla sobbed, "Noooo," and put her hands over her eyes. Martin cracked his knee on a car fender, but he managed to grab Marla and nearly yank her across the hood.

"We're going back up," Martin shouted. His face was next to hers, pressed close. "Get that straight, okay? We're going back up there and get it done. Then it will be over and that's it. They said they'd do it. They said so."

"Martinnnn," Marla screamed.

I put my hands over my ears, but I couldn't block the sound of her crying. I couldn't catch my breath, couldn't think what to do. Martin pulled her up the street, tugging at her arm, although Marla sometimes broke free. More than once they almost fell, and Martin grabbed at anything near, hoisting himself along with the aid of a parking meter, the thin crank of a store's awning. People up and down the block turned to watch, but no one came near, no one said a word.

I ran at Martin. I dived across Marla and hit him with my full force, knocking him back and away. I heard him grunt, the air go out of his lungs. Then we fell. Martin skidded sideways, and I heard his shoes slip, the leather of his boots clump together.

I landed on top. We fell against a mound of snow and ice. Martin hit his head on one jagged piece, and I saw blood start

216

in his hair. I held him as tight as I could. I squeezed and pressed myself closer, wrapping my legs over him, squaring my weight on him whenever he moved. He was crying now, heaving under me, yet I was conscious of the parking meter, the dirty rust color of the nearest hubcap. Above us I saw a narrow ledge on the side of a building, and I remember staring at it as I squeezed Martin's chest, thinking that it was lined with snow and that somehow, I had never seen ledges like that anyplace but New York.

"Oh, oh, oh," Martin wheezed under me. He was a little drunk and completely exhausted. His body finally went still.

"I love you, Martin, but you can't do this," I whispered close to him. "You can't, you can't, you can't."

He nodded and kept crying. I put my forehead against the soft hair at his temple and waited for us to catch our breath.

❖❖ 32 ❖❖

WHEN WE arrived back in Stockton, we left Chris and
Marla almost without a word. I walked with Martin
along the street, both of us tired, the air still bitter cold.

"Well?" he asked once we were alone.

"I don't know, Martin."

"I guess I have to tell someone, huh? It's not going to go away."

"No, I guess it won't."

"This whole thing. This whole shitty thing."

We walked on. Evening was settling in, and already it was
nearly dark. Lights came on in a few houses as we passed.

"We should have taken a taxi," Martin said. "It's too cold for
this."

"Maybe."

"You think I ought to marry her?"

"I think you ought to do what you want. I mean, I think you
have to be fair to her, but I don't think you should let yourself
be bullied into anything. A lot of people have done what you
did; they just didn't get caught. You had a bad break, that's all."

"Yeah, except I knew it could happen. I knew she wasn't using
anything. Right now I can't even stand to look at her. I don't

think I can look at the kid. I hope to hell it doesn't look like me. If it looks like me, I don't know what I'll do."

"How can you get married? Where would you live?"

"Marla says we could live at her house. She says it will work out if we want it to. I think she actually believes it. It's like a fantasy or something to her."

We walked to my house, then separated. I didn't know what Martin was going to do. It was only later, when Stu showed up at the back door, that I found out.

"Is it true then?" Stu asked me. He stood on the back steps. "Is Won Ton really a papa?"

"Shhh."

"What are you shushing me for? Martin spilled the beans. He announced it right at supper. I thought Gil was going to choke on the pot roast. Then he turned all official and yanked Martin into the study. We haven't heard a thing since then. That's why I'm here. Come on out for a minute."

I took my jacket down from behind the door and stepped out. The night was cold and clear. I saw the Kellermans' house through the bare trees.

"So?" Stu asked as soon as we were away from the door. "What's all this about? He knocked up Marla?"

"Yep."

"Christ. Damn Martin. You should have seen Tilly. She started to cry and Marcie started to cry. But old Martin kept sawing away at his pot roast. I don't know where he gets it from."

"So he told everyone?"

"Oh, he told them. He's dead. They said something about a big summit meeting. Marla's folks might be coming over tonight. There's supposed to be some sort of conference call or satellite hookup. I don't know."

We walked across the driveway. Instead of going back toward the dispensary, we walked to the street. Stu plucked at the ice along the bushes.

"Did they yell at him?"

"No. What can they say, really? Hell, Martin didn't do anything immoral. He just got caught. He was stupid, that's all. He was too Martin about it."

"So what will happen?"

"I don't know. You guys tried to fix it, right? Is that what you were doing today?"

"Something like that."

We had reached the street. I saw the Ladds' yard in the distance. The fields beyond Topping Hill were pure white. Now and then I heard a shriek from the kids who went up there to sled.

Stu bent down, picked up a piece of snow crust, and squeezed it. When it crumpled, he picked up another piece and cracked it across his knee.

"Where's Marcie?" I asked.

"It's all so damn predictable," Stu said, ignoring me. "I could have put down odds. Martin wings one with his first bullet."

"It's one of those things."

"No, it isn't," Stu said softly. "I'll tell you this: With Martin you always felt he was saving up for a time when he'd break everyone's heart. He's the smartest, you know? He really has the most potential, even though he gets shitty grades. He's even smarter than Marcie. But I always knew Martin would break everyone's heart."

"I know what you mean, I think. It's just one of those things, though."

"No, it's what Martin's like. The sad thing is that Gil and Tilly aren't even mad at him. They'll act it, just for appearance's sake, but deep down they won't be angry. They'll tell him to go ahead and do what he wants because it's senseless to try anything else. He's just Martin."

"You okay, Stu?"

Stu was crying. I felt myself come close to joining him. We stood on the curb looking straight out. Stu pulled his jacket up around his neck and coughed to clear his throat. He skidded a last piece of ice on the street. It skidded pretty well, rattling back and forth, finally finding a small tire groove that carried it forward.

"Why don't you come over?" Stu asked. "Marcie wants to see you."

"All right."

We cut through a side yard and made our way back to the Kellermans'. Marcie's dispensary light was on, but there was only a thin trail of smoke from the chimney. I walked with Stu to the center of the yard, and there, by leaning a little right and left, we could catch small peeks of the TV room they called the study.

"Can you see him?" Stu whispered.

"No. Just your father once. He's up by the mantel."

"Come on."

We sneaked closer to the house. From ten feet away I finally picked out Tilly. She was holding a cup, and she warmed her hands on it.

"There's Won Ton," Stu said. "He's in the electric chair—the red chair where Dad always puts you when he wants you to sit up straight."

"Is he okay?"

"Won Ton? Looks like he's been crying."

"A lot?"

"I can't tell. Martin doesn't cry much."

Marcie came out then. We heard her step onto the back porch and take a couple of breaths. Stu bent, picked up a piece of ice, and waited for her to step out into the yard. I expected him to lob it, but he rifled it in her direction, and it twanged off the edge of the porch railing.

"Stu?" Marcie asked.

"Pssst. Over here."

"Stu? Is that you? Max?"

Marcie walked with her flashlight. She swept the light across us once or twice before she stepped any closer. Her steps were tentative on the ice, the light down and muffled by her mitten.

"Electric chair," Stu said when she was close enough to hear. "Is he getting it?"

"Marla's father is on the way."

"Damn. What do they want with him right now?"

Marcie shrugged. Her face was red and swollen. I knew she would be going out to her animals later.

Suddenly someone began to shout. I straightened quickly and leaned against Stu. Marcie was next to me, but she didn't look at all. She backed away and looked out across the yard.

It was Gil yelling. He shouted something in a loud, precise cadence, punctuating each word with a little snap of his finger on the mantel. Gil went on about responsibility, about owning up to mistakes, about spending half his life preparing to make a mistake.

221

Tilly got up, but Gil made a quick wave of his hand at her. Then he walked out of the room, giving Martin a wide berth. He slammed the door of the study and walked into the kitchen. As if from far away, I heard the ice trays snap.

"The prosecution rests," Stu said.

"Is Marla's father really coming?" I asked Marcie.

"That's what they said."

The back door opened. We all squatted close to the house. Gil, up on the porch, breathed heavily. He must have needed air, or simply to cool down, because he stood for a long time in complete silence. A couple of times he tapped his boots on the wood, and once I heard him kick at the welcome mat. After a while he came down the steps and stood where the sidewalk curved. He looked up at the moon, at the clear night, then let out a long sigh. He sighed again, and I heard Marcie begin to cry beside me.

I don't know how long he stood there. We stayed in the shadows. Finally he turned and climbed the steps. I heard something break, but I couldn't tell what it was. When I leaned farther out, I saw Gil methodically snapping off the icicles that had formed near the drain. He did not shatter them. He seemed to pry them off intact, slowly applying pressure until they came free in his hand. Then, tapping softly, he knocked one against the other until the one still attached to the house jumped free and shattered on the cement walk.

❖❖ 33 ❖❖

WINTER turned into spring, and through it all the great Martin debates raged on. When Martin and I were accepted to colleges—I to Lehigh, Martin to Springfield College—the celebration was reserved and uneasy. The debates had made us all as cautious about joy as we were about disappointment.

Tilly took much of the worry on herself. She presided from the kitchen, her hip leaning against the sink as she wiped a glass, shook out a place mat, sponged the burners on their electric stove. We all were anxious for new air, anxious for spring, but Tilly kept the door open more than most people during this season, and as a result, her floor turned into a small swamp, which was blotted and dammed by newspapers and loosely knitted throw rugs. Weeks before it was reasonable, she talked Gil into putting the screen doors up, and she took a position there, hovering without real purpose as she watched us working on the kennel. Sometimes, when she became lonely or bored or restless to see Martin, she would come out, a sweater draped over her shoulders, somebody's floppy galoshes over her indoor slippers. She jingled when she walked, the metal snaps clinking together, and she always started the conversation with the same "How's it going?" then stepped out of the wind into the lee of the garage. Her questions, we knew, were directed at Martin. There existed between them a pain that the spring air only made more excruciating. Watching her, I was reminded of an animal, a cat perhaps, checking her young, counting numbers not by sight alone but by smell and shape and the blind knowledge of a mother for its young.

After staying with us for a time, she would go down to the creek and check its thaw. Large patches of ice were gone now, and Tilly reported as she went, telling us what new section had come free, calling back through the branches of the willow and pine clusters in a voice that did not always reach us. Without fail she returned to us with something she had found: an interesting piece of ice; a glazed branch; a frozen leaf, the veined pattern raised and blue. She held these things in her palm for inspection, all the time glancing at Martin, watching him, searching to see the change in him. In the end she went back inside and took up her position by the door.

When the kennel was finally finished, Martin and I were sent to pick up a dog from the Ringlesteins'. Mrs. Ringlestein was an elementary teacher who had heard about Marcie's dispensary through a neighbor. She had come to visit and been so impressed she had called a woman on the local paper, who, in turn, interviewed Marcie, then decided against writing an article for fear of bringing the zoning board down on her head.

A soft rain fell, and it was nearing sundown when we went to pick up the dog. Martin had a piece of paper with the address written on it, and he glanced at the note as we walked. The yards had black patches of snow here and there. One pile of snow still held the remains of a Christmas tree, and I saw where kids had tried to burn the bark. Blackened slabs of newspaper nested beneath the trunk, the snow holed into a dark well.

Martin took out a cigarette. He blew smoke rings in the beams of an early streetlight. He put the cigarette in the middle of his mouth and looked straight up into the drizzle.

"Max?"

"Hmmm."

"I'm getting married. I'd like you to be best man."

"What?"

224

I said it before I could think. I didn't know how to take it. The last time I had talked with him nothing had been decided.

"We decided last night," he said. "I'm getting married."

"Are you serious?"

"Of course, I'm serious."

"Boy," I said. I tried to think of something to say, but most of the things I thought of turned into a question. Finally I asked, "And you'll live?"

"Over at Marla's. They have a rec room downstairs. They're going to turn it into an apartment. It's got a refrigerator and everything. It had a bar in it, but nobody used it. It should be all right."

"How did Marla take it? Was she okay?"

"Sure, she's all for it."

"And her dad?"

"Pretty much," Martin said. He took a long splinter off a telephone pole as we passed. "He wants me to call him by his first name, Fred. I guess that's nice. Anyway, he went on about having a son in the family, but he's angry. I think he hates my guts, to tell the truth, but he's willing to go along with it. It's all momentum. Once one thing happens, everything else seems to follow. Everyone got noble and started saying it would work out fine."

"When's the wedding?"

"I don't know. Soon. She's getting awfully big. Well, you've seen her. She's big."

The rain picked up, but there was no lightning. Martin flicked his cigarette away. I punched him lightly on the shoulder.

"I'd like to," I said.

"Be best man?"

"Yes, I'd like to."

"I'd like it, too. It's going to be a little queer, but I don't know, maybe it won't be too bad. Who knows?"

"You sure you want to get married?"

Martin took another cigarette and lit it.

"Do me a favor, Max. I know you have to ask stuff like that— everyone does—but there comes a time when it doesn't make sense. Does it? You see what I mean? It's decided."

"You're right."

225

"The whole thing isn't ideal. That's Fred's way of putting it. But still, once it's done, you can only second-guess so far. If you can keep people from asking stuff like that, you'd be doing me a real favor. Even Stu and Marcie. They started with the same questions."

"Well, you must be relieved it's all decided."

"I am."

We arrived at the corner of Piedmont and Spruce. The gutters were backed up, and water spread across the road. The trees dripped. More streetlights were coming on, but their light was still dim, not completely heated.

"I'm smoking too much," said Martin, and shook out another cigarette. He lit it off the one he had just finished and tossed the butt away.

"What's the number on the house?" I asked.

"Forty-seven Carol Road."

"Stu said it's one of those split-level jobs. One of the new ones."

We were almost at the end of Piedmont when I heard a horn behind us. A loud splash of water followed, and when I turned, I saw the Kellermans' Biscayne coming toward us. It hit a puddle and shot a large fantail up onto the bordering lawns. The car hesitated, almost went dead, then chugged forward at reduced speed. Stu, at the wheel, honked again.

"Who's walking who?" he asked out the window as he stopped. "Mr. Won Ton slipped his collar, huh?"

"What do you want?" asked Martin.

"We have another dog. He's in the back there. He's the ugliest dog I've ever seen."

"What's his name?" I asked.

"King George."

The dog was in a chrome cage jammed in the back seat. It was a small, overweight pug, a miniature, with a bulldog face lined with folds. Its dog tag stuck out from the side of its head like an exotic earring. A tiny pink tongue darted out of its mouth occasionally, the tip never quite receding all the way.

"Did he stick his tongue out at you?" asked Stu, glancing in the rearview mirror. "This dog beats everything I've ever seen. Every time I look back there he's sticking his tongue out at me. He doesn't even move except to grunt and slobber. What a dog."

226

"Maybe he's gay," Martin said.

"Gay, my foot. Why haven't you guys been to Ringlesteins? They called already."

"We took it slow," I said.

"Well, get in. Come on, we'll pick it up together so I can show you how a master salesman does it. McClintock's the dog's name. I want you to get in the habit of calling dogs by their names. It adds a sense of style."

"Should we call this dog King or George?" Martin asked.

"Whack me. Come on, get in."

We climbed in front. Stu had hung a leash over the rearview mirror, which rocked gently as we pulled away. King George's claws tapped on the metal mesh of his cage. I heard him breathe and grunt softly.

"Hear him?" Stu said. "The dog can't keep its balance. Look at him. He almost falls every time I pull away. What kind of dog is that? What was it bred for . . . being a doorstop? I picture him sitting in a wheelchair with a blanket over his knees. He should go on a cruise and let his owners come to the kennel."

"What kind of dog is McClintock?" I asked. "He's a mutt, isn't he?"

"I think so. He's a paying dog, that's all I care about."

Stu pulled into the Ringlesteins' driveway and shut off the engine. I saw a small head poke out from behind the house. It was a little boy with dark hair. He was dressed in a winter coat, but the coat was almost completely off him, hanging merely by the hood. He must have been using it for a cape, because he ducked behind the garage for a second and reappeared with a bright red party mask over his face.

"Oh, Christ," Stu said. "We've got Superman's dog."

The boy held his hands straight out and pretended to fly toward us. He made a shushing sound. It was the sound effect for flying, and when he looked up to face us, a spray of saliva hissed and flecked the air.

"Hi there. McClintock ready?" Stu asked in his con man voice.

"You from the planet Mars?" the boy asked.

"No, we're from the planet Won Ton, you little wacko. Where's McClintock?"

"You have dugger dites."

227

"What?"

"Dugger dites, dugger dites."

The kid flew toward us again, then shushed his way out onto the lawn. He made a few spastic leaps, then fell down on purpose, his cheeks giving off loud, crashing sounds. He shouted something unintelligible and came up flying again.

"He should go to the kennel," Martin said.

Stu rubbed his eyes, then led us up the flagstone walk. Some of the corner pieces had broken free, but they had been set back in position, ready to be cemented when the thaw finished.

"McClintock, remember," Stu said. "Call the dog by name."

"Yes, sir."

"It's money, Martin. Don't screw around."

Stu looked for the bell. A small mezuzah was nailed to the doorjamb. Stu bent to it, put his lips near, and spoke.

"Hello, God? Are you there? Paging Mr. God, paging the prophet Moses, please report to the courtesy desk."

"You jerk," Martin said.

Behind us, the boy began making machine-gun sounds. When I turned to look at him, he had a stick pointed at my head. I was still watching when Mrs. Ringlestein opened the door.

She was dressed in some sort of tight pants. She had slippers on her feet and bare ankles. A pair of glasses were fastened by a thick blue ribbon around her neck. She had on too much make-up. Her cheeks were bright red, angular, and her eyelashes were caked with mascara. Her voice was partially muffled by the storm door as she opened it.

"Hello, hello. You must be Marcie's brothers. Come in, come in. The dog's ready. Patrick? Patrick! Come around back now. It's time to get ready."

The kid made a machine-gun sound at her. The corners of her mouth went tight. The lines around her eyes bunched.

"Come on, now. You have to get cleaned up."

The kid zoomed off toward the road. He went in exactly the wrong direction.

"Oh, well, I'll get him later," she said, holding the door wide enough for us to step inside. Her lipstick was flaky; her lips looked like wood that had been scraped but not sanded.

"McClintock is right here, all ready," she said.

228

To prove it, the dog ran over and jumped against her legs.

"Down, down," she said, pushing him. "Down, McClintock, down. He's so excitable. Down. It's time for his walk. My husband, Dan, walks him when he gets home, but there wasn't time today. Down! We have to get to Newark by seven."

"We'll walk him," Stu said. "That's our business."

"Yes, it is, isn't it?"

McClintock still jumped up and down, making nervous little hops. Martin rubbed the dog's ears. Stu flicked out a card I had never seen before.

"I thought you might want this in case you need to call or get in touch or anything. We can keep him as long as you like."

"Oh, a card? How nice. Of course, I'll take it with me."

"Then we'll be going."

Stu bent and clipped a silver tag on McClintock's collar. "We put it on so if a dog ever got lost, we'd know whoever found him would know who to call."

"Do you lose many dogs?" asked Mrs. Ringlestein.

"No, it's just a precaution."

"Stu normally wears one," Martin said.

"What's that? I didn't catch it," Mrs. Ringlestein said.

"Never mind."

I opened the door. Patrick was leaning with his forehead pressed flat against the storm door. I jumped back a little, and McClintock barked. Patrick flew off again, running like a maniac across the front lawn.

"Oh, that kid. He's in a dreamworld, I swear. Those damn Saturday morning cartoons . . . that's what does it."

"Good-bye," I said, and went out. Martin followed me. Stu passed me the leash, and McClintock came bounding through the door.

"We'll call when we get back," Mrs. Ringlestein said. Then, shouting over our heads, she said, "Patrick? Patrick? McClintock's leaving, honey. Come and say good-bye. Come on."

Patrick flew toward us. When he was close enough, he bent over McClintock, held out his hand, then rapped McClintock twice on the top of his skull.

"Good-bye . . . good-bye . . . gooodddd." He rattled on until McClintock dodged away.

"Patrick!"

Patrick swooped off again. I walked McClintock to the car. Stu said good-bye one more time; then the door shut. Martin, halfway down the walk, turned and said, "Hey, Patrick? You're a Martian asshole."

"Shut up," Patrick answered. He held his hands in a strange cross. "Dugger dites," he said.

Patrick made louder sounds and circled toward the backyard. I opened the door and let McClintock hop in. As soon as he saw King George, he jumped back out. King George stuck out his tongue.

"Get him in, would you?" Stu said. "Just push him in. King George is nothing to be frightened of."

"Dugger dites," Martin said.

"Oh, Jesus, tell King George to leave McClintock alone. Come on. We look ridiculous out here."

"Who are you worried about?" I asked. "Not that lady, I hope."

Somehow Patrick had worked his way to the back of the car. He bent down and stuck his machine gun up the exhaust pipe. McClintock shied away from the kid and wrapped his leash around Martin's legs.

I reached down, picked up McClintock, and lifted him into the back seat. King George made a strange gargling sound but sat without really moving, his tiny legs nearly crossed, his thick pink tongue now and then appearing between his whiskered lips.

"Close the door and hand me the leash," I told Martin.

I sat in back with the dogs. Martin climbed in front. Stu got behind the wheel, started the engine, and was about to pull out when he realized he couldn't see Patrick anywhere.

"Hey, dugger dite? Come here and let me choke you," he called out the window.

Patrick was silent. I smelled McClintock's fur. It was damp, and whenever he looked up at me or turned his head quickly, his mustache loosed small drops of water.

"Does anybody see him?" Stu asked.

"Can the car explode if he sticks things up the exhaust?" Martin asked. "I mean, if he got the stick way up, what would happen?"

Stu got out. He said something, then disappeared from view. A moment later he stood up with Patrick and led him to the front

230

door. When he climbed back in, he put the car quickly in reverse. The car rocked for a second before it started backward.

"The kid was building little ramps behind the wheels. He thought that would keep it from going. Mrs. Ringlestein just smiled and said he always does things like that. The kid is insane."

It took five minutes to get back to the Kellermans'. Halfway up the driveway I saw Marcie standing outside the dispensary with a man next to her. At first I couldn't tell who he was. Then, easily, he flicked a cigarette onto the grass, and I realized from the motion that it was Mr. Row. Clark, on a long lead, sniffed at the door to the garage.

"Is that Mr. Row?" Martin asked.

"Yep," I said.

"Chris's father?" Stu asked. "He's got a dog, doesn't he?"

Stu got out of the car and went to him. Marcie excused herself and went inside. I didn't know yet whether Mr. Row was here on business or not, but I felt strange seeing him. I hadn't been in touch with Chris, or Janet for that matter, and I felt guilty about the whole thing. I wondered what Mr. Row knew about the situation.

I let McClintock out of the car. Martin picked up King George and lit a cigarette with his free hand. Mr. Row started talking before I could say anything.

"I was just telling Stu that all the women in my family are up in Vermont, trying to get in one last week of skiing, you know, and I have to go to work every morning. I hate to leave a dog alone. Normally I board Clark over at the pound, I know a guy there, but the government's cracking down now. So, when I heard about you guys, I thought it was a natural."

Mr. Row was being expansive. He rocked on his heels as he talked. His raincoat made a whistling sound, and I realized, when I came nearer, that he was on the verge of being very drunk. A corner of a handkerchief poked out of the pocket of his raincoat, and it edged out a little farther as he brought his hand out to shake ours.

"Martin," he said, "and, of course, Max. Max, the heartthrob of my entire household. You were, you know, Max? For quite some time. You have staying power."

I didn't know what to say. To stall, I watched McClintock come forward to sniff Clark. Neither one of them seemed to pay any attention to King George. Instead, they turned quarters and sniffed for a long time at each other, then apparently grew bored. We watched until Stu said, "Would you like to see the facilities, Mr. Row?"

"See them? I'd like to use them. But lead on, Stu. This is a trip to Mecca. You don't know how people are talking about that enterprising young Kellerman boy. You are the coming thing, Stu."

Mr. Row swung close enough to put one hand on my shoulder. My body tensed, but I didn't move away. Clark nuzzled in between our legs. Martin opened the door for all of us.

"This is the animal hospital," Stu said, leading us in.

"Stu, it isn't a hospital," Marcie said from her worktable.

"Well, what is it then?" Stu said, annoyed Marcie wouldn't go along. "Is it the animal morgue? Is that what you expected me to tell people?"

"Just tell the truth."

"Ah, but whose truth, eh, Stu?" Mr. Row asked. His hand slipped off my shoulder. "Dollars have their own truth, don't they, Stu?"

"Sort of."

"Sort of? Absolutely. They absolutely do. Is that a sentence? Anyway, once you've learned that, you've learned everything the business community has to offer. You ever see a stick whittled down? That's what life in the business world does. Years go by, and each one strips a little more bark . . . until you become a sharp, smooth stick."

"Are you all right?" Martin asked him.

"All right? I've been looking at the shavings for a long time now. I'm slowly becoming suitable for only one thing, roasting wienies or maybe cooking marshmallows. That's what happens."

Mr. Row seemed on the verge of collapse. Cigarette ashes drifted down the front of his raincoat; a few burn holes pocked the material near the top button.

Marcie put the lid on the hamster cage and cleared her throat.

"Nice to have met you, Mr. Row," she said, and started to the door.

232

"Charmed," he said. "Charmed by your work, Marcie."

"Thank you."

"Please, have a seat," Stu said to Mr. Row when she was gone. "Why don't you two take the dogs out back? Take Clark along."

We took all the dogs around back. King George was still in his cage. The rain had turned to a fine drizzle. The ground was muddy, and the other two dogs made low, splatting sounds as they walked.

"Three dogs the first day," Martin said. "You have to hand it to him."

"You know who will take care of them, though. He'll be the last one."

"But it's his idea."

Martin opened the gate to the first run and let Clark go in. We put McClintock in the center run. McClintock went right to the common wall and touched noses with Clark. Then he trotted slowly around the entire cage, sniffing at odd intervals, stopping for short periods, then going through the whole routine again.

"You think he's all right?" Martin asked me.

"Who? Mr. Row? Sure, he's okay. He's just that way, I guess."

"He's drunk."

"He's really drunk."

"He seems sad or something. He seems despondent."

"Where'd you dig that one up?"

"You know," Martin said, "whenever I see adults like that, it scares the hell out of me because I realize that they were like us once, so we may be like them someday. I hate thinking about it."

Martin had to tilt King George out for the third run. When Martin shook the cage softly, King George skidded onto the lawn with a jolt. He rolled onto his side, then jumped up barking, his curled tail wagging, his round, fat face bent up in a smile.

"What a dog," Martin said.

"Just let him get used to it."

"Look at him. He doesn't like that rain, I'll tell you that."

Martin squeezed out of the run, but King George stayed right at the door. He sat down and started a long fit of barking. He didn't bark like a normal dog. He barked when he liked, yelping just when you thought he might stop, timing it perfectly so that he was next to impossible to leave.

"Like a windup dog, isn't he?" Mr. Row said from behind us. "That's what he looks like."

Mr. Row came up and leaned on the fence. A moment later Stu rounded the corner. With Mr. Row's back to him, Stu stopped at the corner and pretended to lift a bottle to his lips. He staggered a couple steps and rolled his eyes. As soon as Mr. Row turned, Stu straightened.

"Mrs. Gilchrest said George might be a problem," said Stu. "He's a lap dog. He doesn't like rain."

"He's effeminate, isn't he?" Mr. Row said to no one, and dangled his hand over the fence to pet King George, who backed away.

"So, Martin," Mr. Row said, still staring at George, "I understand you're getting married? Is that right? Stu just said . . . you know I heard some of this through Chris. Well, that's not quite true. I heard all of it."

"I guessed you would."

"Marla's a nice kid. Nicer than most people realize, really. It hasn't been easy at her place. Her dad is a bastard."

"Do you know him?"

"Do you know him? That's the question. Wait and see. He's a brute in the true sense of the word. I've said as much to his face."

"Well, we've gotten along so far."

"Of course. I didn't mean to say you wouldn't. I shouldn't even go on about it. I've just had a few go-arounds with him. I shouldn't even bring it up."

He pushed himself away from the run and patted his pockets for a cigarette.

"Now," he said, and we listened, but he didn't speak until he had located a cigarette and lit it. He shook one out for Martin, and Martin took it.

"Smoking is such a filthy, wonderful habit," Mr. Row said, lighting Martin's cigarette. "I've had certain cigarettes . . . times for cigarettes, if you understand me . . . that I remember so vividly, so clearly—well, now, I already mentioned this to Stu, but I think we should go out right now. I'm on a little bit of a tear, what with everyone gone. I think we should go right this minute, my treat, to have some pizza or Chinese food. Do you like Chinese?"

234

We all looked at one another. I felt embarrassed for Mr. Row, yet there was something kind and friendly about his offer.

"Well?" he asked again. "Let's face it . . . with all respect, no one's going to throw you a bachelor party. Everyone will say you're too young. And I like you, Martin. I like Max, too. I liked Max a lot, and I was damn sorry to see you go off the morning roll call. Stu, you I don't know about yet, but I'm willing to buy you some egg rolls anyway. What do you say? What else are you going to do tonight?"

"I'd like to go," Stu said. He shrugged as he said it, and I couldn't tell if he was being sincere or putting the con on Mr. Row for future business.

"There's one. How about you, Max? Can you go out tonight?"

"Sure, I'd like to."

"There's two. Martin?"

Martin nodded. King George barked. Mr. Row kicked at the screen once, and George shut up.

"What a little pig dog," he said.

We went inside so that Stu and Martin could tell Tilly while I called Gertrude. Then we came back out and climbed into Mr. Row's car. I was worried about his ability to drive, but he backed down the Kellermans' driveway with no difficulty. In fact, he drove a little too fast, a little too smoothly, and he forgot to slow down as he entered the street. The back of the car took a huge dip, and the pan hit the flat plane of the road.

"Christ," Mr. Row said.

Stu, in front, said, "It slows people down. Dad left it like that so no one would roar up the driveway and kill one of his precious children."

"Is that so?"

"Am I supposed to answer that? When you say, 'Is that so?' do you expect me to answer?"

Mr. Row started to laugh. He hit the steering wheel once, then began to cough. He dug in his pocket for a cigarette as he drove through town. We went past the train tracks to the south of town, then pulled over beneath a small trestle. The Chinese restaurant, Chow's, was connected to a bar that had a bad reputation. The bar was called the Bull and Barrel.

"We can eat and order a pitcher. What do you say? Does that sound okay?" Mr. Row asked, already climbing out.

"Sure," Martin said, then began to laugh when it was obvious Mr. Row didn't care what he said.

We followed Mr. Row inside. I'd had the notion he knew the restaurant, but he stopped in the foyer and looked around.

"I just come in here to pick things up. I've never eaten in here. Have any of you?"

"I have," Stu said.

"When?" Martin asked.

"When I arranged for your adoption, that's when. When do you think?"

"How would I know?"

"Do these two always get along like this?" Mr. Row asked me. Then, at the approach of a small Chinese man, he said, "For four."

"Faw faw?"

"Yes. Faw."

We went through a doorway which had beads dangling down. Only one couple sat near the back. The tables were painted mud red. The chairs were constructed of metal, and they had large, heart-shaped backs.

"Here good?" the Chinese waiter asked.

"Good," Mr. Row said. "Excellent. Do you have beer?"

"Nex daw."

"Pitchers?"

"Yeah, pitchers. Yeah, bottles."

"Could we please have two pitchers, please? Very cold."

"Always cold."

"Good. Then it shouldn't be a problem. Now, sit down, boys. Go ahead, take a look at the menu."

During this time Mr. Row hung his coat on a peg near the table. His suit was rumpled, and the tail of his white shirt was loose under his jacket. He turned to us.

"Is it dark in here, or is it my imagination?"

"It's dark," I said.

"I always worry about dark restaurants. They can serve you anything."

The waiter brought two pitchers of beer on a tray. He wore a

236

white towel over his arm, and I noticed he was younger than I had first realized.

"On tab?" he asked.

"What? Oh, yes. Everything's on me. Here we go now, gentlemen. This is for Martin. Martin, who is soon to join the ranks of married men."

Mr. Row poured out four beers. He lifted his glass for a toast.

"To Martin. May he be happy," he said.

"Hear, hear," said Stu.

We clinked glasses and drank. The beer burned my throat, and my eyes watered. I took another gulp. The waiter came back to the table and wiped up a small puddle of beer near the first pitcher.

"Ready to order?" he asked.

"Not ready. Not ready at all," Mr. Row said.

"Okay, no problem."

The couple in the back started to kiss loudly. They bent far over the table. I could only see them in a dim mirror behind Mr. Row, but Stu stared directly at them.

"Is somebody throwing sponges in here?" he asked. "Is somebody eating watermelon?"

"Stop it," Martin told him.

"Stop what?"

"Just stop it."

But the couple didn't seem to notice Stu. If anything, their kissing increased. Their hands locked together in the center of the table. A candle flickered now and then.

"Nice family restaurant, isn't it?" Stu asked.

"It used to be a nice place," Mr. Row said. "It used to be a little saloon when Stockton was bigger. But the people went away, and so did this place. Still, the food's good. It's really very good."

We had a moment of silence then. I suppose we all felt awkward in each other's company. Martin, in the pause, stood and went to buy a pack of cigarettes.

"So, Stu," Mr. Row said, "where did you get the idea for the kennel? It's a good idea, by the way. It was needed in this town."

"I just thought it up."

"Was it Marcie's idea?"

237

"In part. See, the way I figure it, a businessman is at his best when he sees the potential of an idea. Anyone can come up with an idea, but it takes a certain kind of person to take that idea and make something of it."

"It takes a capitalist."

"Right. Whatever you want to call it."

"A capitalist."

"You just said that."

"But that's what I want to call it."

"Okay, call it anything you want."

The waiter came back again. This time Mr. Row picked up the menu and started reading. Stu found his reflection in the back wall. He flexed gently, draping his arm over the back of his chair and making his bicep wiggle.

"I could order for all of us. How would that be?"

"Fine," I said.

"You awdaw fo everyone?" the waiter asked. "Go ahead."

Mr. Row began ordering. I drank some more beer. Two men who looked like bikers came in through the door to the Bull and chose a table across from us. Both of them had large metal chains connecting their wallets to their belts.

"Where's Won Ton?" Stu asked when the waiter left.

"Did you want won ton?" asked Mr. Row.

"No. Martin. Where is he?"

I went to look for him. I became a little uneasy when I saw he had never hung up his jacket. I passed the waiter on the way to the door. Martin wasn't in the foyer, and he wasn't outside. I checked the car, but he wasn't there either.

Back at the table Stu and Mr. Row were discussing capitalism. I heard Stu mention the *Communist Manifesto* and Jeffersonian democracy in one sentence as I slid into the seat.

"Martin took off," I said.

"Oh, did he?" Mr. Row asked, genuinely disappointed.

Stu shook his head.

"I don't know if he's going to make it through this one. You know, it was mostly his idea. No one pushed him into it. Everyone said he was too young."

"Even Fred?" asked Mr. Row.

"Fred was for it. Fred wanted them to get married. He started

238

talking about the pioneer past . . . how young people were when they married back in the old days. All that garbage. But my mom and dad were against it. Especially my mom. Martin, though . . . he just seemed to want to do it just because it didn't make a lot of sense."

"I'm sorry he left, Mr. Row," I said.

"Oh, that's not important. I felt bad when I heard the whole thing. I thought maybe this would get his mind off it or something."

"He's too young," Stu said again.

"Well, I'm sorry, that's all. Really sorry."

The waiter started bringing food. Mr. Row asked if we could drink another pitcher, but our hearts weren't in it. We ate the food quietly, and Mr. Row showed us how to use chopsticks.

❖❖ 34 ❖❖

WHEN Stu and I got back, we found out from Marcie
that Martin had returned. He had taken McClintock
and Clark out for a walk, but that was, she said, more than an
hour ago. He hadn't come back since.

Marcie had been spring-cleaning. The cement floor had been
swept, and all the cages were newly cleaned. King George sat
close to Marcie, his pink tongue still out, his legs almost crossed.
Now and then he struggled to his feet, walked a few paces, then
sat down again with an easy grunt.

"Who asked you to bring George in?" Stu said. "He's supposed
to be a boarder, not a pet."

"I brought him in because I wanted to," Marcie said. "He
started whining as soon as you left. He's been in here ever since."

"He's a homosexual. He's a sissy."

"Oh, Stu, he's just a lap dog. You don't take this sort of dog off
to the Yukon. He's been pampered all his life."

"I don't care. Did Won Ton take both dogs for a walk? Are you
sure?"

"No, he took them out dancing."

"I mean, did he say he was walking them on purpose, or was
he just, you know, walking them around?"

"You have a way with words, Stu."

Just then Tilly called Stu to the phone. He was only gone a few minutes. As soon as he came out, he said, "Won Ton's in trouble."

"Where is he?" I asked.

"He went over to Marla's and had half a snootful. He was drunk."

"He wasn't drunk when he left us. Was he drunk when he came back here?" I asked Marcie.

"No, I don't think so."

"He must have a bottle. Anyway, he and Big Fred had an argument on the front lawn. Marla said they almost started swinging. Big Fred wouldn't let him see Marla."

"Why?"

"Because he was drunk. Mr. Babcock locked the door and took off to the junior high gym or something, and Marla said it looked like Martin followed him. Martin had the two dogs."

"Following him to the gym?"

"That's what she said. Let's go."

"I'm going to tell Mom and Dad," said Marcie. "I don't care what you say."

"Shut up, Marcie."

"I am."

"And who will you help? Quit being Nancy Drew."

"I hate this whole thing."

"So? Tell Mom and Dad if they ask that we had to pick up a dog or something. We'll bring Won Ton back here to sober him up."

Marcie nodded as we left. Stu backed the car out and turned onto the road.

"Marla said he was really stinking drunk. Why didn't he stay with us if he wanted to get drunk?"

"Because he's not going to marry us. I don't know."

We drove to the junior high. I was surprised to see that the parking lot was half full. The gym lights were on, and I heard people shouting and cheering.

"Sounds like a game," I said.

"Maybe they're feeding Martin to the lions. Look, there are the dogs."

241

At first I saw only their eyes. Clark was on the ground, but McClintock was up, jumping against the tether. Eventually he came to a rest against the pull and stood on his back legs, his green eyes shiny in the near darkness.

"What the fuck is Martin up to?" Stu asked as we went to the dogs. They jumped up against us. "Anyone could have taken these dogs."

"He's drunk."

"So? That's no excuse to be sloppy."

Stu gave Clark a quick pat. "Lassie, find Martin," he said, then straightened. A wind blew across the baseball diamond, and a long trail of mist swept off the bleachers along the third base line. Near the parking lot a metal net on a basketball rim hit against its pole.

"Do you want to leave them here or put them in the car?" I asked.

"I'd rather leave Martin chained up."

"He must be inside."

We put the dogs in the car. As we closed the door, we heard a tremendous crack come from the gym.

"What was that?" asked Stu.

"No idea."

We hurried to the door of the school. As soon as we pulled it open, I smelled heat and gunpowder. The smell of gunpowder grew stronger as we approached the gym. I heard another crack, but this time it was much smaller, much softer. Stu looked at me and shrugged.

When we rounded the corner, it finally became clear what was happening. The gym was full of men dressed in Revolutionary War costumes. It took me a few moments to realize the men were shooting at one another. Somewhere near mid-court there was an imaginary boundary, a no man's land. In the very center stood a tall, gruff-looking man dressed in a coonskin cap and leggings. He had a powder horn at his side and a Kentucky long rifle in the crook of his right elbow. He spoke through a bull horn, his voice faint but clear over the gunfire.

"Fire, fire, that's right. Come on, colonials. You'll have to do better, or we'll never . . . There you go, that's better. Fire, fire, faster, go ahead."

242

Behind the two lines of infantry were two encampments com-
prised primarily of women and small children. They made stirring
motions in large black kettles, pretending to camp. Children, some
of them with their hands over their ears to protect them from the
deafening racket, wandered in and out of the makeshift campsite.

"Okay, when you die, make it look real. Come on now, where's
the west? Come on . . . the bleachers are west, remember your
map. Indians? Where? . . . There you go, come on."

At the director's command three Indians came screeching out
of the boys' locker room. It wasn't clear to me whom they were
supposed to represent, but they attacked the British troops, and
the colonials gave a loud cheer.

"Do you believe the smoke?" Stu asked. His face was bright red.
"Where are we?"

"See Mr. Babcock anywhere?"

"No. You really think he goes in for this shit? This is crazy.
What kind of guy does this? And look at the women! For God's
sake, they must be wackier than any of them. What do they get
to do? Stand around and stir pots?"

The director hit a buzzer on the bull horn, and the shooting
suddenly ceased.

"Good, good," he shouted, although there was no longer any
need. He began describing the layout of the land where the mock
battle would be held.

"How about now?" Stu asked me. "You see Big Fred?"

"I can't tell them apart."

"How about the Indians? Weren't they something? That middle
guy must have weighed two fifty. You think they had lard-ass
Indians?"

"No idea."

The director blew the buzzer again, and most of the people
began to fall out. A few of the mens' eyes and foreheads were
stained black from smoke. When the lard-ass Indian walked past,
Stu raised his hand.

"How," he said.

"Don't be a wise ass," the guy said, and went on.

We walked over to the director and asked him if he had seen
Mr. Babcock.

"He's somewhere around here," the director told us.

With a quick motion he brought the bull horn to his mouth and turned it on. The bull horn gave off a squawk, and the director held it away.

"Oh, this thing," he said, then put the bull horn to his lips again. "Marge? Marge?" he called to a woman across the gym. The woman looked up. She had been stirring air soup.

"Marge, have you seen Fred Babcock?"

Marge shook her head no, but a second woman, without benefit of bull horn, yelled back, "He's outside with the equipment people."

"Out back here?" the director asked, pointing.

"Yes."

The director turned to us. "You heard it."

"Thank you."

We went out the way we'd come in. The lard-ass Indian and some friends were outside smoking. As soon as Stu saw him, he said, "Smokum peace pipe?"

"I'll smoke your pecker if you keep it up."

"Anyone see a young guy?" I asked. "Red hair? He was probably here a little earlier."

"With two dogs?" asked the Indian.

"Yes."

"And red hair, you say?"

"Yes."

"Never seen him."

The Indian laughed at his own joke. The men behind him snorted. One of them said, "He was here. I don't know where he went."

"Thanks," Stu said, "or, I mean, how."

We worked our way around back. Two trucks were backed up to the gym, and one, a large step van, seemed to be the center of attention. Several men in white breeches and tricornered hats stood around the back door. I recognized Fred instantly. He was larger than everyone, and somehow his clothes exaggerated his size. The seat of his pants was tight over his rump, and his blue jacket came down in two swallowtails. He had extremely large epaulets, and the gold fringe shimmied when he moved.

Stu stepped up and cleared his throat. "Mr. Babcock?"

Mr. Babcock turned as if from surgery. He held a pistol in his hand, and for the briefest moment I was taken by the illusion that this was really a colonial officer.

"Yes? Can I help?"

"I'm Stu Kellerman."

"Oh, of course. How are you?"

He spread his arms slightly and ushered us off a few steps.

"You're looking for Martin? That's quite a brother you have there, Stu."

His arm was draped over my shoulder. The butt of the pistol dug softly into my collarbone.

"Quite a brother. You know, don't you, that he was very drunk tonight?"

"I didn't know."

"No? Well, he was. He was very, very drunk. He's a sloppy drunk, and I don't care for sloppy drunks. I particularly don't want them in my house."

"I'm sure Martin didn't mean anything by it," I said.

"That isn't the point, is it?"

His arms dropped from our shoulders. He was quite a bit taller than us. I saw the folds in his neck and chin where his stiff collar dug into them.

"Do you know where he is?" Stu asked.

"He was here. I don't know where he is now. I don't care to know where he is until he sobers up."

"He's just a little upset," Stu said.

Fred drew in a long breath. He tapped the pistol against his leg.

"I do not want to hear," Fred said, his voice tight, "about how upset your brother is. I have a seventeen-year-old daughter at home who currently has a child growing in her womb. Perhaps you are too young to understand, but you should not blind yourself to that fact—to the fact that other people have feelings and upsets, as you call them."

Without missing a beat, Stu said, "Fuck you."

"What did you say?"

"I said you could fuck yourself. My brother's seventeen and upset and worried about his whole goddamned life, and if you can't understand that and have a little compassion for it, well then, fuck you. Go play cowboys and Indians some more."

245

Stu spun away and left me standing next to Big Fred. Fred looked to see if the men at the truck had overheard. I was sure they had since Stu hadn't made any attempt to lower his voice.

"Get out of here. Don't ever come around here again."

"This war stuff is ridiculous," I said.

I ran to catch Stu. He was already around the corner, heading to the car. A laugh started in me; then I started to laugh even louder. Stu grinned like a crazy man when I caught him.

We laughed about it all the way to the car, where we found Martin in the back seat asleep, his head lolled back, his clothes dotted with whiskey and vomit. Stu looked in on him and sighed. "Fuck you, too, you idiot."

His shadow fell over Martin's eyes, but Martin didn't respond. Now and then Clark lifted to lick Martin's face, and I saw his hand clutch for an instant in the dog's fur, pulling him closer.

❖❖ 35 ❖❖

MARCIE stood on the other side of the creek on the morning of Martin's wedding. She wasn't aware of my approach until I was almost even with her. She had been watching the water. The sun was bright on the small pool between our yards.

"Marcie?" I asked. "You okay?"

"Oh, it's you, Max. I'm okay. I was just watching the water."

She looked very pretty. Her dress was beige and quite simple. She seemed to have suddenly grown up. I felt funny next to her in my suit and tie.

"How long have you been standing here?"

"Not too long. I keep asking myself why stupid Marla had to go and get pregnant. Have you seen her? She looks enormous. I keep thinking she's going to pop and fly around the room."

"She's okay. I like her."

"You like everyone, Max. It's just the way you are. She isn't so okay in my book."

"She's nice. Besides, Martin was in on it, too. You can't just blame her."

"I can, too. I can do anything I want. I decided that last night. I decided I could make this wedding mean anything I wanted it to mean in my mind. I'm going to do that."

She started to cry. I was going to give her my handkerchief, but I knew she wouldn't like it. When she cried, there was always something functional about it, like a sneeze, and she was quick to be done with it.

"Stu washed the damn car three times," she told me. This started her laughing, and for a few moments she alternated between laughing and crying. "He washed it and then Mom took it downtown and it got dirty so he washed it again; then Martin decided to take two of the dogs for a walk and one got away, so they had to drive the car again. Stu came running out of the house. . . . I'm a terrible storyteller, aren't I?"

"No, not at all."

"Yes, I am. If I could do one thing, well, maybe not one thing . . . See? I fumbled it right here. I was going to say if I could do one thing, I'd like to be able to tell a story, to make people laugh, but my mind always jumps in and edits everything. I always think I'm being stupid."

"You make up for it in other ways."

"Maybe," she said.

We stood for a few minutes watching the water; then she led me up the hill. Stu waited at the door of the dispensary. He wore a suit, and his shirt collar looked terribly tight.

"It's not too late to make it a double ring ceremony," he said. "A double wedding for two little lovebirds like Maxy and Marcie."

"Oh, God, not today," Marcie said, and brushed past him.

"Why not today?" Stu asked, pulling back into the shade. "How wacky can it get? Why not really take the whole thing around the bend? Let's marry King George off to McClintock. Let's bring a cow and a bull into the back pew and let them mate while the organ is going. What do you say, Marcie the vet?"

"Calm down, Stu."

"I'm calm. I could do brain surgery today, are you kidding?"

Stu turned to me.

"Won Ton's upstairs, white as a sheet. Wait until you see him. The only thing I worry about is that when the minister asks if there's any objection, someone is going to stand up and ask if Martin's still breathing."

"Is he all right?"

"All right? What would you be if you were marrying two peo-

248

ple? Think about it . . . family-o-matic. Marla could have that baby out in the desert somewhere if they let her. She's as healthy as a horse. She's going to foal. Believe me, she'll lay down somewhere and presto! Baby Won Ton!"

Stu was in rare form. Even though it was fairly cool, he sweated freely. The ridge of his stomach was dotted with moisture, and the hair around his ears, just beneath his temples, was dark red from perspiration.

"Should I go up? Is he ready for me?" I asked.

"Ready? He needs a shot of lithium, that's what he's really ready for."

"Are you all right, Stu?" Marcie asked. She watered some plants she had set out on the woodstove.

"I'm going up," I said to Stu. "You want to come?"

"Sure. The more the merrier, huh? Maybe you could tell everyone Martin and you plan to run off to Morocco. Maybe we could knock him out or something. If he was in a coma, they might bury him, though. They used to do that. All they ever did was stick a mirror under a guy's nose, and if he didn't fog it up, they'd bury him."

"I know, Stu."

"You do?" he asked, following me across the yard and up the back steps. "How did you know that? Have you learned to read recently?"

I knocked out of nervousness, and Stu jumped on this. He squeezed past me and yanked open the back door.

"You don't knock when you're with someone from the house. What am I supposed to do, wait to be let in by my own mother?"

"I wasn't thinking."

Inside the kitchen Stu stepped to the sink and ran himself a glass of water. He drank it off in a few quick gulps, said, "ahhhhh," then ran another.

"Good food all over," he said when he finished. "It could be a fantastic party if we get rid of Marla and Martin early enough."

Tilly walked in then. She had been crying. She crossed the room and gave me a kiss on the cheek. "Hi, Max," she said. For some reason all I could think of was that I was now much taller than she was.

"Did you give him last rites?" asked Stu.

"Don't start, Stu."

Tilly moved to the sink. She turned the water on, put her hands under the spray, and stared out the window. Stu motioned with his head for us to go upstairs.

"She's been crying," he said on the way up. "She takes one look at Martin, and it's all over. Dad's much better. He starts philosophizing whenever Martin comes into the room. Last night at dinner he was like one of those old Greek guys. He walked around with a glass of scotch, going on about adversity and hardship and the hand life can deal us. It takes a real catastrophe to see how big a jerk people can be."

"Lighten up on him."

Stu shook his head. He looked hotter than before. The hairs on his neck looked pinched by his collar, and his tie, I saw now, stuck straight out from his throat. Even his breathing made his tie bob up and down, and since it was attached by a lobster-shaped tie tack to his shirt, his shirt front also wrinkled and sagged according to whether he inhaled or exhaled.

We stopped outside Martin's door. Stu put his hand in his pocket and rattled his change.

"He's nervous as hell. I won't kid him in here unless you say so."

"I can't tell you what to do, Stu."

"I know, but sometimes I get carried away. If I go too far, just give me a signal, okay? Put your finger in your collar like it's too tight; then I'll know I'm being a jerk. I don't know it otherwise."

"Stu, you don't have to worry."

"Yes, I do. That's just it. You're better at this stuff than I am. You are. I try to goof around, and it ends up being mean or something. I'll take your word for it if you give me the signal."

He patted me on the shoulder and pushed open the door before I could say anything. The room was dark. Only the window provided light, and the curtains moved at every breeze. Martin was on the bed, flat on his back with his hands behind his head.

"You napping?" asked Stu.

"No, I'm yanking my dong for the last time as a single man."

Stu gave off a horse whinny and looked to me as if he had just heard the funniest thing in his life. I was tempted to put my finger in my collar. Instead, I went to the window and propped

250

myself on the sill. The air cooled my back. Stu paced at the foot of the bed.

"What time is it?" Martin asked.

"There's still time for the governor to call," Stu answered. "Don't worry."

"I asked what time it is, that's all."

"Ten," I told him.

"Dad was just in here," Martin asked. He uncrossed his legs, then crossed them the other way. He was careful with the crease of his pants. "He was shaking. I never saw him shake before."

"Was he?" Stu asked.

"Do you think I'm making it up?"

"No, I just meant it like 'Oh, really?' That's all I meant."

Stu turned to me, rolled his eyes, then ran his own finger under his collar. He sat down on the other twin bed and began pulling at a loose thread on the bedspread. I pushed open the window to let in more air.

"Can I do anything for you?" I asked Martin. "Do you need anything?"

"No, I'm okay. Everybody's been nice."

"That's because we want to be remembered in your will, Uncle Won Ton."

"You've been nice, too, Stu."

Stu nodded and looked down. The room suddenly became very close. The wind outside stopped. I tried to hear some other sound, perhaps Tilly running water in the kitchen or Marcie doing work in the dispensary, but everything was silent.

Then, gradually, I began to hear Stu. His shoulders moved just slightly. His hand lifted to his face, and I heard him take a long, deep breath. His other hand covered his left eye, and he sniffed once or twice loudly.

"Stu?" Martin said from his bed. He lifted to one elbow.

But Stu was crying now. I felt my own heart still. I stood up by the window while Martin lifted himself off his bed and, very slowly, moved to sit next to Stu.

"Stu," Martin whispered. "Oh, Stu, come on."

"I'll miss you," Stu said, beginning to sob. His sobs were short. He caught them as soon as they came out.

251

"I'll miss you, too, Stu."

Stu's crying became quiet. He gave several deep sighs, then finally pulled himself out of it. He rubbed his eyes with the tip of his tie and coughed to clear his throat. When he was a little more recovered, he stood and looked at me. He put his hand on Martin's shoulder.

"Actually," he said, "I think it's great you and Max are getting married."

Martin laughed. I shook my head and pulled up the shade. The day was perfect. Stu went to the mirror.

"I feel like we're going to church, that's all," Martin said. "It feels like we're going to church, we're going to listen to a sermon about good acts, then we're going to stop on the way home for the *New York Times* and a bagel. Doesn't it?"

"It does to me," I said.

"Especially the bagel part. It's funny how you remember times through food."

"True, true, oh, Martin, oh, so true," Stu said. He winked at me, then turned his profile to us and began flexing. "Max, you may be best man, but I'm the rock man. I'm the human form poets speak of."

"You're a sweat ball," Martin told him.

"Lather. Simply lather. When you see a great statue, you don't see the marble chips. That's what my sweat is . . . marble chips."

Gill knocked on the door and said it was time.

"Here goes," Martin said, standing.

Stu turned away from the mirror, suddenly serious. I looked out the window and saw Marcie standing in the shade of a small beech tree. Gil was already at the top of the stairs, calling down to Tilly.

"Here goes," Martin said again.

We followed him out the door. All the way down to the kitchen he let his fingers trail over the wall, his nails ticking against the doorjambs and seams of wallpaper.

252

❖❖ 36 ❖❖

MARTIN and Marla were married in the vestry, a small, flower-scented room that opened like a vault in the deep halls of the church. I could not get out of my mind the movie image of backroom marriages. Even the minister, a short, fat man who smelled of lunch and broth, seemed to fit the mold of a movie minister, the rumpled justice of the peace called from bed to marry two hot-blooded youngsters who could not wait out the night. Before the ceremony, in a second back room, he fiddled nervously with the cassock, occasionally talking to himself, mumbling strange rehearsal cues that triggered his memory.

"Music, music, music," he whispered, half facing himself in the mirror, "bride enters, ta-da, music going soft, softer, quiet. Ladies and gentlemen . . . no, pause first, let the music fade. Now."

I worried he wouldn't be a good speaker. He seemed too nervous. He peeked too often into the outer room.

"Almost set. I'm glad we put up the last row of folding chairs . . . it always helps, doesn't it?" he asked us.

"Beats me," Martin said. "This is my first time."

"I didn't mean it that way. But I see what you mean . . . very good, very funny under the circumstances."

In the end a small buzzer went off near the dressing table.

"Ready," he said, and waved us into single file behind him. "Everything okay? You feel all right, Martin?"

"Fine."

"How about the best man?"

"Fine," I said, knowing he had forgotten my name already.

We walked out and stood at the front of the room. The chairs were set out in a small fan pattern, divided by a center aisle with a white carpet. The lights dimmed as the bridal march began. Before Marla entered, I looked up quickly, catching my first glimpse of Chris. She was with her father, who winked when he saw me look in their direction. Cameras started to click. The minister took a few steps forward and rested his hand on Martin's shoulder.

Marla pushed her mother's wheelchair in front of her. The image was wrong for a wedding. Even though I had known Mrs. Babcock was going to be matron of honor, it still unsettled me. They were dressed in similar gowns, pale blue, and they both carried bouquets. Mr. Babcock walked just behind them.

When Marla reached the front row, she parked Mrs. Babcock, kissed her, then took two steps back to join her father. I wondered who had choreographed it.

Marla was too large. She was larger, somehow, than memory could hold. Seeing her, I had to look away, then back in order to understand and take in her size. She was enormous. Her chin was full and flabby, and her breasts, large to begin with, had become those of a large opera singer. In fact, Marla's whole appearance was operatic, reminiscent of wide stages and heavy curtains.

Yet there was also something touching about her. Her bouquet shook as she took her dad's arm. She smiled with assurance as she stepped past her mother.

"Hello," she whispered when she came close enough to speak to Martin. She turned, kissed Fred quickly, then stood before Martin and smiled again.

"Hello," she whispered once more.

Martin nodded and squared his shoulders.

"Marla," he said, his voice choked.

They turned to face the minister. I didn't know what to do. I stood behind them both. I lost track of the ceremony very soon.

Once I heard the minister say, "Here we go now," while Martin and Marla huddled closer. Cameras clicked, and one man I didn't recognize continued to run forward, ambushing us from behind a pot of mums. He hit one of the mums on his last shot and the bud lay bent to the side, its heavy yellow head swinging in the currents of wind.

"I now pronounce you husband and wife," the minister finally said. He whispered some stage directions, then said to himself, "Now, up music."

On cue the music began. The wedding was too small for a formal exit, so people began to clap. Martin kissed Marla. The photographer came forward and crouched near the end of the runner.

I kissed Marla. In the next instant Martin was right beside me. We hugged each other once. Then he hugged me again with a sharp, quick pull.

"What the hell," he said in my ear.

We patted each other on the back; then the whole crowd was around us. I saw Chris work her way to the front, aiming for Marla. She looked very beautiful.

Stu appeared then. He came around the edge of the crowd, his wing tips making a muffled clop. His color had receded a little, but he was still wound up. The veins on either side of his neck were swollen.

"What do you say, Max? You going to dance with Mrs. Babcock? You know how it goes: The bride's father dances with the bride; the groom, with his mother. Maybe Won Ton will have to push Mrs. Babcock all over the lawn to the 'Blue Danube Waltz.' Maybe she'll do the alley cat. I'd give anything to see that."

"Stu, you're nuts."

"No, I'm just sorry he broke up with you, is all."

"We should get going."

The crowd moved slowly out of the room. A small reception line had formed at the door. Far up in the front I saw Gertrude and Uncle Jack. Gertrude kissed Martin. She kissed Marla, too, and her hand went out to protect the child as she leaned over.

When Stu and I got to the vestibule, only a few people remained. The receiving line had broken down. Martin and Marla

255

stood close together. Tilly, hovering, held Marla's purse. Gil and Fred were outside, fetching the cars. Mrs. Babcock talked to Marcie.

"I've always loved animals," she said. "Always. I've fought for years to have pets, a dog, a cat, but my husband says no. He says pets are as bad as a child, but I always say, 'As good as a child is what you mean.' I finally talked him into a bird. Just a little budgie . . . I call it Cloud, because it's white and soft and it flies. Oh, my, you should see it fly."

We all listened to her go on. She stopped only when the two cars pulled up.

Martin ended up wheeling Mrs. Babcock. Marla directed him, her gown lifted in one hand. He bounced Mrs. Babcock down the steps backward, then rolled her along the sidewalk. Mr. Babcock came around to arrange the lift into the car. He was good at it but abrupt, folding the wheelchair with hard slaps and tossing it in the trunk.

"All set?" he asked too often.

In the end I knew what would happen. Gil and Tilly and Marcie and Stu and I climbed in the Kellermans' car. Martin and Marla, giving in to Fred, climbed into the back seat of the Babcocks' car.

Stu and Marcie and I were in back. Tilly, as soon as our door shut, leaned onto Gil's shoulder and began sobbing. Gil lifted her gently and rolled the window up just as the Babcocks passed. He didn't honk back as Fred began slamming their horn. We sat in the spring sunshine and watched Martin fade away, taken from us long before we were ready.

PART
❖❖ 4 ❖❖

❖❖ 37 ❖❖

I ARRIVED in Westfield in late evening. I took my time driving. I slowed the car, a cheap Volkswagen I had bought secondhand from a friend of Stu's, and cranked down the windows. The warm spring air poured in, causing a plastic cleaner's bag to chatter gently against the back window.

The front of the house was dark and a little somber, almost as if it had been built for harder times, heavier winters. Rising up behind it, in the distance, I saw the outline of the Watchung Mountains and the deep woods that flowed from the crest of the hill down almost to the backyard.

I pulled close to the garage and turned off the engine. Crickets started chirping almost at once. I stepped out of the car and started unloading. The yard was growing darker and darker.

I waited for a moment, then went to the back door and unlocked it. I took a step into the kitchen, my eyes slowly moving over the surfaces. The shape of the table was unchanged. The lines and height of the counters were a comfort; I knew where my father's waist hit the sink. I could imagine how I might have seen the line of his pants leg over his boot, his heavy legs knotted and rocking as he sat at the kitchen table, reading his charts, his journal.

I went to the edge of the kitchen light. The living room was just beyond. The steps rose toward the second floor, toward my father's room.

"Hello," I said into the quiet. "Hello, my name is Max Darrigan."

The next morning I was up at sunrise. The house was very quiet. I made myself several slices of toast, smeared them with butter and honey, then carried them outside.

The yard, as Uncle Jack had suggested, was more field than lawn. The grass rose to my thigh. I leaned back against the wall of the house and ate the bread slowly, listening to the bees drift in and out of the weeds. A low wind moved over the yard, sending waves through the grass, stretching the stalks like fur pulled back.

The dig, I knew, was somewhere beneath it all. I did not look to see where it had been, though I sensed it there, the rise of its edges no higher than a mole's run in a summer garden.

After a while I went to the garage and yanked open the door. The grass-stained mower leaned against the wall. It wouldn't work on the backyard; it would clog and refuse to cut. Instead, I pulled down an old scythe and carried it outside. It was rusted red, almost rusted to clay. I found some oil and rubbed the blade until it looked like metal.

I went to the southeast corner to begin. The old rail fence that used to run along the border was still there, though one post was sagged and splintered. Ants had bored into the wood, and their brown mounds flaked a little in the wind.

I began to cut. I tested the blade on small clumps of grass, and the scythe did not work well. Most of what I hit bent to one side. Now and then I reached out my free hand and took an awkward swing with the blade, trying to chop between my hand and the earth. Normally I ended up missing or skimming the blade off the strip of grass.

I worked for an hour before I heard footsteps on the driveway. The sound frightened me. The steps were steady and cautious, though they never paused. I took a step to my left in order to see who it was and spotted Honey standing near the back door, watching me.

"Max?" she said, taking her own step to the side and bringing her hand up to shade her eyes. "Is that you? I wouldn't have recognized you . . . you're so big suddenly."

260

I tossed the scythe down and went to meet her. She held up her arms. She was skinnier now, and her face was much more angular. I hugged her hard, and she hugged me back. We held each other for a long time until she tapped my shoulder blade and pushed me away.

"It's like hugging a horse. Look at how sweaty you are."

"I didn't think."

"And if you had thought, what then? You wouldn't have hugged me?"

She took my hand and held it in hers. She looked at me for a long time, then clapped her open palm on the top of my wrist.

"You're still my Max, I can see that. You're all grown up, but you're still there."

"You look the same."

"No, I'm older."

"No, you look the same to me."

"Then I must have looked pretty awful."

She touched my wrist again, then let me go. She pulled open the back door and stepped into the kitchen. Her hand went to her chest momentarily. She shook her head, then walked to the sink and put her purse on the counter.

"This old house always gives me a start," she said. "Does it ever do that to you?"

"A little last night."

"Sit down, sit down. Look at that grass all over you."

She reached to the table and pulled out a chair for me. I sat and felt grass press against my back. I stood quickly and went to the back door to brush it off.

"You never were neat, were you?" said Honey.

"No, I guess not."

"I think people are born neat or not. There's no teaching them really."

"I don't know," I said, and came back to the table. "How are you? How's Zeke?"

"First things first. Hold on now. I'm going to make us some lemonade. Do you have ice up here? I told Zeke to put some water in the trays when he came to turn everything on. . . . Gertrude packed you all this food?"

She lifted out two trays of ice. She had to scout for a couple of minutes through the old cupboards to find a decent pitcher. She settled on a martini shaker.

"Here," she said to me after she had rinsed it out, "shake this until it gets good and slushy. Go ahead."

She dumped the ice into the shaker and gave it to me. I shook it for a while, my sweat flying off and marking the floor. While I worked, I tried to see what had changed about Honey. Her hair was certainly grayer, and her weight was down. Her legs were stiff; she wore an Ace bandage over her right ankle. But it was her eyes that had really grown older. The sockets seemed more pronounced. She watched me from a greater distance.

She took the shaker back, added the contents to a pitcher she had finally found, then stirred the whole thing together. She looked at me.

"You remember how you liked to draw pictures on the window? In the cold? Right where you're sitting now."

"I don't remember."

"You did. Picture windows, you called them. You'd spend hours doing it. Now, there it is. That should do it."

She poured us each a glass. Finally she sat down.

"I can't believe how grown-up you are. Is that your car?"

"Yes."

"Nice-looking little thing. Does it run all right?"

"So far. Now, how's Zeke? You haven't said."

"Oh, Zeke's fine. Working hard."

Honey drank. She leaned back in her chair and took a long look at the kitchen. She examined it, her eyes actually roaming from top to bottom, her hand still holding the lemonade.

"You remember the house?" I asked.

"Of course I do. I was just thinking about this room, about how many days I spent in it. How well do you remember it?"

"Pretty well. I'm remembering I remember it more, if you know what I mean. It's coming back to me that I can remember it."

"I can understand that. We had some nice times here. I recall plenty of good mornings here, for one thing."

She took another sip and leaned forward. She rolled her forearm on the tabletop to rid it of a few flecks of water.

"Have you gone up to that room yet?" she asked.

"No."

262

"But you will?"

"Probably. Yes, I guess so."

Honey sighed. It was warm in the kitchen. The faucet dripped, and the refrigerator made a low, humming sound.

"I wish you wouldn't," she said.

"Wouldn't go in the room?"

"Yes."

"Why?"

"Why should you? You can't find your daddy up there."

"That's not fair, Honey."

"This is no good. I don't know why Jack let you come back here."

"The place needs work. You can see that for yourself."

"Of course it does. But will you do it and leave that room alone?"

"I don't know."

"You'll be inviting more pain."

"I don't want pain. You know that, Honey."

"You forgiven your dad for leaving you yet?"

"I think so."

"He was just sick, Max. He wasn't responsible."

"I know that."

"Do you believe it?"

"As much as I can."

She nodded and drank more lemonade. She took my hand and held it while she talked about Zeke, about relatives of hers I remembered dimly, about changes in the area. She asked me questions about Jack and Gertrude. After a few minutes I stopped listening to her exact words and relied on the gentle sound of her voice. Her voice was an old sound to me, and I felt safe listening to it, as calm as a child in bed hearing the slide of his parents' dresser drawers announcing they were near.

❖❖ 38 ❖❖

ABOUT TWO weeks later I returned from grocery shopping and heard a sound from the backyard as I unlocked the door. I looked around the corner and saw Stu standing in the center of the lawn, swinging the scythe like a golf club. He raised his hands high in a follow-through and kept his eyes down until the last second to make sure he hit the ball properly.

When he saw me, he raised his hand and put a finger to his lips.

"Ladies and gentlemen, Stu Kellerman is leading the U.S. Open. If he sinks this putt, which he will, of course, being the world's greatest golfer, he will win fifty thousand dollars, and a free date with Maxy One Ball to the love tunnel."

"What are you doing here, Stu? How'd you get here?"

"By golf cart. Shhhhh. Here's the putt, ladies and gentlemen. The putt goes, it's breaking left . . . no, no, it rimmed the cup, but wait, it's coming back, it's in! Stu Kellerman has won the U.S. Open!"

Stu threw the scythe down and ran toward me with both hands in the air. He blew kisses to an imaginary crowd. When he reached me, he squeezed me and took the jar of peanut butter out of the bag. He used it for a microphone.

"Here he is, the runner-up, Maxy One Ball. Nice try, Maxy, but

of course, you couldn't compete with that legend of the long iron
Stu Kellerman. Let's have a big hand for him anyway, huh, folks?
Let's hear it for this handicapped player!"

He was all wound up. I still didn't know how he had arrived,
but it was good to see him. I nodded at the back door and asked
him to open it.

He held it open for me, saying, "Isn't it nice to be married like
this? Isn't it just divine?"

I put the groceries on the counter. Stu followed me and looked
in the refrigerator.

"How did you get here, Stu? Seriously."

"By car, how did you think?"

"So where's the car?"

"Mr. Won Ton has it."

"Where is he? Is he here?"

Stu took a big fingerful of peanut butter.

"Mr. Won Ton had his baby. Or rather, Marla exploded. The
baby came out like it was going down a sliding board. She had
something like a five-minute labor."

"A boy or girl?"

"A boy. His name is David.

"And everything's okay?"

"Everything's okay with the baby and Marla, but we'll have to
wait to see about Martin."

"Where is he?"

"He thought we should get some steaks or something. He went
to the grocery store. He's probably lost. He has a terrible sense
of direction."

"Wait, Stu, how big was the baby?"

"Fifty-five pounds."

"Seriously. You say Marla is okay? Everything's fine? What did
you mean about Martin just then?"

I finished putting the groceries away and sat at the kitchen
table. Stu kept eating peanut butter. He climbed onto the counter
and tapped his heels against a cupboard door.

"The baby was baby-sized. . . . How do I know? Why do people
ask that anyway? What does it tell them?"

"It just gives you a sense of how the baby is, I guess. Now,
what's this about Martin?"

265

Stu contemplated one last fingerful, decided against it, and screwed on the lid. He skidded the jar far enough away from him so he wouldn't be tempted.

"Fred and Martin went a few rounds the other day."

"They actually fought?"

"No, Fred fought. Martin took it. He has an eye out to here. I don't know exactly what happened, but Martin showed up at Marcie's dispensary with his eye bleeding and his nose bleeding and I think something wrong with his ribs. Marcie just about had a cow, of course, but Martin made her swear to be quiet about it and just fix him up."

"Fred actually punched him?"

"Do you have your hearing aid on?"

"I just can't believe it, that's all."

"I think it had something to do with Martin's drinking again. When he got to Marcie's, he still smelled to high heavens, but he was sure as hell sobered up. Marla went into the hospital the next morning."

"What a fuck head."

"Who, Marla?"

"No, Fred."

"So what else is new? Marcie was surprised, too, but hell, I knew what it was going to be like."

Stu leaned across the counter and retrieved the peanut butter. He started to unscrew the lid, thought better of it, then skidded it back. He turned the water on next to him and bent to drink from the tap.

"It's a cute kid," he said afterward. "Really pretty cute."

"How's Martin with him?"

"Martin loves kids. That's no surprise either, is it? You know, all the while everyone was complaining about Martin's situation, I never heard him complain about having a baby. The rest of it, sure, but not the kid part."

A car pulled into the driveway. Stu jumped down.

"I got a new station wagon. Take a look," he said.

I wasn't prepared for Martin's eye. It was worse than Stu's description. It was angry and red and swollen. His brow and temple were yellow and purple, and the entire eye seemed several inches thick. When Martin looked at me, he had to turn sideways.

266

"Jesus, what an eye," I said.

"You like it? Here, Stu, take this stuff. You have a barbecue grill, Max?"

"I think so. How are you? Congratulations on the baby," I said, still staring at the eye.

"Thanks. He's beautiful. He really is."

"And Marla's okay?"

"She's fine, a little crazy.

All this time Martin unloaded the car. I recognized a few boxes that Gertrude must have sent. The car itself was a second-hand station wagon with STU ENTERPRISES stenciled on the side.

"How do you like it?" Stu asked when he saw me looking. "I got this guy to paint it on; it's hand-painted, not just blown through some stencil grid."

"Who's Stu?" I asked.

"Funny, Max. Seriously, how do you like it?"

"Is this the name for all the future companies?"

"Stu Enterprises is the corporate name. Underneath it there's still Dog Tags, the kennel. And the lawn company, of course. I'm calling the lawn company Who's Next Lawn Cutters. Handy Dandies has been absorbed."

"You're insane, Stu," Martin said.

"Is the kennel making money? How's Marcie doing with it?"

"You talk like you've been to Africa," Stu said. "It's fine, but Marcie misses her big, strong lover boy. She misses her Maxy honey bun."

We carried everything inside. Martin put his groceries on the counter. He had gone overboard. There were steaks, potatoes, dinner rolls, carrots, celery, and pretzels. Stu took three beers out of the bag and opened them.

"To little Stu," he said.

"It's not Stu," Martin told him.

"To little Stu from Unky Wunky Stu."

Stu raised his bottle and gulped down a third of it. He burped afterward and slapped his stomach. Martin and I clinked bottles. I stared at his eye.

"Something else, huh?" he asked.

"Why did he hit you?"

"I guess I deserved it."

"Everyone deserves an eye like that," Stu said, jumping back on the counter. "With a little effort, maybe you could deserve a broken skull."

"No, seriously, I wasn't the best."

"Were you drunk?" I asked.

Martin took the steaks out of their cellophane wrappers. He put them on an old cutting board and scored the fat.

"It was like this. Big Fred was dressed for one of the musters that he's always going to. You know, white pants and a tri-cornered hat . . . you've seen it. Well, I can't stand seeing him in it. I always want to make a sarcastic remark. Anyway, it's got a lot to do with him coming into our place whenever he wants. He just walks in, and I know it's his house, but if he expects us to live there, then he's got to give us some privacy."

"So he walked in one night?"

"He walked in and I was a little drunk."

"A lot or a little?" asked Stu.

"A lot. A little. Who knows? Marla was out to here, and I was just sitting having a beer, and he started in about how he didn't want me to drink in the house. So I finally asked him if I was in his house or in our apartment. He got all pissed off and asked me if I was paying rent. It was stupid. I think he had had a couple of belts himself before he came down, and it must get to him some-times to have us sitting down there, and his nutty wife upstairs, and a baby coming and all his Revolutionary War friends whisper-ing. So he hit me."

"Just like that?" I asked.

"Pretty much. I didn't see the punch. I hit my head against one of the stools, and Marla screamed. Fred walked out after that. He went to war practice."

"Does he really call it war practice?"

"Yep. He's wacko. He has every book ever written on any American battle. You name it and he'll tell it to you. He's a brigadier or something in the colonial army. I've seen other guys salute him, and I couldn't quite tell if they were serious or not."

Stu grabbed a celery stalk and chomped it. Martin rubbed some salt and pepper onto the steaks. I still couldn't believe the size of his eye.

"I'd sneak up on him and punch him back," Stu said.

"Punch your wife's father? Doesn't exactly add up to domestic tranquillity, does it?"

"He punched you."

"So maybe I should stab him then, just to get back? Maybe we should escalate the whole thing so that we jump out at each other with machetes, huh?"

"You have a rational approach to discussion, you know that, Martin?"

We carried everything outside. I found an old grill in the back of the garage. The bottom was almost rusted away. We cleaned it as well as we could, then added charcoal and lit it. A black beetle, hidden somewhere near the bottom, scurried away as soon as it felt the heat.

"You want to bring the table out?" Martin asked. "We could eat out here."

"Sure, why not?"

Stu and I brought out the kitchen table and set it on the grass. The kitchen chairs sank in the soil, but eventually we settled them in positions where they didn't wobble. I brought out a transistor radio and we tuned to WABC. Cousin Brucie was on, playing the top twenty-five. We watched the fire and drank beer.

"How about you, Max?" Martin asked. "You've been working around here, huh?"

"Pretty much. The place needs it."

"They keep the house for your dad?" asked Stu.

"Uncle Jack never wanted to sell it."

"Of course not," Martin said, wrapping potatoes in tin foil and tossing them on the fire. "Selling it would be like giving up."

"Still, it's worth something," Stu said.

"Shit, it's worth more this way," Martin told him.

Stu, sitting at the table, suddenly said, "Why don't you get Won Ton to move in here? Maybe just for the summer, but it would get him out of Big Fred's mitts. What do you say, Max?"

"Stu . . ." Martin started, but I saw at once that the idea appealed to him. He smiled as he bent over the grill and turned the potatoes. He had to tilt his head to see clearly.

"You could, you know," I said.

"No."

"You really could," I said again. "The house is big enough. Do you think Marla would? Do you think Fred would let her?"

"She hates him, too. I don't know what you guys think of Marla, but she hasn't had it easy. I think he's hit her."

"While she was pregnant?" asked Stu.

"No, earlier. Growing up and everything."

It was getting darker. Cousin Brucie shouted something about summer and necking in cars. There was an ad for Rockaway Playland and another for Raceway Park. Underneath it, the crickets chirped. I smelled grass letting off the heat of the day. The gutters expanded against the side of the house.

Martin drank his beer and worked around the fire.

"I'd like you to move in," I said.

"Well, that's nice of you, but think about it. It isn't just me."

"I know that."

"I'm not even sure it would work out. I mean, I don't even know if we could get free. We're sort of captives."

"Bull," Stu said.

"We are a little."

"This would be the best thing in the world for you," Stu said. "You don't even have a chance where you are now. That's the truth, and you know it. If Max will let you, you should get here as soon as you can. I'll even arrange to move you. For a price, of course."

"What about the baby?"

"Do you want the kid growing up with Fred? What if he hurt little Stu?"

"Cut the crap, Stu."

"Okay, but you see what I mean. He might punch you again. The whole thing is nuts the way it is."

We ate dinner in the darkness. Stu kept us all supplied with beer. After we were finished, Stu carried the dishes inside. He used the dish drainer, stacking everything in the appropriate slot.

"Genius at your service," he said, going into the kitchen.

Martin turned to face the grill. I took a long look at his eye.

"Move in," I said again.

"We'll see."

Stu came out in about ten minutes. He had on an old fedora,

270

which he wore when he cut lawns. The fedora, I knew, was soaked with mosquito repellent and crusted by salt and sweat.

"Let's go to this Trailside you're always talking about," he said to me. "Let's go for a walk or something."

"You want to, Martin?" I asked.

"Sure, I don't care. Whatever."

We moved the fire away from the house and locked the doors. Stu had a bottle of whiskey he had kept out of sight until then. He cracked the top and took a drink, then passed it around.

"Which way?" Stu asked me. "Are we supposed to guess, or what?"

"This way."

It took only a few minutes to get to the bridle path. The trail was very dark. I heard the stream long before we reached it. I felt the colder air on my bare ankles first.

Martin started running. He angled up along the path and began going back and forth, zigzagging as Honey did. In a second we were all jogging, running slowly up the hill. It was a drunken thing to do, but it felt good all the same. Each time I approached the stream I felt its coolness. Then, when I veered away from it, I felt the insects fold over me, the heat press up from the pine of the forest.

We ran nearly to the top. Martin ran faster than Stu or I. We saw his silhouette when he crested the hill, but then he was gone. As soon as he disappeared, Stu stopped and grabbed me. He looked crazy in the darkness, in his hat, but he pressed toward me, and I felt the power in his arms, the strength of his hands.

"Listen," he said, his breath warm with whiskey, "I'll help pay if he moves in here."

"Who?" I asked stupidly. "What do you mean?"

"I'm saying Fred hits him more than that. I'm saying Fred punched him more than once. Martin's drinking, too. It's a bad situation. I don't think any of us knows what it's like, and Martin's headed for something. If you can let him move in, maybe it would work."

"He can move in."

"I'll help with the money. He's got to get work. He's changed, you know? He's bitter now."

"It's only been a couple of weeks. A month or so."

271

"You don't think you can change that quick? You better take a closer look at him."

"He can move in. I already said so."

Stu put his arms around me and hugged me. Martin appeared at the top of the ridge and blew through his hands to make an owl call. The sound came down hollow and beautiful. Stu cupped his hands and called back.

❖❖ 39 ❖❖

I WENT to Stockton for the christening the following
Saturday. When I arrived, Stu was out shoveling the
kennels. He leaned the shovel against the fence and came over.
He hadn't changed into a suit yet. His muscles looked enormous.

"Hi, Stu," I said.

"Hi, Max."

"Where's Marla and Martin?"

"In Portugal."

"Seriously."

"Seriously they're living in that clump of bushes over there.
They've decided to go back to nature."

Martin and Marla pulled in a few minutes later. They drove
one of the Babcocks' cars. Martin, dressed in a suit and tie, looked
like a family man behind the wheel. Marla held the baby, David,
in her arms.

Stu hurried to help her. As Marla climbed out, David began to
kick and cry. Stu took a blanket from Martin and helped Marla
wrap the baby in it. He squeezed Marla's elbow as he moved away.

"You have it? You okay?" he kept asking.

I walked over and kissed Marla; then she smiled. "Want to hold
him?" she asked.

"Sure."

She handed me the baby. It weighed next to nothing. I touched its cheek with my finger while Marla held back the blanket.

"Who does he look like?" asked Marla.

"I think like you."

"Really? I think he looks like Martin."

Martin came around the car and patted my shoulder. He bent very close to the baby and kissed its forehead, his darkened eye blue and yellow now with healing.

"What do you think, Uncle Max?" he asked.

"He's beautiful."

"I think so, too. He's sleeping better, too. We almost made it all the way through last night, didn't we, Davey?"

Marcie came out then, already dressed for church. She had on a dress similar to the one she had worn to the wedding; only this time I noticed there was a provocative slit along her right thigh.

Stu saw it, too.

"Your dress is ripped, Marcie," he said.

He went past her, carrying two bags. Martin kissed her.

"Hello, hello, hello," she said. She came over and stood beside me so she could see the baby.

Tilly came hurrying out behind Marcie. She wore a bathrobe and slippers. The powder at her throat was streaked by tiny drops of water.

"There you are," she said, her eyes on the baby. "There you are. We have to hurry; the christening is at ten. Can I hold him, Max? I'll just hold him a second; then I have to get dressed. Hello, precious. That's right . . . hello."

"Did somebody give her a script upstairs?" asked Stu. "Who talks like that?"

Tilly didn't listen. She kissed each of us, her head craning over the small body of the baby. Afterward she stood in the warm sunlight, her finger touching the baby's cheek.

We carried everything inside. Gil was out getting provisions for the small party that would follow the christening. Marla and Marcie carried the baby upstairs. Tilly went to finish dressing.

Stu gave us each a beer, and for a time we stood in the kitchen. It was cool there. A nice breeze moved through the house.

"Come on," Stu suddenly said, pushing away from the counter. "Come on, I almost forgot."

"Where? I don't want to get all dirty," said Martin.

"Back behind the garage. Come on."

Stu led us out. We went around the kennel runs, and Stu nodded at three dogs. Then he turned to face us and walked backward so he could watch our expressions.

"Wait until you see this. This is not to be believed," he said.

"What is it?"

"Wait."

He led us to the willow. At first I didn't see what he was so excited about, but then, gradually, I made out the form of a small pony. The pony had markings like a pinto, black flanks and a piebald face. The colors blended with the shade of the willow branches. His hooves knocked on the packed dirt as we approached. He trotted back and forth, his sides making the willow branches ripple as he passed. He was like a ghost in the dimness, and several times I actually lost him in the shade.

"Is it a pony or a horse?" Martin asked.

We stopped a few yards away.

"That's Ivan the Impaler. He's a fucking maniac horse. He almost killed a little kid. Wait and see. Step a little closer."

We took a few steps. The pony let out a snorting sound and stopped to our left. Something changed in the air because I saw him become rigid. He moved slowly toward the center of the tree, the willow wands lifting and falling like a skirt.

"A little closer," said Stu.

As soon as we moved, the horse stuck out his head and tried to bite Stu. It was an impossible reach, but the pony didn't seem to care. He snapped his teeth at us once, twice, then shook his head with a wild, angry shiver. Just as quickly he shied to one side and the willow branches lifted and poured over his back. He whinnied and began snapping again.

"Just the thing for a kids' party," Stu said. "Rent a bronco."

"You're not serious. Is he always like this?" asked Martin.

"No, sometimes he's worse. Sometimes he curls up into a fetal position and rolls around in the dirt. He has an identity crisis."

"Where did you get him?" I asked.

I took a few steps sideways, and the pony drifted still farther around the tree.

"The SPCA. Marcie heard about him. Somebody kept him in a little garage stall—you know the type of thing. It was dark, and the horse didn't have any room to move."

"Is it a horse or a pony, for God's sake?" asked Martin, taking a sip of beer.

"A pony, I think. Anyway, he was locked up for a long time. They had pictures of him in the paper. He had shit all over him, and his hooves were about two feet long. They curled up, you know, just like a court jester or some Ali Baba. That's how the SPCA found him, and they put a picture in the paper."

"And Marcie saw it?" I asked.

"Saw it? Are you kidding me? She heard the pony got cast—fell down in the stall and couldn't get up. She went crazy. She bawled like a siren the whole way down to the SPCA. She knows all the people there. You should see it. She knows everyone. They all told her the pony was scheduled to be destroyed, and that set her off again. After that she became very calm, very clear that she wanted the horse to be brought here. The people at the SPCA didn't care."

"So now what?"

"So now she's playing shrink. She comes out here and talks to Ivan. The thing whirls around the tree, but Marcie doesn't mind. It almost bit her hand off once, but she always says she wants it to have at least as much time under this tree as it did in that dark garage. It eats up half her profit from the kennel. Dad's worried someone is going to come over and try to pet the thing and get trampled."

The pony stuck his head out again and gnashed his teeth. His eyes looked unfocused. Stu took a few steps forward, and the horse pulled back, looking like someone ducking through the shower curtain after listening for the phone.

"Wily's buried there," Martin said.

"Who?" asked Stu.

"Wily. Marcie's imaginary friend, remember?"

We turned away from the tree. Ivan whinnied one long call, then snorted. I heard him trotting again as we circled the garage.

"I thought of making him a security pony," Stu said. "You

276

know, lock him up over night in somebody's yard. He'd attack anyone who came in."

"How would you collect him each morning?" I asked.

"I'd send Won Ton in for him, right, Wonny Tonny? Or maybe I'd rope him, maybe Marcie would come over and talk him down each day."

"Maybe you could headlock him," I said.

"Oh, is that right?"

His arm shot out quicker than I could dodge. Oddly I found myself bending to accept it, ducking under it like an ox taking on a familiar yoke. His arm cupped my head, and he gave me a short, hard bop, then let me go.

"Still not ripe," he said.

Stu went up to dress as soon as we got back to the house. His door slammed, and I heard him yell to Marcie that Ivan the Impaler had been trying to take an overdose of sleeping pills.

Martin listened and held his beer bottle a long time at his mouth. Now and then he turned to catch some new noise. Once he stretched his hand to let it warm in a patch of sunlight.

"I'd like to move in," he said finally.

"You know you're welcome."

"Only for the summer. I wrote Deado a letter and asked if there's any work out there."

"Where did you get his address?"

"From the manager down at the Y. They have a mailing list type of thing."

"Did Deado answer?"

"Not yet. I just wrote it. I don't know if it will even get to him."

"And if it does?"

"Then we go," he said.

"What would you do?"

"Change tires. Something. We have to get out of here. Here we're known as a mistake. Marla and I talked about it. We'll always be known as the people who screwed up. It's a black mark."

"What about school? Will you take courses?"

"With what? I took a job over at the Esso station this week just to pay for some of the baby's doctor bills and everything else."

Martin tilted his beer back and finished it. Afterward he put his finger in the top of the bottle and plucked it a few times. He began speaking again as he put the bottle on the counter.

"Maybe I'll take courses, I don't know. We'll see. But if I could, I'd like to move in just for the summer. Say no if you want to. Marla and I talked it over. Stu thinks he can get me work at an Esso station down by Westfield. I'll wait and see what Deado says."

"You can move in today."

"Well, next week will be good enough. I'll give you a call."

It took ten minutes for everyone to come down. I drove Stu and Marcie. We had the windows all the way down, but it didn't help. Marcie sat in one corner looking out. We were only halfway there when Stu turned to her.

"Did you see Martin's hands?" he asked.

"What about them?"

"See his nails? I saw them against the baby's blanket. That's what gets me. He couldn't even get them clean."

I could tell this was a conversation they had had before. Marcie continued looking out the window, her hair whipping around her head. She didn't talk. She looked very tired.

"If the dirt gets in too deep, you can't get it out," Stu said.

"You're being dramatic, Stu," Marcie told him.

"No, I'm not."

"Yes, you are."

"No, I'm not. I've seen guys like that. It gets in their knuckles, under their nails. They never get clean again."

Marcie wouldn't get into it with him. She leaned forward and put her chin on the back of our seat. Once or twice she opened her mouth, flexed her jaw, then let her teeth click shut without saying a word.

278

❖❖ 40 ❖❖

THE CHRISTENING went off without incident. Fred and Marla's mom sat on the other side of the aisle. We were as segregated as we had been at the wedding, but at least now there were other people mixed in—ladies with children, baby carriages, diaper bags, young mothers appearing tired and happy. At any given moment one or two babies cried. Their cries bounced off the walls, echoed until they caught in still another voice.

After the ceremony we went back to the Kellermans'. I visited with Uncle Jack and Aunt Gertrude. Aunt Gertrude stayed very close to me. She filled my plate with cold cuts and thick sandwiches from the table. Each time she returned she put her hand on my forearm as if to reestablish a connection.

In the late afternoon Uncle Jack pulled me aside. He led me down to the willow and stood quietly, looking at our house. The pony snorted, then calmed down. Uncle Jack sipped at the last of a glass of scotch.

"How are you doing on the house?" he asked after a while. "Things shaping up?"

"The yard's better. I can paint the house if you want me to."

"You know how?"

"I think so. I'm pretty sure."

"Did I hear something about Martin and Marla moving in? That's what's on the drum."

"I think they will. They're having a hard time at Mr. Babcock's."

The pony moved. It walked slowly, the branches lifting and falling over it quietly. It made a low, hissing sound. Jack tilted his head toward it. He swirled the ice cubes at the bottom of his glass.

"The other thing is," he said, although there was no other thing except perhaps in his rehearsal of what he was about to say, "the other thing is your dad's been found."

"What?"

"Your dad's been located."

"Where?"

"There was another vagrancy charge. He's still in Colorado, someplace near Denver. I have the address. The man there, a social worker, called me. Your father had to give them the name of a relative to get out—I didn't get it all."

"Is he still there?"

"Yes, he's still there. This social worker helped get him a job sweeping up in a library. Your father's worked there for about three weeks."

"When did this man call?"

"Last night. We figured we'd wait and tell you in person."

I couldn't think. All I could remember of him at that moment was the smell of grapefruit, the shine of tape cassettes on the hump of the station wagon.

Jack looked straight at the creek and didn't say anything for a long time. A crow called from a nearby tree. A soft wind blew off the creek, cooling us and carrying the smell of rain. Jack picked up a leaf and stroked it several times. Then he spun it by the stem, letting it turn against his lips.

"I made two reservations for a flight tomorrow. We can get into Denver around one. Gertrude and I have talked this over. We can do it any way you like. I don't have to go if you don't want. I'm not going to bring him back against his will, and it might be painful for him if I simply show up."

"You think I should go alone?"

"I don't know, Max. I keep thinking that he's the only thing that kept him away. He could have come home anytime he wanted. Think of that when you're making up your mind. We build things. We dream them up. It's hardly ever like you think it will be."

"I have to go, though, Uncle Jack."

"I understand."

"I have to see him."

"I thought you would. It's okay. You're entitled to it."

Uncle Jack stayed with me for a little while, talking about the house, then went back to the party. He walked very slowly and stopped once to catch his breath. When he passed the willow, he turned back to me.

"Is this thing a horse or a pony?" he asked.

"I don't know, Uncle Jack."

Jack nodded and kept walking, turning the glass up to let the ice spill out.

❖❖ 41 ❖❖

UNCLE JACK came with me to Newark Airport, but he did not take the plane. Standing near the gate, he gave me two hundred dollars and a pack of gum.

"I'm not going," he said. "Not this time."

"Are you sure?"

"Yes. I'm sure now."

"Do you want me to tell him anything?"

"Tell him he's welcome back here. Tell him I love him."

"I will."

"Rent a car at the airport. There'll be a desk right there, Avis or Hertz, it doesn't matter. Go to Mr. Corwin's office. I'll phone to say you're coming."

"All right."

"Be careful, Max. Protect yourself, you understand me?"

"Yes."

We hugged and I left. I had never flown before.

I found Mr. Corwin's office in a modern building on the outskirts of Denver. The mountains rose behind it to the west, but they were mostly covered with clouds and smog. Only occasionally did I see a peak as I drove from the airport.

A line of men waited across the hall from Mr. Corwin's office, most of them smoking. The men were dressed in winter clothing, heavy overcoats and thick boots; some wore gloves, some ski caps and surplus army pants. They were silent for the most part. Two younger men, a little older than I was, occasionally lifted the black rubber hose of a fire extinguisher and let it twang against the steel canister.

Mr. Corwin's desk was one of about twenty in a large, poorly lighted room. It was a government desk, gray and nondescript. A computer monitor was stationed on the left-hand corner. A straight-backed steel chair stood on the right, positioned so that whoever sat there could see the job list on the monitor. It was a chair chosen deliberately to be uncomfortable.

"You must be Max," Mr. Corwin said when I was buzzed past the receiving counter. He was short. His hair was thin on top. He wore a white shirt without a jacket, and the shirt had an old, faded ink stain on the pocket.

"My uncle, Jack Darrigan, called you."

"Yes, about your father, Mr. Darrigan. I'm glad you came out. Please, sit down."

I sat in the straight-backed chair. The job monitor scrolled slowly, listing openings around the state. The same jobs moved across all the screens on all the desks in the office.

"I called the library where your father works. He's still there. The librarian, Mrs. Eberhardt, is satisfied. It seems to be working out."

"Would he be there now?"

"Yes, I suppose so. I can call."

"No, that's all right. I'd rather just go over."

Mr. Corwin glanced at the monitor. He reached forward and touched a button, and the scroll moved faster. He slowed it and took down the address of the library.

"Here you are," he said. "I hope this all works out."

"Was my father all right?"

"I didn't get to know him, honestly. I called your uncle simply as part of procedure. I'm sorry. I wish I could tell you more. He does have a record of some confinement."

"In prison?"

"In prison and in some hospital wards. The terms weren't long. They were for general disorientation."

283

He looked over my shoulder toward the reception counter. Then he glanced at the clock. My father's case wasn't anything special.

I asked him for directions and left with the address. It didn't take me long to find it. The library was an extension of the Denver city library system. The building was constructed of red brick.

It took me a long time to go inside. I checked the address twice, walking both ways down the block until I verified the cross streets. There could be no mistake; it was the right library.

It was four o'clock when I finally went to the door. I pushed through a turnstile and walked past the reference section. Somebody was using a Xerox machine near the check-out desk, and the light occasionally flashed across the room.

I spotted my father standing with his back toward me on the second floor. The ordinariness of seeing him stopped me. He was reading something and didn't notice me. He looked older and thinner. His hair was gray, and his body seemed hunched and stooped. He wore a green custodian's uniform.

I stepped behind a card catalogue and watched him. For a long time I considered leaving, just turning around and walking away. But then he made a small motion, one I recognized, and I found myself moving toward him. He did not turn, did not even notice my approach. I ran the last few steps.

"Dad?" I said.

He did not turn at first, probably thinking the word could not be for him. He squinted at the book open in front of him.

"Dad?" I said again.

This time he turned. As soon as he saw me, one hand went to his forehead and wavered there, shaking, lightly touching his eyebrow.

"Max?" he asked.

"Hello, Dad."

"Oh," he said, and sat.

"Dad, I didn't know . . ."

"Oh, Max."

His hand trembled at his eyebrow. I saw that he was much more frail than I had thought. A very slight palsy, a small permanent shake, had entered all his movements. His head now shook in minuscule tremors, like the twitching of a badly injured finger.

284

I sat down next to him. We still hadn't touched. He covered his eyes for a moment and breathed into his hands.

"You know," he said, nodding to himself, "you know, don't you, that there was another case identical to the one we found? It was here, just outside Denver."

"I didn't know."

"Two similar cases substantiates it. I think it proves the whole thing, don't you?"

"I guess it does, Dad."

"There was no shackle, but the boy used to catch small things up in the attic and put the bones under the floorboards—he actually worked on the bones first. It was like scrimshaw, like the whalers used to do, and they're really quite marvelous to look at. Pictures of strange creatures, wonderful creatures the boy imagined. We could see them."

"I'd like that."

"I don't think the museum is open today."

"That's okay. Some other time."

My voice broke on the last word, and I started to cry. I cried uncontrollably. There was nothing I could do to stop it, and even after I felt his hand on my shoulder, the flutter of his fingers drumming quietly, I couldn't stop.

"I'm so sorry, Max. So sorry."

"No, it's all right."

I cried into my hands for a long time. My father's hand rested on my shoulder, the stutter of his pulse and nerves typing his memory into me.

"Maybe we should just get out of here for a little," he said. "Just for a little. I have to work, you see. This is a new job, and I have to give the right impression."

I nodded. We went out slowly. The light from the Xerox machine flashed twice. He showed me the different sections of the library, introducing them almost as friends.

"I'm reading more and more history. But of course, it's a little like being a bloodhound—you see, a bloodhound is never caught up with the present, is he? He's always behind because that's his function. Exactly that. He's got his nose to the ground, and he can't see just in front of him."

"Do you read dog books anymore?" I asked.

"You remember those, Max?"

"Yes, I remember them."

"Oh, they were something, weren't they? We had something then, didn't we? Old Spitz—wasn't it?—going down in the Arctic twilight, the dogs gathered around, and Buck, I think it was Buck, making that feint for Spitz's throat, then biting his legs and cracking the bone. I'm glad you remember that."

"I do."

"Are you hungry?" I asked him when we stood in the late-afternoon sun. "I could buy you some dinner."

"Do you have a car?"

"Yes. I rented one."

"Well, that's fine."

"I'd like to buy you dinner if you're hungry."

"Well, all right. I guess so then."

I walked him to the car. He had trouble finding the door button, and I bent in front of him to open it. He smiled and climbed in, then hunched his shoulders together as if to make room for me to close the door. I walked behind the car to the driver's side. His eyes remained straight ahead, staring at the mountains. He did not say anything while I started the car. It took him two or three blocks to get his seat belt buckled.

❖❖ 42 ❖❖

I DROVE up into the mountains, following my father's directions. We had a bag of hamburgers between us. We didn't say anything at all. The sun was almost down behind the mountains, but they were still beautiful.

We drove for twenty minutes; then my father told me to pull off into a small picnic area. The picnic area, back from the road, looked out on a huge meadow and the corner of a lake. It was clearer now. The mountains stood in a ring around us.

"It's pretty, isn't it?" my father asked as we walked to the tables.

We sat at a gray table on the edge of the meadow. My father busied himself with spreading out the waxed paper for the hamburgers, laying out napkins. His hands shook continually, causing the paper to rattle, the napkins to bunch. When he took a bite from his hamburger, onions and pickles pattered on the paper. They quivered in his fingers on the way to his mouth.

"You're not hungry?" he asked me.

"No, not really."

He pushed some french fries at me. I took a few and gave them back to him. He seemed very hungry, unaccustomed to eating as much as he wanted.

"Uncle Jack says hello," I said.

"How is he?"

"He's fine."

"And Gertrude?"

"She's fine, too."

"How about Honey and Zeke? They both living?"

"They're both fine. Honey asked to be remembered to you."

He nodded. He finished his first hamburger and opened a second one. A drop of ketchup rested on the corner of his mouth. His head shook; his hands touched just the edge of the waxed paper. For the first time since seeing him, I actually saw what time had done to him. His eyes were rimmed with black, and his skin was white, pale white, indoor white.

I watched him for a while, then said softly, "You're welcome to come home."

"It all collapsed, Max, and I can't explain it to you," he said suddenly.

"I know. It's all right."

He began to cry then. His tears came from deep inside, as if his body were almost too dry to yield any more. I watched him and forgave him and reached forward to hold his hand. He pulled my hand to his face and cried against the back of it, sometimes kissing it, saying in a whisper, "Forgive me, Max. Forgive me."

We sat like that until the elk came into the meadow. At first only one came down off the side of the mountain, tentative and unsure, its spring antlers turning to test the wind. Then others followed, stepping across the meadow in search of tender grass, in search of forage along the rim of the lake. The wind was to our advantage, and they did not see us. The herd grazed across the field, grouping and breaking apart, the males sometimes lifting their heads to listen.

My father watched for a long time, then led me down into the meadow. The grass was high, but dry already for summer. In two or three months there would be snow. Summer would end, and it would be time to start school again, Stu would be leaving, and Martin would go west. Marcie would be left alone with her animals. And even as I thought this, I felt my father's hand take mine, tremulous and old, and I understood he would not come back, that it was unfair even to ask.

So I let him go and watched him walk through the meadow

288

toward the elk. He did not walk well any longer, but there remained still a trace of his old eagerness, his joy at seeing a live thing. The sun was down, and the night just beginning. And when he raised his voice and yelled into the night, I heard it echo up and down the meadow. And I held him there in my mind, held him with the deep, haunting sound of a hundred elk running into winter.

Having grown up in Westfield, New Jersey, Joseph Monninger lives in Vienna, Austria. This is his third novel.